Soledad Brother

Soledad Brother

The Prison Letters
of George Jackson

Foreword by Jonathan Jackson, Jr.

Lawrence Hill Books

Chicago

Copyright © 1994 by Jonathan Jackson, Jr.
Letters originally published 1970

Published by Lawrence Hill Books
An imprint of Chicago Review Press Incorporated
814 North Franklin Street
Chicago, Illinois 60610
ISBN 978-1-55652-230-7

Library of Congress Cataloging-in-Publication Data
Jackson, George, 1941–1971
Soledad brother: the prison letters of George Jackson /
foreword by Jonathan Jackson, Jr. ; introduction by Jean Genet.
p.   cm.

Originally published: New York: Coward-McCann, [1970].
Includes bibliographical references.
ISBN 1-55652-230-4: $14.95

1. Jackson, George, 1941–1971 Correspondence.
2. Afro-American prisoners—California—Correspondence.   I. Title.
HV9468.J3A4   1994
365'.6'092—dc20
[B] 94-28264
CIP

Printed in the United States of America

To the Man-Child,

Tall, evil, graceful, brighteyed, black man-child—Jonathan Peter Jackson—who died on August 7, 1970, courage in one hand, assault rifle in the other; my brother, comrade, friend—the *true revolutionary,* the black communist guerrilla in the highest state of development, he died on the trigger, scourge of the unrighteous, soldier of the people; to this terrible man-child and his wonderful mother Georgia Bea, to Angela Y. Davis, my tender experience, I dedicate this collection of letters; to the destruction of their enemies I dedicate my life.

ontents

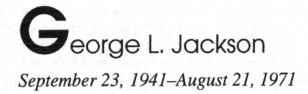

George L. Jackson

September 23, 1941–August 21, 1971

In 1960, at the age of eighteen, George Jackson was accused of stealing $70 from a gas station in Los Angeles. Though there was evidence of his innocence, his court-appointed lawyer maintained that because Jackson had a record (two previous instances of petty crime), he should plead guilty in exchange for a light sentence in the county jail. He did, and received an indeterminate sentence of one year to life. Jackson spent the next ten years in Soledad Prison, seven and a half of them in solitary confinement. Instead of succumbing to the dehumanization of prison existence, he transformed himself into the leading theoretician of the prison movement and a brilliant writer. *Soledad Brother*, which contains the letters that he wrote from 1964 to 1970, is his testament.

In his twenty-eighth year, Jackson and two other black inmates—Fleeta Drumgo and John Cluchette—were falsely accused of murdering a white prison guard. The guard was beaten to death on

January 16, 1969, a few days after another white guard shot and killed three black inmates by firing from a tower into the courtyard. The accused men were brought in chains and shackles to two secret hearings in Salinas County. A third hearing was about to take place when John Cluchette managed to smuggle a note to his mother: "Help, I'm in trouble." With the aid of a state senator, his mother contacted a lawyer, and so commenced one of the most extensive legal defenses in U.S. history. According to their attorneys, Jackson, Drumgo, and Clutchette were charged with murder not because there was any substantial evidence of their guilt, but because they had been previously identified as black militants by the prison authorities. If convicted, they would face a mandatory death penalty under the California penal code. Within weeks, the case of the Soledad Brothers emerged as a political cause célèbre for all sorts of people demanding change at a time when every American institution was shaken by Black rebellions in more than one hundred cities and the mass movement against the Vietnam War.

August 7, 1970, just a few days after George Jackson was transferred to San Quentin, the case was catapulted to the forefront of national news when his brother, Jonathan, a seventeen-year-old high school student in Pasadena, staged a raid on the Marin County courthouse with a satchelful of handguns, an assault rifle, and a shotgun hidden under his coat. Educated into a political revolutionary by George, Jonathan invaded the court during a hearing for three black San Quentin inmates, not including his brother, and handed them weapons. As he left with the inmates and five hostages, including the judge, Jonathan demanded that the Soledad Brothers be released within thirty minutes. In the shootout that ensued, Jonathan was gunned down. Of Jonathan, George wrote, "He was free for a while. I guess that's more than most of us can expect."

Soledad Brother, which is dedicated to Jonathan Jackson, was released to critical acclaim in France and the United States, with an introduction by the renowned French dramatist Jean Genet, in the fall of 1970. Less than a year later and just two days before the opening of his trial, George Jackson was shot to death by a tower guard inside San Quentin Prison in a purported escape attempt. "No Black person," wrote James Baldwin, "will ever believe that George Jackson died the way they tell us he did."

Soledad Brother went on to become a classic of Black literature and political philosophy, selling more than 400,000 copies before it went out of print twenty years ago. Lawrence Hill Books is pleased to reissue this book and to add to it a Foreword by the author's nephew, Jonathan Jackson, Jr., who is a writer living in California.

Foreword

I was born eight and a half months after my father, Jonathan Jackson, was shot down on August 7, 1970, at the Marin County Courthouse, when he tried to gain the release of the Soledad Brothers by taking hostages. Before and especially after that day, Uncle George kept in constant contact with my mother by writing from his cell in San Quentin. (The Department of Corrections wouldn't put her on the visitors' list.) During George's numerous trial appearances for the Soledad Brothers case, Mom would lift me above the crowd so he could see me. Consistently, we would receive a letter a few days later. For a single mother with son, alone and in the middle of both controversy and not a little unwarranted trouble with the authorities, those messages of strength were no doubt instrumental in helping her carry on. No matter how oppressive his situation became, George always had time to lend his spirit to the people he cared for.

A year and two weeks after the revolutionary takeover in Marin, George was ruthlessly murdered by prison guards at San Quentin. Both he and my father left me a great deal: pride, history, an unmistakable name. My experience has been at once wonderful and incredibly difficult. My life is not consumed by the Jackson legacy, but my charge is an accepted and cherished piece of my existence. It is out of my responsibility to my legacy that I have come to write this Foreword to my uncle's prison writings.

Today I read my inherited letters often—those written from George to my mother with a dull pencil on prison stationery. They are things of beauty, my most valuable possessions, passionate pieces of writing that have few rivals in the modern era. They will remain unpublished. However, the letters of *Soledad Brother* demonstrate the same insight and eloquence—the way George's writings make his personal experience universal is the mainstay of his brilliance.

When this collection of letters was first released in 1969, it brought a young revolutionary to the forefront of a tempest, a tempest characterized by the Black Power, free speech, and antiwar movements, accompanied by a dissatisfaction with the status quo throughout the United States. With unflinching directness, George Jackson conveyed an intelligent yet accessible message with his trademark style, rational rage. He illuminated previously hidden viewpoints and feelings that disenfranchised segments of the population were unable to articulate: the poor, the victimized, the imprisoned, the disillusioned. George spoke in a revolutionary voice that they had no idea existed. He was the prominent figure of true radical thought and practice during the period, and when he was assassinated, much of the movement died along with him. But George Jackson cannot and will not ever leave. His life and thoughts serve as the message—George himself is the revolution.

The reissue of *Soledad Brother* at this point in time is essential. It appears that the nineties are going to be a telling decade in U.S. history. The signposts of systemic breakdown are as glaringly obvious as they were in the sixties: unrest manifesting itself in inner-city turmoil, widespread rise of violence in the culture, and international oppression to legitimize a state in crisis. The fact that imprisonments in California have more than tripled over the last decade, supported by the public, is merely one sign of societal decomposition. That systemic change occurred during the sixties is a myth. The United States in the nineties faces strikingly analogous problems. George spoke to the issues of his day, but conditions now are so similar that this work could have been written last month. It is imperative that George be heard, whether by the angry but unchanneled young or by the cynical and worldly mature. The message must be carried farther than where he bravely left it in August of 1971.

Over the past twenty-five years, why has George Jackson not been an integral part of mainstream consciousness? He has been and still is underexposed, reduced to simplistic terms, and ultimately misunderstood. Racial and conspiracy theory aside, there are rational reasons for his exclusion. They stem not only from the hard-line revolutionary aspects of George's philosophy, but more importantly from the nature of the political system that he existed in and under.

Howard Zinn has pointed out in *A People's History of the United States* that "the history of any country, presented as the history of a family, conceals fierce conflicts of interest (sometimes exploding, most often repressed) between conquerors and conquered, masters and slaves, capitalists and workers, dominators and dominated." U.S. history is essentially that type of hidden history. Without denying important mitigating factors, the United States of today is strongly linked to the values and premises on which it was founded. That is, it is a settler colony founded primarily on two basic pillars, upheld by the Judeo-Christian tradition: genocide of indigenous peoples and slave labor in support of a capitalist infrastructure. Although the Bible repeatedly exalts mass slaughter and oppression, Judeo-Christian morality is publicly held to be inconsistent with them. This dissonance, evident within the nation's structure from the beginning, informs the state's first function: to oversimplify and minimize immoral events in order to legitimize history and the state's very existence simultaneously.

Ironically, traditional Judeo-Christian morality is a perfect vehicle for genocide, slavery, and territorial expansion. As a logical progression from biblical example, expansion and imperialism culminated in the United States with the concept of Manifest Destiny, which held that it was the colonists' inherent right to expand and conquer. Further it was a duty, the "white man's burden," to save the "natives," to attempt to convert all heathens encountered. Protestant Calvinism provided a set of ethics that fit perfectly with the colonists' conquests. Max Weber, in his definitive study on religion, *The Sociology of Religion*, wrote, "Calvinism held that the unsearchable

God possessed good reasons for having distributed the gifts of fortune unevenly"; it "represented as God's will [the Calvinists'] domination over the sinful world. Clearly this and other features of Protestantism, such as its rationalization of the existence of a lower class,* were not only the bases for the formation of the United States, but still prominently exist today. "One must go to the ethics of ascetic Protestantism," Weber asserts, "to find any ethical sanction for economic rationalism and for the entrepreneur." When a nation can't admit to the process through which it builds hegemony, how can anything but delusion be a reality? "The monopoly of truth, including historical truth," stated Daniel Singer in a lecture at Evergreen State College (Washington) in 1987, "is implied in the monopoly of power."

Clearly, objective history is an impossibility. This understood, the significant problem lies in how the general population defines the term; *history* implies that truth is being told. It is an unfortunate fact that history is unfailingly written by the victors, which in the case of the United States are not only the original imperialists, but the majority of the "founding fathers," dedicated to uniting and strengthening the existing mercantile class among disjointed colonies. There can be no doubt that from the creation of this young nation, history as a created and perceived entity moved further and further away from the objective ideal. Genocide, necessary for "the development of the modern capitalist economy," according to Howard Zinn, was rationalized as a reaction to the fear of Indian savages. Slavery was similarly construed.

The personalization of history, the process by which we construct heroes and pariahs, is a consequence of its dialectical nature. Without fail, an odd paradox is created around someone who, by virtue of his or her actions, becomes prominent enough to warrant the designation "historical figure." There is a leap on the part of the general public, sparked by the media, to another mindset. Sensational deeds are glorified, horrible acts reviled. A few points are selected as defining characteristics. The media, conforming to their restrictions of con-

---

* Called bootstrap ideology, this tenet holds that all the poor need to do is "pull themselves up by their bootstraps" to be materially successful. Accordingly, those who do not do so deserve to be in their situation and are considered unworthy.

cision (which make accuracy nearly impossible to attain), reiterate these points over and over. Schools and textbooks not only teach these points but drill them into young minds. Howard Zinn comments that "this learned sense of moral proportion, coming from the apparent objectivity of the scholar, is accepted more easily than when it comes from politicians at press conferences. It is therefore more deadly."

A few tidbits, factual or not, incomplete and selective, are used to describe the entirety of a person's existence. They become part of mainstream consciousness. We therefore know that Lincoln freed the slaves, Malcolm X was a black extremist, and Hitler was solely responsible for World War II and the Holocaust. All half-truths go unexplained, all fallacies go unchallenged, as they appear to make perfect sense to the everyday, noncritically thinking American. The paradox has been created: The more famous a person becomes, the more misunderstood he or she is. This accepted occurrence is incredibly counterintuitive: the public should know more, not less, about a noteworthy individual and the sociopolitical dynamics surrounding him or her.

This historical mythicization is not, for the most part, a consciously created phenomenon. The media don't go out of their way to mislead the public by constructing false heroes and emphasizing the mundane. Fewer "dimly lit conferences" take place than conspiracy theorists believe. It is the existing political system that is responsible for the information that reaches the general public. The state's control of information created the system, and it continually re-creates it. Propagated by schooling and the media, information that reaches the public is subject to three chief mechanisms of state control: denial, self-censorship, and imprisonment.

Denial is the easiest control mechanism, and therefore the most common. If events do not follow the state's agenda or its ecumenical ideology and might bring unrest, they are denied. Examples are plentiful: prewar state terrorism against the people of North and South Vietnam and later the bombing of Cambodia; government funding and military aid to the Nicaraguan Contras; and support of UNITA and South Africa in the virtual destruction of Angola, among many others.

Denial goes hand in hand with self-censorship. The media emphasize certain personal characteristics and events and de-emphasize others, in a pattern that supports U.S. hegemony. The information that reached the public after the U.S. invasion of Panama in 1989 is telling. It was not until much later, after the heat of controversy, that the average citizen had access to the scope of the devastation. The effectiveness of self-censorship in this case was maximized, as the full details of the Panama invasion were patchwork for years.

While we may assume that the media have an obligation to accurately convey such an event to the public, the media in fact perpetuate the government's position by engaging in their own self-censorship. Noam Chomsky points out in *Deterring Democracy*, "With a fringe of exceptions—mostly well after the tasks had been accomplished—the media rallied around the flag with due piety and enthusiasm, funnelling the most absurd White House tales to the public while scrupulously refraining from asking the obvious questions, or seeing the obvious facts."

Denial and self-censorship create a comfort zone for the U.S. citizenry, generally uncritical and willing to accept digestible versions of historical personalities and world events. The reasoning behind denial and self-censorship: do not make the public uncomfortable, even if that means diluting, sensationalizing, or lying about the truth.

Ultimately, when denial and self-censorship may not be sufficient for control of information, the state resorts to imprisonment. All imprisonment is political and as such all imprisonments carry equal weight. Society does, however, distinguish two categories of imprisonment: one for breaking a law, the other for political reasons. A difference is clear: American Indian Movement leader Leonard Peltier, serving a federal sentence for his supposed role at Wounded Knee, is considered a different type of prisoner than an armed robber serving a five-to-seven-year sentence.

State policy reflects institutional needs. When the state as an institution cannot tolerate an outside threat, real or perceived, from an individual or group, the consequences at its command include isolation, persecution, and political imprisonment. All may occur in greater or lesser form, depending on the degree of threat.

Political incarceration removes threats to the political and economic hegemony of the United States. Even though in 1959 George Jackson initially went to prison as an "everyday lawbreaker" with a one-year-to-life sentence, it was his political consciousness that kept him incarcerated for eleven years. In 1970 George wrote:

> International capitalism cannot be destroyed without the extremes of struggle. The entire colonial world is watching the blacks inside the U.S., wondering and waiting for us to come to our senses. Their problems and struggles with the Amerikan monster are much more difficult than they would be if we actively aided them. We are on the inside. We are the only ones (besides the very small white minority left) who can get at the monster's heart without subjecting the world to nuclear fire. We have a momentous historical role to act out if we will. The whole world for all time in the future will love us and remember us as the righteous people who made it possible for the world to live on. If we fail through fear and lack of aggressive imagination, then the slaves of the future will curse us, as we sometimes curse those of yesterday. I don't want to die and leave a few sad songs and a hump in the ground as my only monument. I want to leave a world that is liberated from trash, pollution, racism, nation-states, nation-state wars and armies, from pomp, bigotry, parochialism, a thousand different brands of untruth, and licentious usurious economics.

Nothing is more dangerous to a system that depends on misinformation than a voice that obeys its own dictates and has the courage to speak out. George Jackson's imprisonment and further isolation within the prison system were clearly a function of the state's response to his outspoken opposition to the capitalist structure.

Political incarceration is a tangible form of state control. Unlike denial and self-censorship, imprisonment is publicly scrutinized. Yet public reaction to political incarceration has been minimal. The U.S. government claims it holds no political prisoners (denial), while any notice given to protests focused on political prisoners invariably takes the form of a human interest story (self-censorship).

The efficacy of political incarceration in the United States cannot be denied. Prison serves not only as a physical barrier, but a communication restraint. Prisoners are completely ostracized from society, with little or no chance to break through. Those few outside who might be sympathetic are always hesitant to communicate or protest past a certain point, fearing their own persecution or imprisonment. Also, deep down most people believe that all prisoners, regardless of their individual situations, really did do something "wrong." Added to that prejudice, society lacks a distinction between a prisoner's actions and his or her personal worth; a bad act equals a bad person. The bottom line is that the majority of people simply will not believe that the state openly or covertly oppresses without criminal cause. As Daniel Singer asked at the Evergreen conference in 1987, "Is it possible for a class which exterminates the native peoples of the Americas, replaces them by raping Africa for humans it then denigrates and dehumanizes as slaves, while cheapening and degrading its own working class—is it possible for such a class to create a democracy, equality and to advance the cause of human freedom? The implicit answer is, 'No, of course not.'"

How does a person—inside or outside prison—confront the cultural mindsets, the layers of misinformation propagated by the capitalist system? Sooner or later, what can be called the "radical dilemma" surfaces for the few wanting to enter into a structural attack/analysis of the United States. Culturally, educationally, and politically, all of us are similarly limited by these layers of misinformation; we are all products of the system. None of us functions from a clean slate when considering or debating any issue, especially history as it pertains to the United States.

George Jackson struggled against the constraints of denial and self-censorship, to say nothing of his physical and communicative distance from society. Political prisoners are inherently vulnerable to an either/or situation: isolating silence or elimination. For George, his vociferous revolutionary attitude was either futile or self-exterminating. He was well aware of his situation. In *Blood in My Eye*, his political treatise, he wrote:

> I'm in a unique political position. I have a very nearly closed future, and since I have always been inclined to get disturbed over organized injustice or terrorist practice against the innocents— wherever—I can now say just about what I want (I've always done just about that), without fear of self-exposure. I can only be executed once.

George was equally aware that revolutionary change happens only when an entire society is ready. No amount of action, preaching, or teaching will spark revolution if social conditions do not warrant it.

My father's case, unfortunately, is an appropriate indicator. He attempted a revolutionary act during a reactionary time; elimination was the only possible consequence.

The challenge for a radical in today's world is to balance reformist tendencies (political liberalism) and revolutionary action/ideology (radicalism). While reformism entails a legitimation of the status quo as a search for changes within the system, radicalism posits a change of system. Because revolutionaries are particularly vulnerable, a certain degree of reformism is necessary to create space, space needed to begin the laborious task of making revolution.

George's statement "Combat Liberalism" and the general reaction to it typify the gulf between the two philosophies. George was universally misunderstood by the left and the right alike. As is the case with most modern political prisoners, nearly all of his support came from reformists with liberal leanings. It seems that they acted in spite of, rather than because of, the core of his message.

The left's attitude toward COINTELPRO is a useful illustration. COINTELPRO, the covert government program used to dismantle the Black Panther Party, and later the American Indian Movement, is typically cited by many leftists as a damning example of the government's conspiratorial nature. Declassified documents and ex-agents' testimonies have shown COINTELPRO to be one of the most unlawful, insidious cells of government in the nation's history. COINTELPRO, however, was really a symptomatic, expendable entity; a small police force within a larger one (FBI), within a branch of government (executive), within the government itself (liberal democracy), within the economic system (capitalism). Reformists in radicals' clothing unknowingly argued against symptoms, rather than the roots, of the entrenched system. Doing away with COINTELPRO or even the FBI would not alter the structure that produces the surveillance/elimination apparatus.

In George's day, others who considered themselves left of center, or even revolutionary, concerned themselves with inner-city reform issues, mostly black ghettos. The problem of and debate about inner cities still exists. However, recognition of a problem and analysis of that problem are two very different challenges. The demand to better only predominantly black inner-city conditions is unrealistic at best. In the capitalist structure, there must be an upper, middle, and especially a lower class. Improving black neighborhoods is the equivalent of ghettoizing some other segment of the population—poor whites, Hispanics, Asians, etc. Nothing intrinsic to the system would change, only superficial alterations that would mollify the liberal public. As Chomsky asserts in *Turning the Tide*:

> Determined opposition to the latest lunacies and atrocities must continue, for the sake of the victims as well as our own ultimate survival. But it should be understood as a poor substitute for a challenge to the deeper causes, a challenge that we are, unfortunately, in no position to mount at the present though the groundwork can and must be laid.

Failure to understand the radical, encompassing viewpoint in the sixties led to reformism. In effect, the majority of the left completely deserted any attempt at the radical balance required of the politically conscious, leaving only liberalism and its narrow vision to flourish.

Nobody comprehended the radical dilemma more fully than George Jackson. Indeed, he developed his philosophy not out of mere happenstance, but with a very conscious eye upon maintaining his revolutionary ideology. He writes in *Blood in My Eye*:

> Reformism is an old story in Amerika. There have been depressions and socio-economic political crises throughout the period that marked the formation of the present upper-class ruling circle, and their controlling elites. But the parties of the left were too committed to reformism to exploit their revolutionary potential.

George's involvement with the prison reform movement should therefore be seen as a matter of survival. Unlike the reformist left, prison oppression was *directly* affecting him. His balanced reform activities—improving prisoners' rights while speaking out against prison as an entity—were required to make living conditions tolerable enough for him to continue on his revolutionary path. Simply, he did what he had to do to survive—created space while simultaneously pursuing his radical theory.

The reform George Jackson did accomplish was and still is incredible, transforming the prison environment from unlivable to livable hell, from encampments that he called reminiscent of Nazi Germany to at least a scaled-down version of the like. With his influence, these changes occurred not only in California, but throughout the nation. Only now is his influence beginning to slip, with reactionary politics bringing about torture and sensory depriva- tion facilities such as Pelican Bay State Prison in California, as well as the reintroduction for adoption of the one-to-life indeterminate sentence. This type of sentence is fertile ground for state oppression, as it is up to a parole board to decide if an inmate is ever to be let go. A prison can easily and effectively create situations that transform a one-to-life into a life sentence. (Tellingly, the indeterminate sen- tence is being promoted not by the right, but by a California senator formerly associated with mainstream liberal causes.)

Politically, George Jackson provided us all with a radical educa- tion, a viable alternative to viewing not only the United States but the world as a political entity. He gave the disenfranchised a lens through which they could clearly see their situation and become more conscious about it. He wrote in April 1970:

> It all falls into place. I see the whole thing much clearer now, how fascism has taken possession of this country, the interlock- ing dictatorship from county level on up to the Grand Dragon in Washington, D.C.

Crucially, George's treatment is a concrete, undeniable example of political oppression. Race is more times than not the easy answer to a problem. Among people of color in the United States, the quick fix, "blame it on whitey" mentality has become so prevalent that it shortcuts thinking. Conversely, stereotypes of minorities act as simple-minded tools of divisiveness and oppression. George ad- dressed these issues in prison, setting a model for the outside as well: "I'm always telling the brothers some of those whites are willing to work with us against the pigs. All they got to do is stop talking honky. When the races start fighting, all you have is one maniac group against another." On the surface, race has been and is still being put forth as an overriding issue that needs to be addressed as a prereq- uisite for social change. In fact, although it seems to loom as a large problem, race as an issue is again a symptom of capitalism. Of course, on a paltry level and among the relatively powerless, race does play a part in social structure (the racist cop, the bigoted landlord, etc.), pitting segments of the population against each other.

But revolutionary change requires class analysis that drives appropriate actions and eliminates race as a mitigating factor. Knowing these socioeconomic dynamics, George Jackson was first and foremost a people's revolutionary, and he acted as such at all times without compromise. His writings clearly reflect his belief in class-based revolutionary change.

Considering the many structural elements affecting him, it is easy to see why George and his message have been misinterpreted. The quick takes on him are abundant: it's assumed that he was imprisoned and oppressed because he was black, because he had publicized ties with the Black Panther Party and was a well-known organizer within the prison reform movement. Although George became a "prison celebrity," a status that certainly didn't help him in terms of acquittal and release, ignorance of the actual forces responsible for his prolonged imprisonment is inexcusable. The radical viewpoint is absolutely indispensable when regarding both George's life circumstance and philosophy. His life serves not as a mere individual example of prison cruelty, but as a scalding indictment of the very nature of capitalism.

In these times, there are two very different ways to be born into privilege. First and most obvious in the system of capital is to be born into wealth. Second, and not precluding the first, is to have an intellectual, politically conscious base from which to grow as a person philosophically and spiritually. Radical figures in modern society—Lenin, Trotsky, Ché Guevara, my father, Jonathan Jackson, and my uncle George Jackson—have the capability of providing this base through their examples and writings.

Those not born into privilege can achieve a politically conscious base in different ways. No veils separate the lower class from the realities of everyday life. They have been given the gift of disillusion. Bourgeois lifestyle, although perhaps sought after, is in most cases not attainable. Daily survival is the primary goal, as it was with George. Of course, when it finally becomes more attractive for one to fight, and perhaps die, than to live in a survival mode, revolution starts to become a possibility. Not a riot, not a government takeover by one or another group, but a people's revolution led by the politically conscious.

This consciousness doesn't simply appear. Individuals must grow and work into it, but it's an invaluable gift to have insight into and access to an alternative to the frustration, a goal on the horizon.

The nineties are an unconscious era. The unimportant is all-important, the essential neglected. What system than capitalism, what time period than now, is better suited to naturally create the scapegoat, the seldom-heard political prisoner, misunderstood in his cult-of-personality status, held back in a choke hold from society? It is not only our right, but our duty, to listen to and comprehend George Jackson's message. To not do so is to turn our backs on one of the brilliant minds of the twentieth century, an individual passionately involved with liberating not only himself, but all of us.

> Settle your quarrels, come together, understand the reality of our situation, understand that fascism is already here, that people are dying who could be saved, that generations more will die or live poor butchered half-lives if you fail to act. Do what must be done, discover your humanity and your love in revolution. Pass on the torch. Join us, give up your life for the people.
>
> —*George Jackson*

Jonathan Jackson, Jr.
San Francisco
June 1994

Recent Letters and an Autobiography

JUNE, 1970
10

Dear Greg,*

     I probably didn't work hard enough on this but I'm pressed for time—all the time.

I could play the criminal aspects of my life down some but then it wouldn't be me. That was the pertinent part, the thing at school and home I was constantly rejecting in process.

All my life I pretended with my folks, it was the thing in the street that was real. I was certainly just pretending with the nuns and priests, I served mass so that I could be in a position to steal altar wine, sang in the choir because they made me. When we went on tour of the rich white catholic schools we were always treated very well—fed—rewarded with

*The editor who asked for the author's autobiography.

3

gifts. Old Father Brown hated me but always put me down front when we were on display. I can't say exactly why, I was the ugliest, skinniest little misfit in the group.

Blackmen born in the U.S. and fortunate enough to live past the age of eighteen are conditioned to accept the inevitability of prison. For most of us, it simply looms as the next phase in a sequence of humiliations. Being born a slave in a captive society and never experiencing any objective basis for expectation had the effect of preparing me for the progressively traumatic misfortunes that lead so many blackmen to the prison gate. I was prepared for prison. It required only minor psychic adjustments.

It always starts with Mama, mine loved me. As testimony of her love, and her fear for the fate of the man-child all slave mothers hold, she attempted to press, hide, push, capture me in the womb. The conflicts and contradictions that will follow me to the tomb started right there in the womb. The feeling of being captured . . . this slave can never adjust to it, it's a thing that I just don't favor, then, now, never.

I've been asked to explain myself, "briefly," before the world has done with me. It is difficult because I don't recognize uniqueness, not as it's applied to individualism, because it is too tightly tied into decadent capitalist culture. Rather I've always strained to see the indivisible thing cutting across the artificial barricades which have been erected to an older section of our brains, back to the mind of the primitive commune that exists in all blacks. But then how can I explain the runaway slave in terms that do not imply uniqueness?

I was captured and brought to prison when I was 18 years old because I couldn't adjust. The record that the state has compiled on my activities reads like the record of ten men. It labels me brigand, thief, burglar, gambler, hobo, drug addict, gunman, escape artist, Communist revolutionary, and murderer.

I was born as the Great Depression was ending. It was ending because the second great war for colonial markets was

4

beginning in the U.S. I pushed out of the womb against my mother's strength September 23, 1941—I felt free.

My mother was a country girl from Harrisburg, Illinois. My father was born in East St. Louis, Illinois. They met in Chicago, and were living on Lake Street near Racine when I was born. It was in one of the oldest sections of Chicago, part ghetto residential, part factory. The el train passed a few yards from our front windows (the only windows really). There were factories across the street and garage shops on the bottom level of our flat. I felt right in the middle of things.

Our first move up the social scale was around the corner to 211 North Racine Street, away from the el train. I remember every detail of preschool days. I have a sister 15 months older than myself, Delora, a beautiful child and now a beautiful woman. We were sometimes *allowed* to venture out into the world, which at the time meant no further than fenced-off roof area adjoining our little three-room apartment built over a tavern. We were allowed out there only after the city made its irregular garbage pickups. The roof area was behind the tavern and over an area where prople deposited their garbage. But, of course, I went out when I pleased.

Superman was several years old about then, I didn't really confuse myself with him but I did develop a deep suspicion that I might be Suppernigger (twenty-three years ahead of my time). I tied a tablecloth around my neck, climbed the roof's fence, and against my sister's tears would have leaped to my death, down among the garbage barrels, had she not grabbed me, tablecloth and all, and kicked my little ass.

Seeing the white boys up close in kindergarten was a traumatic event. I *must* have seen some before in magazines or books but never in the flesh. I approached one, felt his har, scratched at his cheek, he hit me in the head with a baseball bat. They found me crumpled in a heap just outside the school-yard fence.

After that, my mother sent me to St. Malachy catholic mission school. It was sitting right in the heart of the ghetto

5

area, Washington and Oakley streets. All of the nuns were white; of the priests (there were five in the parish) I think one was near black, or near white whichever you prefer. The school ran from kindergarten to 12th grade. I attended for nine years (ten counting kindergarten). This small group of missionaries with their silly costumes and barbaric rituals offered the full range of Western propaganda to all ages and all comers. Sex was never mentioned except with whispers or grimaces to convey something nasty. You could get away with anything (they were anxious to make saints) but getting caught with your hand up a dress. Holy ghosts, confessions, and racism.

St. Malachy's was really two schools. There was another school across the street that was more private than ours. "We" played and fought on the corner sidewalks bordering the school. "They" had a large grass-and-tree-studded garden with an eight-foot wrought-iron fence bordering it (to keep us out, since it never seemed to keep any of them in when they chose to leave). "They" were all white. "They" were driven to and from school in large private buses or their parents' cars. "We" on the black side walked, or when we could afford it used the public buses or streetcars. The white students' yard was equipped with picnic tables for spring lunches, swings, slides, and other more sophisticated gadgets intended to please older children. For years we had only the very crowded sidewalks and alley behind the school. Years later a small gym was built but it just stood there, locked. It was only allowed to be used for an occasional basketball game between our school and one of the others like it from across the city's various ghetto areas.

Delora and I took the Lake Street streetcar to school each morning, and also on Sundays when we were forced to attend a religious function. I must have fallen from that thing a hundred times while it was in motion. Each time Delora would hang on to me, trying to save me, but I was just too determined and we would roll down Lake Street, books and all, miraculously avoiding the passing cars. The other black

6

children who went to public school laughed at us. The girls had to wear a uniform, the boys wore white shirts. I imagined that the nuns and priests were laughing too every time they told one of those fantastic lies. I know now that the most damaging thing a people in a colonial situation can do is to allow their children to attend any educational facility organized by the dominant enemy culture.

Before the winter of my first-grade year, my father, Lester, prepared a fifty-gallon steel drum to store oil for our little stove. As I watched, he cleaned the inside with gasoline. When he retreated from his work temporarily for a cigarette he explained to me about the danger of the gas fumes. Later when he had completed work on the barrel, I sneaked back out to the roof with my sister Delora trailing me like a St. Bernard. I had matches and the idea of an explosion was irresistible. As soon as my sister realized what I was going to do, she turned her big sad eyes on me and started crying. I lit a match as I moved closer and closer to the barrel. The I lit the whole book of matches. By now Delora was convinced that death was imminent for us both. She made a last brave effort to stop me but I was too determined. I threw the matches across the last few feet. Delora shielded my eyes with her hand as the explosion went off. She still carries her burns from that day's experiences. I was injured around the lower face but carry no sign of it. Our clothes were burned and ripped away. I would probably be blind if not for this sister.

My parents had two more children while we were hanging on there at North Racine, Frances and Penelope. Six of us in the little walk-up. The only thing that I can think of that was even slightly pleasant about the place was the light. We had plenty of windows and nothing higher about us to block off the sun. In '49 we moved to a place in the rear on Warren near Western that was the end of the sun. We had no windows that opened directly on the street, even the one that faced the alley was blocked by a garage. It was a larger place but the neighborhood around the place was so vicious that my mother

7

never, never *allowed* me to go out of the house or the small yard except to get something from one of the supermarkets or stores on Madison and return immediately. When I wanted to leave I would either go by a window, or throw my coat out the window and volunteer to take out the garbage. There was only one door. It was in the kitchen and always well guarded.

I spent most of the summers of those school years in southern Illinois with my grandmother and aunt, Irene and Juanita. My mother, Georgia, called it removing me from harm's way. This was where my mother grew up and she trusted her sister Juanita, whose care I came under, completely. I was the only man-child and I was the only one to get *special* protection from my mother. The trips to the country were good for me in spite of the motive. I learned how to shoot rifles, shotguns, pistols. I learned about fishing. I learned to identify some of the food plants that grow wild in most areas of the U.S. I could leave the house, the yard, the town, without having to sneak out of a window.

Almost everyone in the black sector of Harrisburg is a relative of mine. A loyal, righteous people; I could raise a small army from their numbers. I had use of any type of rifle or pistol on those trips downstate and everyone owned a weapon. My disposition toward guns and explosions is responsible for my first theft. Poverty made ammunition scarce and so . . . I confess with some guilt that I liked to shoot small animals, birds rabbits, squirrels, anything that offered itself as a target. I was a little skinny guy; scourge of the woods, predatory man. After the summer I went back up north for school and snowball (sometimes ice-block) fights with the white kids across the street.

I don't remember exactly when I met Joe Adams, it was during the early years, but I do recall the circumstances. Three or four of the brothers were in the process of taking my lunch when Joe joined them. The bag was torn, and the contents spilled onto the sidewalk. Joe scrambled for the food and got all of it. But after the others left laughing, he returned and

8

stuffed it all into my pockets. We were great friends from then on in that childish way. He was older by a couple of years (two or three years means a lot at that tender age), and could beat me doing everything. I watched him and listened with John and Kenny Fox, Junior, Sonny, and others sometimes. We almost put the block's businessmen into bankruptcy. My mother and father will never admit it now, I'm sure, but I was hungry and so were we all. Our activities went from stolen food to other things I wanted, gloves for my hands (which were always cold), which I was always wearing out, marbles for the slingshots, games and gadgets for outdoorsmen from the dime store. Downtown, we plundered at will. The city was helpless to defend against us. But I couldn't keep up with Joe. Jonathan, my older brother, was born about this time.

My grandfather, George "Papa" Davis, stands out of those early years more than any other figure in my total environment. He was separated from his wife by the system. Work for men was impossible to find in Harrisburg. He was living and working in Chicago—sending his wage back to the people downstate. He was an extremely aggressive man, and since aggression on the part of the slave means crime, he was in jail now and then. I loved him. He tried to direct my great energy into the proper form of protest. He invented long simple allegories that always pictured the white politicians as animals (jackasses, toads, goats, vermin in general). He scorned the police with special enmity. He and my mother went to great pains to impress on me that it was the worst form of niggerism to hook and jab, cut and stab at other blacks.

Papa took me to his little place on Lake and fed me, walked me through the wildest of the nation's jungles, pointing up the foibles of black response to crisis existence. I loved him. He died alone in southern Illinois the fifth year that I was in San Quentin, on a pension that after rent allowed for a diet of little more than sardines and crackers.

After Racine Street we moved into the Troop Street projects, which in 1958 were the scenes of the city's worst

9

riots. (The cats in those projects fell out against the pig with heavy machine guns, 30s and 50s that were equipped with tracer ammunition.)

My troubles began when we were in the projects. I was caught once or twice for mugging but the pig never went much further than to pop me behind the ear with the "oak stick" several times and send for my mortified father to carry me home.

My family knew very little of my real life. In effect, I lived two lives, the one with my mama and sisters, and the thing on the street. Now and then I'd get caught at something, or with something that I wasn't supposed to have and my mama would fall all over me. I left home a thousand times, never to return. We hoboed up and down the state. I did what I wanted (all my life I've done just that). When it came time to explain, I lied.

I had a girl from Arkansas, finest at the mission, but the nuns had convinced her that love—touching fingertips, mouths, bellies, legs—was nasty. Most of my time and money went to the other very loose and lovely girls I met on the stairwells of the projects' 15-story buildings. That was our hangout, and most of the time that's where we acted out the ritual. Jonathan, my new comrade, just a baby then, was the only real reason that I would come home at all; a brother to help me plunder the white world, a father to be proud of the deed—I was a fanciful little cat. But my brother was too young of course. He's only seventeen now while I'm twenty-nine this year. Any my father, he was always mortified. I stopped attending school regularly, and started getting "picked up" by the pigs more often. The pig station, a lecture, and oak-stick therapeutics. These pickups were mainly for "suspicion of" or because I was in the wrong part of town. Except for once or twice I was never actually caught breaking any laws. There just wasn't any possibility of a policeman beating me in a footrace. A target that's really moving with evasive tactics is almost impossible to hit with a short-barreled revolver. Through a gangway with a gate that only a few can operate with speed

10

(it's dark even in the day) up a stairway through a door. Across roofs with seven- to ten-foot jumps in between (the pig is working mainly for money, bear in mind, I am running for my life). There wasn't a pig in the city who could "follow the leader" of even the most timid ghetto gang.

My father sensed a need to remove me from the Chicago environment so in 1956 he transferred his post-office job to the Los Angeles area. He bought an old '49 Hudson, threw me into it, and the two of us came West with plans to send for the rest of the family later that year. I knew nothing of cars. It was the first car our family had ever owned. I watched my father with great interest as he pushed the Hudson across the two thousand miles from Chicago to Los Angeles in two days. I was certain that I could handle the standard gearshift and pedals. I asked him to let me try upon our arrival in Los Angeles that first day. He dismissed me with an "Ah—crazy nigger lay dead" look. We were to stay with his cousin Johnny Jones in Watts until the rest of the family could be sent for. He went off with Johnny to visit other relatives, I stayed behind with the keys and the car. I made one corner, down one street, waited for a traffic light, firmed my jaw, dry-swallowed—took off around the next corner, and ended the turn inside the plate-glass window and front door of the neighborhood barbershop. Those cats in the shop (Watts) had become so immune to excitement that no one hardly looked up. I tried to apologize. The brother that owned the shop allowed my father to do the repair work himself. No pigs were called to settle this affair between brothers. One showed up by chance, however. I had to answer a court summons later that year. But the brother sensed that my father was poor, like himself, with a terribly mindless, displaced, irresponsible child on his hands, probably like his own, and didn't insist upon having the gun-slinging pig from the outside enemy culture arbitrate the problems we must handle ourselves.

My father fixed the brother's shop with his own hands, after buying the materials. No charges were brought against me

11

for the damages. My father straightened out the motor bed, plugged the holes in the radiator, hammered out some of the dents and folds from the fender, bought a new light, and taped it into place on the fender. He drove that car to and from work, to the supermarkets with my mother, to church with my sisters, for four years! It was all he could afford and he wasn't the least bit ashamed of the fact. And he never said a word to me about it. I guess he was convinced by then that words wouldn't help me. I've been a fool—often.

Serious things started to happen after our settling in L.A. but this guy never abandoned me. He felt shame in having to bail me out of encounters with the law but he would always be there. I did several months in Paso Robles for allegedly breaking into a large department store (Gold's on Central) and attempting a hijack. I was 15, and full grown (I haven't grown an inch since then). A cop shot me six times point-blank on that job, as I was standing with my hands in the air. After the second shot, when I was certain that he was trying to murder me, I charged him. His gun was empty and he had only hit me twice by the time I had closed with him—"Oh, get this wild nigger off me." My mother fell away from the phone in a dead faint when they informed her that I had been shot by the police in a hijack attempt. I had two comrades with me on that job. They both got away because of the exchange between the pigs and me.

Since all black are thought of as rats, the third degree started before I was taken to the hospital. Medical treatment was offered as a reward for cooperation. At first they didn't know I had been hit, but as soon as they saw the blood running from my sleeve, the questions began. A bullet had passed through my forearm, another had sliced my leg, I sat in the back of the pig car and bled for two hours before they were convinced that lockjaw must have set in already. They took me to that little clinic at the Maxwell Street Station. A black nurse or doctor attended. She was young, full of sympathy and advice. She suggested, since I had strong-looking

12

legs, that instead of warring with the enemy culture I should get interested in football or sports. I told her that if she could manage to turn the pig in the hall for a second I could escape and perhaps make a new start somewhere with a football. A month before this thing happened a guy had sold me a motorcycle and provided a pink slip that proved to be forged or changed around in some way. The bike was hot and I was caught with it. Taken together these two things were enough to send me to what California calls Youth Authority Corrections. I went to Paso Robles.

The very first time, it was like dying. Just to exist at all in the cage calls for some heavy psychic readjustments. Being captured was the first of my fears. It may have been inborn. It may have been an acquired characteristic built up over the centuries of black bondage. It is the thing I've been running from all my life. When it caught up to me in 1957 I was fifteen years old and not very well-equipped to deal with sudden changes. The Youth Authority joints are places that demand complete capitulation; one must cease to resist altogether or else . . .

The employees are the same general types found lounging at all prison facilities. They need a job—any job; the state needs goons. Chino was almost new at the time. The regular housing units were arranged so that at all times one could see the lockup unit. It think they called it "X". We existed from day to day to avoid it. How much we ate was strictly controlled, so was the amount of rest. After lights went out, no one could move from his bed without a flash of the pigs' handlight. During the day the bed couldn't be touched. There were so many compulsories that very few of us could manage to stay out of trouble even with our best efforts. Everything was programmed right down to the precise spoonful. We were made to march in military fashion everywhere we went—to the gym, to the mess hall, to compulsory prayer meetings. And then we just marched. I pretended that I couldn't hear well or understand anything but the simplest directions so I was never given anything but the simplest work. I was lucky; always when my mind failed me I've had great luck to carry me through.

All my life I've done exactly what I wanted to do just when I wanted, no more, perhaps less sometimes, but never any more, which explains why I had to be jailed. "Man was born free. But everywhere he is in chains." I never adjusted. I haven't adjusted even yet, with half my life already spent in prison. I can't truthfully say prison is any less painful now than during that first experience.

In my early prison years I read all of Rafael Sabatini, particularly *The Lion's Skin*. "There once was a man who sold the lion's skin, while the beast still lived, and was killed while hunting him" This story fascinated me. It made me smile even under the lash. The hunter bested, the hunted stalking the hunter. The most predatory animal on earth turning on its oppressor and killing it. At the time, this ideal existed in me just above the conscious level. It helped me to define myself, but it would take me several more years to isolate my real enemy. I read Jack London's, "raw and naked, wild and free' military novels and dreamed of smashing my enemies entirely, overwhelming, vanquishing, crushing them completely, sinking my fangs into the hunter's neck and never, never letting go.

Capture, imprisonment, is the closest to being dead that one is likely to experience in this life. There were no beatings (for me at least) in this youth joint and the food wasn't too bad. I came through it. When told to do something I simply played the idiot, and spent my time reading. The absentminded bookworm, I was in full revolt by the time seven months were up.

I went to school in Paso Robles and covered the work required for 10th-year students in the California school system, and entered Manual Arts for the 11th year upon my release. After I got out I stopped in Bakersfield, where I planned to stay no more than a week or two. I met a woman who felt almost as unimpressed with life as I did. We sinned, I

14

stayed. I was 16 then, just starting to get my heft, but this wonderful sister, so round and wild, firm and supple, mature . . . in one month she reduced my health so that I had to take to the bed permanently. I was ill for eleven days with fevers and chest pains (something in the lungs). When I pulled out of it I was broke. I'd collected a few friends by that time. Two of them would try anything. Mat and Obe. We talked, borrowed a car, and went off.

A few days later we were all three in county jail (Kern County) on suspicion of committing a number of robberies. Since the opposition cleans up the books when they find the right type of victim, they accused us of a number of robberies we knew nothing about. Since they had already identified me for one, I copped out to another and cleared Mat and Obe on that count. They "allowed" Obe to plead guilty to one robbery instead of the three others they threatened him with. They cleared Mat altogether. Two months after our arrest Mat left the county jail free of charges.

I was in the "time tank" instead of the felony tank because they had only two felony tanks (that was the old county jail) and they wanted to keep the three of us separated. After Mat left, a brother came into the time tank to serve 2 days. The morning he was scheduled to leave I went back to his cell with a couple of sheets and asked him if he would aid me in an escape attempt. He dismissed me with one of those looks and a wave of the hand. I started tearing the sheet in stripes, he watched. When I was finished he asked me, "What are you doin' with that sheet?" I replied, "I'm tearing it into these strips." "Why you doin' that?" "I'm making a rope." "What-chew gonna do with ah rope?" "Oh—I'm going to tie you up with it."

When they called him to be released that morning, I went out in his place. I've learned one very significant thing for our struggle here in the U.S.: all blacks do look alike to certain types of white people. White people tend to grossly underestimate all blacks, out of habit. Blacks have been over-

15

estimating whites in a conditioned reflex.

Later, when I was accused of robbing a gas station of seventy dollars, I accepted a deal—I agreed to confess and spare the county court costs in return for a light county jail sentence. I confessed but when time came for sentencing, they tossed me into the penitentiary with one to life. That was in 1960. I was 18 years old. I've been here ever since. I met Marx, Lenin, Trotsky, Engels, and Mao when I entered prison and they redeemed me. For the first four years I studied nothing but economics and military ideas. I met black guerrillas, George "Big Jake"Lewis, and James Carr, W.L. Nolen, Bill Christmas, Torry Gibson and many, many others. We attempted to transform the black criminal mentality into a black revolutionary mentality. As a result, each of us has been subjected to years of the most vicious reactionary violence by the state. Our mortality rate is almost what you would expect to find in a history of Dachau. Three of us were murdered several months ago by a pig shooting from 30 feet above their heads with a military rifle.

I am being tried in court right now with two other brothers, John Clutchette and Fleeta Drumgo, for the alleged slaying of a prison guard. This charge carries an automatic death penalty for me. I can't get life. I already have it.

When I returned to San Quentin Prison last week from a year in Soledad Prison where the crime I am charged with took place, a brother who had resisted the logic of proletarian-people's revolutionary socialism for the blackman in America sent me these lines in a note:

"Without the cold and desolation of winter there
could not be the warmth and splendor of spring!
Calamity has hardened my mind, and turned it to steel!!
Power to the People"

George

16

APRIL, 1970

*Dear Fay,**

On the occasion of your and Senator Dymally's tour and investigation into the affairs here at Soledad, I detected in the questions posed by your team a desire to isolate some rationale that would explain why racism exists at the prison with "particular prominence." Of course the subject was really too large to be dealt with in one tour and in the short time they allowed you, but it was a brave scene. My small but mighty mouthpiece, and the black establishment senator and his team, invading the state's maximum security row in the worst of its concentration camps. I think you are the first woman to be allowed to inspect these facilities. Thanks from all. The question was too large, however. It's tied into the question of why all these California prisons vary in character and flavor in general. It's tied into the larger question of why racism exists in this whole society with "particular prominence," tied into history. Out of it comes another question. Why do California joints produce more Bunchy Carters and Eldridge Cleavers than those over the rest of the country?

I understand your attempt to isolate the set of localized circumstances that give to this particular prison's problems of race is based on a desire to aid us right now, in the present crisis. There are some changes that could be made right now that would alleviate some of the pressures inside this and other

*Mrs. Fay Stender, the author's lawyer.

17

prisons. But to get at the causes, you know, one would be forced to deal with questions at the very center of Amerikan political and economic life, at the core of the Amerikan historical experience. This prison didn't come to exist where it does just by happenstance. Those who inhabit it and feed off its existence are historical products. The great majority of Soledad pigs are southern migrants who do not want to work in the fields and farms of the area, who couldn't sell cars or insurance, and who couldn't tolerate the discipline of the army. And of course prisons attract sadists. After one concedes that racism is stamped unalterably into the present nature of Amerikan sociopolitical and economic life in general (the definition of fascism is: a police state wherein the political ascendancy is tied into and protects the interests of the upper class—characterized by militarism, *racism*, and imperialism), and concedes further that criminals and crime arise from material, economic, sociopolitical causes, we can then burn *all* of the criminology and penology libraries and direct our attention where it will do some good.

The logical place to begin any investigation into the problems of California prisons is with our "pigs are beautiful" Governor Reagan, radical reformer turned reactionary. For a real understanding of the failure of prison policies, it is senseless to continue to study the criminal. All of those who can afford to be honest know that the real victim, that poor, uneducated, disorganized man who finds himself a convicted criminal, is simply the end result of a long chain of corruption and mismanagement that starts with people like Reagan and his political appointees in Sacramento. After one investigates Reagan's character (what makes a turncoat) the next logical step in the inquiry would be a look into the biggest political prize of the state—the directorship of the Department of Correction.

All other lines of inquiry would be like walking backward. You'll never see where you're going. You must begin with directors, assistant directors, adult authority boards, roving

18

boards, supervisors, wardens, captains, and guards. You have to examine these people from director down to guard before you can logically examine their product. Add to this some concrete and steel, barbed wire, rifles, pistols, clubs, the tear gas that killed Brother Billingslea in San Quentin in February 1970, while he was locked in his cell and the pick handles of Folsom, San Quentin, and Soledad.

To determine how men will behave once they enter the prison it is of first importance to know that prison. Men are brutalized by their environment—not the reverse.

I gave you a good example of this when I saw you last. Where I am presently being held, they never allow us to leave our cell without first handcuffing us and belting or chaining the cuffs to our waists. This is preceded always by a very thorough skin search. A force of a dozen or more pigs can be expected to invade the row at any time searching and destroying personal effects. The attitude of the staff toward the convicts is both defensive and hostile. Until the convict gives in completely it will continue to be so. By giving in, I mean prostrating oneself at their feet. Only then does their attitude alter itself to one of paternalistic condescension. Most convicts don't dig this kind of relationship (though there are some who do love it) with a group of individuals demonstrably inferior to the rest of the society in regard to education, culture, and sensitivity. Our cells are so far from the regular dining area that our food is always cold before we get it. Some days there is only one meal that can be called cooked. We *never* get anything but cold-cut sandwiches for lunch. There is no variety to the menu. The same things week after week. One is confined to his cell 23½ hours a day. Overt racism exists unchecked. It is not a case of the pigs trying to stop the many racist attacks; they actively encourage them.

They are fighting upstairs right now. It's 11:10 A.M., June 11. No black is supposed to be on the tier upstairs with anyone but other blacks but—mistakes take place—and one or two blacks end up on the tier with 9 or 10 white convicts

19

frustrated by the living conditions or openly working with the pigs. The whole ceiling is trembling. In hand-to-hand combat we always win; we lose sometimes if the pigs give them knives or zip guns. Lunch will be delayed today, the tear gas or whatever it is drifts down to sting my nose and eyes. Someone is hurt bad. I hear the meat wagon from the hospital being brought up. Pigs probably gave them some weapons. But I must be fair. Sometimes (not more often than necessary) they'll set up one of the Mexican or white convicts. He'll be one who has not been sufficiently racist in his attitudes. After the brothers (enraged by previous attacks) kick on this white convict whom the officials have set up, he'll fall right into line with the rest.

I was saying that the great majority of the people who live in this area of the state and seek their employment from this institution have overt racism as a *traditional* aspect of their characters. The only stops that regulate how far they will carry this thing come from the fear of losing employment here as a result of the outside pressures to control the violence. That is O Wing, Max (Maximum Security) Row Soledad—in part anyway.

Take an individual who has been in the general prison population for a time. Picture him as an average convict with the average twelve-year-old mentality, the nation's norm. He wants out, he wants a woman and a beer. Let's say this average convict is white and has just been caught attempting to escape. They may put him on Max Row. This is the worst thing that will ever happen to him. In the general population facility there are no chains and cuffs. TVs, radios, record players, civilian sweaters, keys to his own cell for daytime use, serve to keep his mind off his real problems. There is also a recreation yard with all sorts of balls and instruments to strike or thrust at. There is a gym. There are movies and a library well stocked with light fiction. And of course there is work, where for 2 or 3 cents an hour convicts here at Soledad make paper products, furniture, and clothing. Some people actually like this work

20

since it does provide some money for the small things and helps them to get through their day—*without thinking* about their real problems.

Take an innocent con out of this general population setting (because a pig "thought" he may have seen him attempting a lock). Bring him to any part of O Wing (the worst part of the adjustment center of which Max Row is a part). He will be cuffed, chained, belted, pressured by the police who think that every convict should be an informer. He will be pressured by the white cons to join their racist brand of politics (they *all* go under the nickname "Hitler's Helpers"). If he is presidposed to help black he will be pushed away—by black. Three weeks is enough. The strongest hold out no more than a couple of weeks. There has been *one* white many only to go through this O Wing experience without losing his balance, without allowing himself to succumb to the madness of ribald, protrusive racism.

It destroys the logical processes of the mind, a man's thoughts become completely disorganized. The noise, madness streaming from every throat, frustrated sounds from the bars, metallic sounds from the walls, the steel trays, the iron beds bolted to the wall, the hollow sounds from a cast-iron sink or toilet.

The smells, the human waste thrown at us, unwashed bodies, the rotten food. When a white con leaves here he's ruined for life. No black leaves Max Row walking. Either he leaves on the meat wagon or he leaves crawling licking at the pig's feet.

Ironic, because one cannot get a parole to the outside prison directly from O Wing, Max Row. It's positively not done. The parole board won't even consider the Max Row case. So a man licks at the feet of the pig not for a release to the outside world but for the privilege of going upstairs to O Wing adjustment center. There the licking process must continue if a parole is the object. You can count on one hand the number of people who have been paroled to the streets

21

from O Wing proper in all the years that the prison has existed. No one goes from O Wing, Max Row straight to the general prison population. To go from here to the outside world is unthinkable. A man *must* go from Max Row to the regular adjustment center facility upstairs. Then from there to the general prison population. Only then can he entertain throughts of eventual release to the outside world.

One can understand the depression felt by an inmate on Max Row. He's fallen as far as he can into the social trap, relief is so distant that is very easy for him to lose his holds. In two weeks that little average man who may have ended up on Max Row for *suspicion* of *attempted* escape is so brutalized, so completely without holds, that he will never heal again. It's worse than Vietnam.

He's dodging lead. He may be forced to fight a duel to the death with knives. If he doesn't sound and act more zealous than everyone else he will be challenged for not being loyal to his race and its politics, fascism. Some of these cons support the pigs' racism without shame, the others support it inadvertently by their own racism. The former are white, the latter black. But in here as on the street black racism is a forced *reaction*. A survival adaptation.

The picture that I have painted of Soledad's general population facility may have made it sound not too bad at all. That mistaken impression would result from the absence in my description of one more very important feature of the main line—terrorism. A frightening, petrifying diffusion of violence and intimidation is emitted from the offices of the warden and captain. How else could a small group of armed men be expected to hold and rule another much larger group except through *fear*?

We have a gym (inducement to throw away our energies with a ball instead of revolution). But if you walk into this gym with a cigarette burning, you're probably in trouble. There is a pig waiting to trap you. There's a sign "No Smoking." If you miss the sign, trouble. If you drop the

22

cigarette to comply, trouble. The floor is regarded as something of a fire hazard (I'm not certain what the pretext is). There are no receptacles. The pig will pounce. You'll be told in no uncertain terms to scrape the cigarette from the floor with your hands. It builds from there. You have a gym but only certain things may be done and in specified ways. Since the rules change with the pigs' mood, it is really safer for a man to stay in his cell.

You have work with emoluments that range from nothing to three cents an hour! But once you accept the pay job in the prison's industrial sector you cannot get out without going through the bad conduct process. When workers are needed, it isn't a case of accepting a job in this area. You take the job or you're automatically refusing to work, even if you clearly stated that you would cooperate in other employment. The same atmosphere prevails on the recreation yard where any type of minor mistake could result not in merely a bad conduct report and placement in adjustment center, but death. A fistfight, a temporary, trivial loss of temper will bring a fusillade of bullets down on the darker of the two men fighting.

You can't begin to measure the bad feeling caused by the existence of one TV set shared by 140 men. Think! One TV, 140 men. If there is more than one channel, what's going to occur? In Soledad's TV rooms there has been murder, mayhem, and destruction of many TV sets.

The blacks occupy one side of the room and the whites and Mexicans the other. (Isn't it significant in some way that our numbers in prison are sufficient to justify the claiming of half of all these facilities?)

We have a side, they have a side. What does your imagination envisage out of a hypothetical situation where Nina Simone sings, Angela Davis speaks, and Jim Brown "splits" on one channel, while Merle Haggard yodels and begs for an ass kicking on another. The fight will follow immediately after some brother, who is less democratic than he is starved for beauty (we did vote but they're 60 to our 40), turns the station to see Angela Davis. What lines do you think the fighting will be along? Won't it be Angela and me against Merle Haggard?

But this situation is tolerable at least up to a point. It was worse. When I entered the joint on this offense, they had half and we had half, but out half was in the back.

In a case like the one just mentioned, the white convicts will start passing the word among themselves that all whites should be in the TV room to vote in the "Cadillac cowboy." The two groups polarize out of a situation created by whom? It's just like the outside. Nothing at all complicated about it. When people walk on each other, when disharmony is the norm, when organisms start falling apart it is the fault of these whose responsibility it is to govern. They're doing something wrong. They shouldn't have been trusted with the responsibility. And long-range political activity isn't going to help that man who will die tomorrow or tonight. The apologists recognize that these places are controlled by absolute terror, but they justify the pig's excesses with the argument that we exist outside the practice of any civilized codes of conduct. Since we are convicts rather than men, a bullet through the heat, summary execution for fistfighting or stepping across a line is not extreme or unsound at all. An official is allowed full range in violent means because a convict can be handled no other way.

Fay, have you ever considered what type of man is capable of handling absolute power. I mean how many would not abuse it? Is there any way of isolating or classifying generally who can be trusted with a gun and *absolute* discretion as to who he will kill? I've already mentioned that most of them are KKK types. The rest, all the rest, in general, are so stupid that they shouldn't be allowed to run their own bath. A *responsible* state government would have found a means of weeding out most of the savage types that are drawn to gunslinger jobs long ago. How did all these pigs get through?! Men who can barely

24

read, write, or reason. How did they get through!!? You may as well give a baboon a gun and set him loose on us!! It's the same in here as on the streets out there. *Who* has loosed this thing on an already suffering people? The Reagans, Nixons, the men who have, who own. Investigate them!! There are no qualifications asked, no experience necessary. Any fool who falls in here and can sign his name might shoot me tomorrow from a position 30 feet above my head with an automatic military rifle!! He could be dead drunk. It could really be an accident (a million to one it won't be, however), but he'll be protected still. He won't even miss a day's wages.

The textbooks on criminology like to advance the idea that prisoners are mentally defective. There is only the merest suggestion that the system itself is at fault. Penologists regard prisons as asylums. Most policy is formulated in a bureau that operates under the heading Department of Corrections. But what can we say about these asylums since *none* of the inmates are ever cured. Since in every instance they are sent out of the prison more damaged physically and mentally than when they entered. Because that is the reality. Do you continue to investigate the inmate? Where does administrative responsibility begin? Perhaps the administration of the prison cannot be held accountable for every individual act of their charges, but when things fly apart along racial lines, when the breakdown can be traced so clearly to circumstances even beyond the control of the guards and administration, investigation of anything outside the tenets of the fascist system itself is futile.

Nothing has improved, nothing has changed in the weeks since your team was here. We're on the same course, the blacks are fast losing the last of their restraints. Growing numbers of blacks are openly passed over when paroles are considered. They have become aware that their only hope lies in resistance. They have learned that resistance is actually possible. The holds are beginning to slip away. Very few men imprisoned for economic crimes or even crimes of passion

25

against the oppressor feel that they are really guilty. Most of today's black convicts have come to understand that they are the most abused victims of an unrighteous order. Up until now, the prospect of parole has kept us from confronting our captors with any real determination. But now with the living conditions of these places deteriorating, and with the sure knowledge that we are slated for destruction, we have been transformed into an implacable army of liberation. The shift to the revolutionary antiestablishment position that Huey Newton, Eldridge Cleaver, and Bobby Seale projected as a solution to the problems of Amerika's black colonies has taken firm hold of these brothers' minds. They are now showing great interest in the thoughts of Mao Tse-tung, Nkrumah, Lenin, Marx, and the achievements of men like Che Guevara, Giap, and Uncle Ho.

Some people are going to get killed out of this situation that is growing. That is not a warning (or wishful thinking). I see it as an "unavoidable consequence" of placing and leaving control of our lives in the hands of men like Reagan.

These prisons have always borne a certain resemblance to Dachau and Buchenwald, places for the bad niggers, Mexicans, and poor whites. But the last ten years have brought an increase in the percentage of blacks for crimes that can *clearly* be traced to political-economic causes. There are still some blacks here who consider themselves criminals—but not many. Believe me, my friend, with the time and incentive that these brothers have to read, study, and think, you will find no class or category more aware, more embittered, desperate, or dedicated to the ultimate remedy—revolution. The most dedicated, the best of our kind—you'll find them in the Folsoms, San Quentins, and Soledads. They live like there was no tomorrow. And for most of them there isn't. Somewhere along the line they sensed this. Life on the installment plan, three years of prison, three months on parole; then back to start all over again, sometimes in the same cell. Parole officers have sent brothers back to the joint for selling newspapers (the

26

Black Panther paper). Their official reason is "Failure to Maintain Gainful Employment," etc.

We're something like 40 to 42 percent of the prison population. Perhaps more, since I'm relying on material published by the media. The leadership of the black prison population now definitely identifies with Huey, Bobby, Angela, Eldridge, and antifascism. The savage repression of blacks which can be estimated by reading the obituary columns of the nation's dailies, Fred Hampton, etc., has not failed to register on the black inmates. The holds are fast being broken. Men who read Lenin, Fanon, and Che don't riot, "they mass," "they rage," they dig graves.

When John Clutchette was first accused of this murder he was proud, conscious, aware of his own worth but uncommitted to any specific remedial action. Review the process that they are sending this beautiful brother through now. It comes at the end of a long train of similar incidents in his prison life. Add to this all of the things he has witnessed happening to others of our group here. Comrade Fleeta spent eleven months here in O Wing for possessing photography taken from a newsweekly. It is such things that explain why California prisons produce more than their share of Bunchy Carters and Eldridge Cleavers.

Fay, there are only two types of blacks ever released from these places, the Carters and the broken men.

The broken men are so damaged that they will never again be suitable members of any sort of social unit. Everything that was still good when they entered the joint, anything inside of them that may have escaped the ruinous effects of black colonial existence, anything that may have been redeemable when they first entered the joint—is gone when they leave.

This camp brings out the very best in brothers or destroys them entirely. But none are unaffected. None who leave here are normal. If I leave here alive, I'll leave nothing behind. They'll never count me among the broken men, but I can't say that I am normal either. I've been hungry too long. I've gotten

27

angry too often. I've been lied to and insulted too many times. They've pushed me over the line from which there can be no retreat. I *know* that they will not be satisfied until they've pushed me out of this existence altogether. I've been the victim of so many racist attacks that I could never relax again. My reflexes will never be normal again. I'm like a dog that has gone through the K−9 process.

This is not the first attempt the institution (camp) has made to murder me. It is the most determined attempt, but not the first.

I look into myself at the close of every one of these pretrial days for any changes that may have taken place. I can still smile now, after ten years of blocking knife thrusts and pick handles; of anticipating and faceless sadistic pigs, reacting for ten years, seven of them in Solitary. I can still smile sometimes, but by the time this thing is over I may not be a nice person. And I just lit my seventy-seventh cigarette of this 21-hour day. I'm going to lay down for two or three hours, perhaps I'll sleep . . .

Seize the Time.

JUNE, 1970
12

You know I had a visit yesterday from an old friend, Joan. They told her she couldn't come back again, an economy move. It costs the state too much to supervise my half-hour visits, so I'll be held incommunicado it seems. They turned my sister away today. Someone is going to have to come up with some guts. These fools must be stopped.

28

Absolute power in the hands of idiots! It makes me think of Rome and England. Do you know where the barbarians and guerrillas are going to come from to destroy Imperial Amerika, from the black colonies and these concentration camps. The three of us are the only convicts in this joint who have to accept half-hour visits, with a special guard, handcuffed and chained. Now it seems we won't even get that. My sister, my brother can't visit me in what could be the last days of my life! Well, one good thing comes from this experience; no question remains in the minds of any member of my family as to where their energies would best be spent. My father will have a whole den of Panthers there to feed.

With each attempt the pigs made on my life in San Quentin, I would send an SOS out to my family. They would always respond by listening and writing letters to the joint pigs and Sacramento rats, but they didn't entirely accept that I was telling them the truth about the pig mentality. I would get dubious stares when I told them the lieutenants and the others who propositioned some of the most vicious white convicts in the state: "Kill Jackson, we'll do you some good." You understand, my father wanted to know why. And all I could tell him was that I related to Mao and couldn't kowtow. His mind couldn't deal with it. I would use every device, every historical and current example I could reach to explain to him that there were no-good pigs. But the task was too big, I was fighting his mind first, and his fear of admitting the existence of an identifiable enemy element that was oppressing us because that would either commit him to attack that enemy or force him to admit his cowardice. I was also fighting the establishment's public relations and propaganda machine. The prisons all use the clean, straight faces, or the old, harmless-looking pigs to work in areas where they must come in contact with free people. And these pigs are never allowed to use their tusks. Regarding the racism, my father would remind me that there were black pigs too. But, of course, that means nothing at all. They simply work around the blacks when necessary.

29

One guard or two guards working together is all that's needed to murder any con in the joint. But it isn't really necessary to work around the black pigs. They'll all cooperate or turn their heads.

The black cop could be a large factor in preventing our genocide. But no help can be expected from that quarter. The same stupidity and desperation that brought him to the gates prevents him from interceding. The job, the wage means too much to him. Often he feels compelled to prove himself, prove that he is loyal to the force, prove that he is not prejudiced in favor of us, prove that he is honest. His honesty prevents him from dealing in contraband as every white pig does. Look, I was in San Quentin for seven straight years. I knew *everything* that was brought in and by whom. The white pig actually considers it his privilege to supplement his income by bringing in and selling narcotics, weapons, and, of course, pornography. The black pig is afraid, too unsure of his position to be dishonest.

This same fear will cause him to show more zeal in the "club therapy" sessions than even the whites manage. If the victim is black, he's going to get so mad that the white pigs will have to stand back and let him swing. If they don't have murder planned for that session, they'll have to pull that nigger off of you. A pig—is a pig.

It all falls into place. I see the whole thing much clearer now, how fascism has taken possession of this country. the interlocking dictatorship from country level on up to the Grand Dragon in Washington, D.C.

The solidarity between the prison here and the court in Salinas, between the judge and grand jury, the judge and the D.A. and other city officials. The institution has effectively cut me off from any relief. The *un*meek have taken over this whole county, the state, the entire country. They work together, to the same end, effective control.

I knew of these links before this, long before this, but

seeing it in operation is pretty frightening. What force binds them together? I'm referring to the intermediary, the physical thing, not the ideal. What is it that really ties that fat rat with a chain of department stores to a uniformed pig? The fat rat wants the country and world policed, made safe for his business to expand. But how does he sell the ideal to the man who must do the policing? Money is the bond I think. They're in it for the money, these pigs and skinny rats. The fascist ideal doesn't really take hold until one gets into the upper levels of the power pyramid. Then any ideal that preserves becomes attractive.

People's government would decentralize this power that they hold over us—these men must be stopped.

Power to the People.

George

JUNE, 1970
13

Dear Fay,

No one here knows about the scheduled court hearing. They say we're not going. The prison doesn't like moving us, so somehow they have managed to arrange with the judge to *leave us out of our own trial*! Or pretrial. Can they try us in absentia (is that the term??)? Some bull (pig I mean) just

31

said that the judge under no circumstances wants us in his court. In that case they shouldn't mind dropping the whole thing or sending us to another county for trial. Berkeley perhaps. But as you've said more than likely it'll be Orange County.

Why do we accept this sort of thing? We have numerical superiority—but they have guns and money. And then the righteous don't like to cut throats, so we languish in misery.

When you finally get me out of this mess, you'll have to send me away somewhere for a while, somewhere like Cuba or China or Tanzania, so that I can reorient myself. My understanding had been strained to the utmost.

JUNE, 1970
14

I don't think we can afford to be nice much longer, the very last of our protection is eroding from under us. There will be no means of detecting when that last right is gone. You'll only know when they start shooting you. The process must be' checked somewhere between now and then, or we'll be fighting from a position of weakness with our backs against the wall. (I think we still have the advantage now.) We of the black colony know about that kind of action, fighting off of the wall. It's not the best way to get down.

It's getting tighter here, they're taking our visits. It looks as if they're stopping our court appearances. They also made a mistake concerning our "money draw" this month. This means we'll be without the little things even.

You may never read this letter either, our mail is being held back, returned, thrown away somewhere. Nice people aren't they? They richly deserve anything we can do to them. This man who just passed my cell counting, he'll never listen to reason. His mind isn't constructed that way. While we reason with him in ideals and ideas, he isn't listening. He is thinking about which rule he'll quote to dismiss us. When he walks away, you'll see the little code book protruding from his ass pocket. That's where he carries his mind, in his ass pocket. When we attack the problem with intellectualism we give away the advantage we have in numbers.

I'm with Bobby! We are going to have to kick him where he keeps his brain, in the region of the ass.

Power.

George

Letters
1964-1970

JUNE, 1964*

Dear Mother,

Are you well? I think of you often and would write more regularly than I do if I could but find the time. The things that I am working on demand a great deal of time. I guess this is so because it is my lot to have no one to help me.

Mama, and I mention this without vanity, I have made some giant steps toward acquiring the things that I personally will need if I am to be successful in my plans; aside from the factual material acquired from books and observations there is, as you know, a certain quality of character needed to perform the thing that I have in mind. I have completely repressed all

*All previous letters were accidentally destroyed. They were described by the author as "extremely bitter."

37

emotion; have learned to see myself in perspective, in true relation with other men and the world. I have enlarged my vision so that I may be able to think on a basis encompassing not just myself, my family, my neighborhood, but the world. I have completely arrested the susceptibility to think in theoretical terms, or give credence to religious, supernatural, or other shallow unnecessary things of this nature that lock the mind and hinder thinking.

When a man does something or possesses something that is complementary to his character, it is virtually impossible for him to hide this thing, keep it to himself, keep from telling it to those he wishes to impress; this is natural egoism, the need for attention and flattery asserting itself. I have quietly removed this need; neglect and loneliness have no effect whatever on me anymore. I feel no pain of mind or body, and the harder it gets the better I like it. I must rid myself of all sentiment and remove all possibility of love. Though I owe allegiance to no one other than myself I clearly understand that my future rests with the black people of the world. I am trying in every way possible to adjust my thinking habits so that their ways of life won't seem as strange and alien to me as these people over here would have it. After I am finished with myself, an observer who could read my thoughts and watch my actions would never believe that I was raised in the United States, and much less would he believe that I came from the lowest class, the black stratum of slave mentality.*

I have been meaning to ask you how Delora was doing with her husband in jail. I sincerely hope she is not finding it too hard, but life on the treadmill can be expected to be hard; if

*During his early years in prison, the author explained to the editor that he had completely lost faith in American blacks and their ability to become a truly revolutionary force. The only thing he wanted was to get out of prison and fight for Roberto in Angola or Lumumba in the Congo.

you will send me her address and ask her if she wants to write me, I will send the necessary forms to her.

Hang on, I'm going to make everything all right.

Your son,

George

SEPTEMBER, 1964

Dear Mother,

I went up yesterday and I'll have to say that it does not look too hopeful. I think my black brother crossed me, the one you met when you were here last. They made mention of my going to school. One of them told me in so many words to bring back a diploma. Maybe this was his meaning, maybe not. I will not know for sure until my official results come in on Friday of this week. I'll write you again then.

Lavera* came to see me this weekend, and said she will come again next weekend. I will tell her Saturday what I got at the board; she can contact you. But there is no need for that much disquiet; if I should get an immediate release there would still be weeks of formalities to go through.

We have birthdays this week. Though I have lost all of my sentimentality, I know you people still cling to the old, so I'll observe the social amenities by wishing you health on your

*The author's mother's niece.

birthday. Really though, is it not silly, the little pat phrases, Merry Christmas, Happy New Year, etc.? They (the Europeans) have reduced all life to a very dull formula. All natural feelings have been lost.

I have work here in my cell to do, see you soon.
Love,

George

DECEMBER, 1964

Dear Father,

I guess you are right in what you say about Mother's position. If she wishes to occupy the corner set aside for us in this society and be happy with such then let it be. I merely speak of better and different things in a society greater (in my humble opinion) and more conducive to advancement for people of my kind. Always bear in mind that though I may sound intolerant and pressing at times, all I say is by way of discourse and nothing by way of advice. You see I understand you people clearly. You are afflicted by the same set of principles that has always governed black people's ideas and habits here in the U.S. I know also how we arrived at this appalling state of decadence. You see, my father, we have been "educated" into an acceptance of our positions as national scapegraces. Our acceptance of the lie is consciously based on the supposition that peace can and must be preserved at any price. Blacks here in the U.S. apparently do not care how well they live, but are only concerned with how long they are able to live. This is odd indeed when considering that it is possible

40

for us all to live well, but within the reach of no man to live long! My deepest and most sincerely felt sympathies go out to all of you who are not able to resolve your problems because of this fundamental lack of spirit. The morass of illusionment has claimed your souls completely. I do not care about the other millions of blacks here in the land of tears, their fate is of their own choosing; but because you and the others of our family have always been close to me whatever successes I wring from the eternal foe you will share. Until I do this I know it is expecting too much for you to be impressed with the ideals I put forward. It's always been this way I imagine. One has to be shown the fruits and feel the rewards of a new or different thing before perceiving its merits.

In the airmail letter you sent it is not altogether clear to me what you were trying to say, so I won't leap to any conclusions but let me state that I have a singular incapability, which is my strongest point, my first principle. I could never in this existence betray my kind. Love of self and kind is the first law of nature, my father. What N. did to me in 1958 I can never forgive.* I can understand why she betrayed me to the whites and can even explain why she thought herself right in doing so, but I can't forgive her because she has not made any effort to change her completely backward sympathies. It is the same thing today with her as it was yesterday. She would betray me a second time if I allowed it. You know that I love

*"In 1958 I escaped from Kern County Jail and fought the pigs, all the way back to the midwestern area of my birth, '.45 smokeless' in hand. I lost them altogether in Chicago. The pigs gave up on me after about three months. I ended up in Harrisburg to await the return of my mother's half-brother, Amide Walker. I was hoping that he would help me get out of the country. While I was waiting for him, my aunt discovered through my family in California that I was on the run from the law. She turned in my name and I was recaptured."

41

my mother dearly for many reasons, she always (through your labor of course) provided for me materially the best she knew how, but she failed me bitterly in matters of the mind and spirit. My education she put in the hands of the arch-foes of my kind. This is a betrayal of the worst kind, because of this I've had to learn everything I now know on my own by trial and error. I have almost arrived but look at the cost. I would not be in prison now if she hadn't been reading life through those rose-colored glasses of hers, or if you would have had time and the wisdom to tell me of my enemies, and how to get the things I needed without falling into their traps. She kept telling me how wrong I was and making me feel guilty. All of this I now understand, but again cannot forgive because she is still doing this same sort of thing!!

I got the nuts and cake today thanks, socks and handkerchiefs also. Take care.

Son

DECEMBER, 1964

Dear Father,

Everything was in order, concerning the package that is. They brought it right in front of the cell and opened it.

Mama sent me a card with a picture of some white people on the front of it. I guess she just can't perceive that I don't want anything to do with her white god.

I am still confined to this cell. It is nine by four. I have left it only twice in the month I've been here for ten minutes each time, in which I was allowed to shower. Did I tell you? They have assured me that I have not been given a bad-conduct report. It is just that they felt I was about to do some wrong. It's always suspicions. What I was supposed to have done or was about to do, never, never what they caught me doing as it should be. The last time I was in a cell like this three months, from February to May (1964) for reasons that are not altogether clear yet! I have had no serious infraction in almost three years now. You know I had at least $125 on me when I was arrested in 1960 and they took it. I assume it was to cover the $70 that was missing as the result of the robbery. So I'm thinking that I shouldn't owe them too much more. You know in fact I'm fast awakening to the idea that I may not owe anyone anything and that they even might owe me. I have given four-and-a-half years of life, during which I have had to accept the unacceptable, for $70 that I didn't take—I protest. I protest.

If you knew how much I protested, how seriously I felt about the matter, you and Mother and anyone who has a natural affinity with me would surely be trying to convince me that you were on my side.

The events of the Congo, Vietnam, Malaya, Korea, and here in the U.S. are taking place all for the same reason. The commotion, the violence, the struggles in all these areas and many more spring from one source, the evil and malign, possessive and greedy Europeans. Their abstract theories, developed over centuries of long usage, concerning economics and sociology take the form that they do because they suffer under the mistaken belief that a man can secure himself in this insecure world best by ownership of great personal, private wealth. They attempt to impose their theories on the world for obvious reasons of self-gain. Their philosophy concerning government and economics has an underlying tone of selfishness, possessiveness, and greediness because their character is made up of these things. They can't see the merit in socialism and communism because they do not possess the qualities of

43

rational thought, generosity, and magnanimity necessary to be part of the human race, part of a social order, part of a system. They can not understand that "From each according to his abilities, to each according to his needs" is the only way men can live together without chaos. There is a species of fly that lives only four hours. If one of these flies (June fly I believe they are called), if one of these flies was born at twelve o'clock midnight in darkness and gloom, there would be no way possible for him in his lifetime to ever understand the concept of day and light. This is the case with the Europeans.

They are small men with their petty intrigues and prejudices. "In shallow men the fish of small thoughts cause much commotion, in magnanimous oceanic minds the whales of inspiration cause hardly a ruffle" (Mao Tse-tung).

George

FEBRUARY, 1965

Dear Mother,

I promised myself that I wouldn't write you again from here. I only take pen in hand when feeling moves me to do so. My feeling seems to be wasted on you. You know beyond question what my feelings are, I never think of anything trite or inconsequential anymore. I've forgotten the feeling of joy. I've long since had my last smile wrung unceremoniously from my hollow soul. I write home to you people, my people, the closest of my kind for understanding and advice. I attempt to advise you in areas of which experience has made me better informed. I get no understanding. If I followed the advice I receive it would only serve to enslave me further to this madness of our times. My advice falls upon deaf ears!

This is my reason for not wanting to write. What can I say further? It is clear you don't love me when you refuse to aid me the only way you can, the only way I expect! By telling me I am right and that I have your blessings. You see I am being frank: though I care about your feelings, I care more for your well-being. There are things brewing now that could ruin you completely if, when they break, you are in sympathy with wrong. Robert is the same way, he pretends or he may earnestly not feel the effects of the circumstances I attempt to explain. He is sympathetic to wrong. But I can overlook him more readily because of his almost complete lack of mental training. His past experiences have been very limited regarding the stimulus of academic learning, he is innocent. But not so with you, though your exposure was not all that it should have been, you are equipped with the basic fundamentals needed to guide one to the truth, should it be truth one favors. When I consider my own experience bought at the cost of these terrible years, supplemented in love and concern by your own experience and learning, what am I to think but that something is radically wrong, that I am being betrayed and have been betrayed. The question is one of grave proportions to me. I cannot stress this point too clearly. I mean to make sure this doesn't happen to me again or to my seed. If a person doesn't stand with me, he stands against me to my way of thinking. I feel that you have failed me Mama. I know that you have failed me. I also know that Robert has never held an opinion of his own. You have influenced his every thought ever since you have known him. You have always had the running of things. You have done him a disservice. You are doing Jon a disservice now. You are a woman, you think like a bourgeois woman. This is a predatory man's world. The real world calls for a predatory man's brand of thinking. Your way of viewing the world is necessarily bourgeois and feminine. How could I, Robert, Jon, or any of the men of our kind

45

accomplish what we must as men if we think like bourgeois women, or let our women think for us. This is what's happening all over this part of the world! Robert should have been stronger, should have had more time and freedom of movement. So should Grandfather, and Great-Grandfather. But they didn't and it isn't their fault. The cruelest and most suppressive treatment has always fallen to the males because they have not that tender defense the woman is born with. So understand me once and for all. I speak no further on the matter. You conceived and Robert sired a man. Nothing can turn me from my resolve. Make no further attempts. I am going to give my all to this thing, and if the victory is to fall to me, you and people like you must stand beside me, not lean or lie on me.

Robert tells me you are sick. I am writing to ask about the nature of your illness. I know a hope will not aid you any, but by whatever gods there be I hope and wish you well. There is much sickness and tears to come, some will fall to me also I guess, but my condition can only improve from where I stand now.

Fare you well.

Son

FEBRUARY, 1965
25

Dear Mother,

Your letter reached me late for some unknown reason. Has your health improved? I think you should relax; all has not been said or done yet. You are a little confused now for understandable reasons; things will be made clear before long. I should be out of here this year. I have complied with all of their demands: group counseling, school, clean conduct record. I go to board next time they meet. You could start writing letters to the Adult Authority now, the more the better. You know what to say: that I was young then and you see a vast change in my character now. Also say that you can and will help me with a place to stay.

I asked Robert to send me some shoes. Check with him on it. They have to be sent from Sears by the salesman, cost no more than $25, have the price or sales slip in the box, and in the way of type and size I want some old folks' comforts with high tops, 9–B. Nothing else, my feet need therapy in the worst way. Soon as you can on this, I want to get rid of these corns and sores before I get out.

I'm glad you weren't a singer or dancer. Pop was wise in that. The image held of the blacks in this part of the world is that we are proficient in but one or two areas only, the service trades or the physical entertainment fields (singers, dancers, boxers, baseball players).

Would you like to support the theory that we are good for nothing but to serve or entertain our captors?

In the society of our fathers and in the civilized world today, women feel it their obligation to be ever yielding and obedient to their men. Life is purposely made simple for them because of their nature, and they are happy. When the women outnumber the men in the black societies, the men take as many wives as they can afford, and care for them all equally. In the white for some nebulous reason the men can take only one . . . the rest are left to become prostitutes, nuns, or lesbians. In the civilized societies the women do light work, bear children, and lend purpose to the man's existence. They train children in the ways of wisdom that history has shown to be correct. Their job is to train the children in their early life to be men or women, not confused psychotics! This is a big job, to train and propagate the race!! Is this not enough? The rest is left to the men: government administration, the providing of means of subsistence, and defense, or maintenance of life and property against any who would deprive us of it, as the barbarian has and is still attempting to do. The white theory of "the emancipated woman" is a false idea. You will find it, as they are finding it, *the factor* in the breakdown of the family unit. Mama, all this struggle is unnecessary. Let's not create an atmosphere of competition among ourselves as they have done. Life is too short. There is too much for us to restore to its proper order and we are too wise. What do you think made the white guy write that life is "a tale told by an idiot, full of sound and fury, signifying nothing"—he felt frustrated and stupid.

Son

MARCH, 1965
12

Dear Mama,

The things you speak of are uppermost in my mind and my heart. I am not too manly or sophisticated to say that I love you and all the rest with a devotion and dedication that will continue to grow until I pass from this existence. Anything that will please you, and that falls within human accomplishment, I will carry out. I say this with confidence because of my certainty that you would never ask me to please you by surrendering my mental liberty and self-respect; I wouldn't want to live were these, my last two real possessions, to be lost.

Any confidence you put in me, Mama, will be well placed. This is not mere talk, my ego is nowhere involved. If we are to surmount these barriers standing between us, and finally work things around to our advantage, on a few points we must be agreed. You must listen to me. I've been trying to say something. Stop closing my voice off from your mind! My hair has started to turn gray and I'm beginning to look like an old man. My best efforts up to now have all fallen far short of their intended goals. I know, however, just as sure as day follows night that I will win the last round. That is the one I always win, the important one.

I feel that you understand the situation better than most who live on your level. From your last letter, I know you are

49

intelligent enough to understand. I have it before me now and I glean much to indicate that this is so. But there is much that has escaped your understanding, and it is quite reasonable that this be true. You have no way of learning and bettering. However, if you will honor my humble voice, I would very much like to pass on to you just a thought or two I have had. All that I ask is that you hear me, and think about what I say. Do not just read over the lines. Think of what I say in relation to things past, and the vague possibility that is our future. I'm not just another convict or "Negro." I'm one who really loves you and who has been observing with a practiced eye and an almost photographic memory. But first let me clear up one other incidental thing. Robert has never said anything unattractive or belittling about you. Each of his letters expresses almost total grief for the condition of your health. He blames me even, then himself, but never the right people. He feels he has failed you, me, and all the others, and he keeps trying to learn if I also blame him. Of course I do not blame him or you, or myself. I place the blame for the social ills that have caused us discomfort and unhappiness squarely upon the shoulders of those responsible: the people in control!!

It is mainly on this subject that I am going to speak now. To get it across I am going to write two letters, this one and another sheet also tonight. This should be read first for the idea to follow in logical order.*

I am going to do exactly as you say concerning the show of good conduct here. I have never raised my hand against any man, since I've been an adult that is, except in self-defense, but there has been an element of aggressiveness in the way that I have handled these incidents. I'll have to always defend my person, but I promise you that unless there is a direct threat to my existence I will never have another bit of trouble here. Understand though that you do not live in the real rip-and-tear

*California prison regulations limit the length of convict letters to both sides of one standard 8½ by 11 ruled sheet.

50

world. You have escaped it by surrendering your self-determination and freedom of thought in a tranquilizing conformity to the wishes of whoever may hold the strings. Consequently you do not know how hard it is to live in peace even for a short period with people who defy violence, and vilify peace and harmony.

George

MARCH, 1965
12

Dear Mama,

I will try what you advised. I know it to be the best way at this point in the little game. But should I fail you are not to say, "George is no good." You must try to understand that now, just as in the past, there are other considerations and influences that enter into the course of events that turn our lives one way or the other.

Have you ever wondered how you and I and all our kind lost their identity so fast? The last blacks were brought into this country only 75 to 80 years ago, three generations at most. This is too short a time for us to have lost as much as we have. No other people have completely been divorced from their own as we have in such a short period. I don't even know my name. Have you ever wondered about this? The answer is found in the fact that we lost control of the circumstances surrounding our lives. We were alienated from our sources,

51

isolated, and remolded to fit in certain forms, to fill a specific purpose. No consideration was or has ever been given to our being anything other than what we were originally intended to be (I ask for electronics or drafting and I'm told to be practical). You must realize, understand fully, that we have little or no control over our lives. You must then stop giving yourself pain by feeling that you failed somewhere. You have not failed. You have been failed, by history and events, and people over whom you had no control. Only after you understand this can you then go on to make the necessary alterations that will bring some purpose and value to your life; you must gain some control! I have said this to Robert a hundred times but it makes no impression at all. He writes back in the same vein as he did the time before I said anything. He just doesn't have the mental equipment. Will you look deeper and think on the matter and then explain to him? I was born knowing exactly nothing. I had no one, no one, to teach me the things of real value. The school systems are gauged to teach youth what to think, not how to think. Robert never had the time to say even hello, and neither of you really knew anything to give my anyway, because your parents knew nothing. Do you see where the cycle brings us, to the real source of the trouble, the alienation and the abandonment, the pressure from without, the system and its supporters? I didn't know either. So we must look to the people whose responsibility it is to see to it that the benefits of society pass down to all concerned for an answer. If a good god exists then they are the ones who must make an appeal to him for forgiveness: forgiveness for relinquishment and dereliction of duty! I don't need god, religion, belief, etc. I need control, control of the determining factors relating to the unquestioning support and loyalty of my mother, father, brothers, sisters. You need Robert and I need him and he needs you. We all need each other. The standards and emotions we have used in the past to regulate our relations defy all nature and run contrary to all known precedent. When did blood cease to be thicker than and more binding than all else? We must look to each other and destroy the barriers placed between us with trust, and love. I am committed and I will do all that I have to. I am equal to anything that is required. Help me when you can, the only way you can, by trying to understand.

I don't want a package this year; save the money; save all you can. I am living very badly now and just to stay alive is an ordeal, but I see something better. It is vague, and is a possibility at best, but I know a place, a refuge where people love and live.

George

MARCH, 1965
16

Dear Father,

I've been going through final examinations at school. Had to use all of my available time in study and have not been able to write like I should, but forgive me. They are over now and I did well.

I go before the board next week.

I didn't know about L.'s husband. That is too bad. She seems to be extremely unlucky in that area. She told me that the last husband she had was worse. Since that is the case I can feel nothing against her, but as you said, she should have explained. People are odd indeed, about money that is. The best method of testing a person's character is through money. The shocks and strains of this money-mad society are enough to ruin the purest of minds. Men are so deeply engaged in making a living that their very existence is shaped and dominated by the system of production. I'm thoroughly tired already, Pop. When I obtain what I need to work with, nothing could stop me from going home. That is where I will invest my money, resources, and talents. My labor shall be expanded where it will be appreciated. My taxes will go to an order and system of government that will in turn protect me and my interests. I shall not, as long as I call myself a man, compromise with tyranny. There are a few things that mean more to me than life. Though I must think of and plan for tomorrow, I cannot, I must not surrender for tomorrow all that I possess today. I can repair this loss, this morbid depression that owns a little more of my mind each day that passes. The pale and almost indistinguishable glow of the future may yet materialize to disperse the gloomy stupor that has encompassed me completely. I have been purposely kept ignorant, I have been taught *what* to think, instead of *how* to think. I have been subjected to the ordeal of hunger, thirst, name-calling, and other uncountable indignities. Danger comes even from those of my own kind. Their lack of response and unyielding adherence to ineffectual thought and action is an obstacle to my plans. I may yet surmount it, but only if I follow my call. I must obey the dictates of my mind.

Give my regards to all.

Son

MARCH, 1965
30

Dear Father,

I haven't read anything or studied in a week now. I have been devoting all my time to thought. I trust you are all in health. I think of my personal past quite often. This is uncomfortable sometimes but necessary. I try not to let my past mistakes bother me too much, though some seem almost unpardonable. If it were not for the few intermixed little victories, my confidence in my ability would be irreparably shaken.

Though I know I am a victim of social injustice and economic pressure and though I understand the forces that work to drive so many of our kind to places like this and to mental institutions, I can't help but know that I proceeded wrong somewhere. I could have done a lot worse. You know our people react in different ways to this neoslavery, some just give in completely and join the other side. They join some christian cult and cry out for integration. These are the ones who doubt themselves most. They are the weakest and hardest to reach with the new doctrine. Some become inveterate drinkers and narcotic users in an attempt to gain some mental solace for the physical depravity they suffer. I've heard them say, "There's no hope without dope." Some hire on as a janitor, bellboy, redcap, cook, elevator boy, singer, boxer, baseball player, or maybe a freak at some sideshow and pretend that all is as well as is possible. They think since it's always been this way it must always remain this way; these are the fatalists, they serve and entertain and rationalize.

Then there are those who resist and rebel but do not know what, who, why, or how exactly they should go about this. They are aware but confused. They are the least fortunate, for they end where I have ended. By using half measures and failing dismally to effect any real improvement in their condition, they fall victim to the full fury and might of the system's repressive agencies. Believe me, every dirty trick of deception and brutality is employed without shame, without honor, without humanity, without reservation to either convert or destroy a rebellious arm. Believe me, when I say that I begin to weary of the sun. I am by nature a gentle man, I love the simple things of life, good food, good wine, an expressive book, music, pretty black women. I used to find enjoyment in a walk in the rain, summer evenings in a place like Harrisburg. Remember how I used to love Harrisburg. All of this is gone from me, all the gentle, shy characteristics of the black men have been wrung unceremoniously from my soul. The buffets and blows of this have and have-not society have engendered in me a flame that will live, will live to grow, until it either destroys my tormentor or myself. You don't understand this but I must say it. Maybe when you remember this ten or twenty years from now you'll comprehend. I don't think of life in the same sense that you or most black men of your generation think of it, it is not important to me how long I live, I think only of how I live, how well, how nobly. We think if we are to be men again we must stop working for nothing, competing against each other for the little they allow us to possess, stop selling our women or allowing them to be used and handled against their will, stop letting our children be educated by the barbarian, using their language, dress, and customs, and most assuredly stop turning our cheeks.

George

APRIL, 1965
18

Dear Father,

Did you get my letter of April 11, last Sunday? I fear you may not have gotten that letter since therein I set down some important matters in an almost too direct manner* I did so thinking that if it was allowed to go through, you would have in your possession knowledge of the singular events that seem to rush upon me menacing and evil from all directions at once. You would have this information in as complete a form as the space of that single page allows, or if they had sent it back or destroyed it, nothing. This was logical in that I wanted you to know immediately. It is best to have such matters done, and related, and over with. Here in my position you know I'm not supposed to be critical, nor am I supposed to attempt to convey what goes on in here. So please acknowledge my letter. I have from you only the letters you wrote on April 1 and April 2. Have you sent others?

They are sending me to Folsom soon, so they told me. The assault charge was referred to the district attorney. He will in turn refer it to the grand jury, which will then bring what they call legal proceedings against me. Let me say here that all of

*All of Jackson's correspondence had to pass through the rigors of prison censorship. Much of it was completely destroyed or mutilated. Only his last letters to his lawyer passed through uncensored.

this is a well-thought-out effort to frighten me and maybe even do me whatever harm they can without alarming or shocking those around me, you included, too much. I guess they want to show me and those around me here how powerless I am in their hands. But they must do this without giving rise to feelings of total insecurity on the part of the little people which could serve as stimulus to some act which would lead toward changing conditions or circumstances that threaten not just our well-being but our very existence. Thus if I or any of my kind should suffer the final hurt, it would be by accident, heart attack instead of poisoning, malnutrition instead of beating, suicide by hanging instead of being shot, or legal proceedings instead of foul play.

But I have much to say about any matter that concerns me in spite of their wishes. Fear, the emotion that stiffens and inhibits the minds of most men, causing them to be incapable of acting in their defense at the moment of trial, is totally lacking in me. I could look upon my total ruin with as detached an unconcern as I look upon theirs. The payment for life is death. I have written many a page in the book of life in spite of my limited years, and I intend to write many more. I'll come out of this as I have everything else. I'll see Ghana yet.

Folsom is a better prison than this. There will be found many older inmates who are more stable and less inclined to mind others' business. I can also obtain a parole faster there or a transfer to some minimum security camp. On the assault charge I don't think they will convict me. Maybe won't even try me. The D.A. has to accept the case, and then the grand jury must be convinced to accept what evidence they may concoct against me.

Give Mother my regards.

Fare you well.

Son

MAY, 1965
2

Dear Mother and Father,

I am still in isolation. Nothing has changed since I wrote you last, Robert.* You have a remarkable method for relieving yourself of unpleasant or weighty problems that can almost be admired, were it just a little less chancy and not so slow. You seem to just ignore the matter or pretend it doesn't exist, hoping maybe others with more time or brains or perhaps more to lose will work something out. I have tried several times over the last few years to adopt this means of rationalization for my own relief. I tried it at the start of this last attack upon my well-being. Like you, I go to bed each night hoping that the morrow will bring about the needed change. I simply force all my awareness, all my many and monumental problems, from my remembrance. Without plans or forethought, without a hint of uneasiness, I go to bed each night, hoping, trying to avert the storm that is now coming on. I find each morning, as I found this one, freighted with possibilities of my own disaster. I still see the poverty among plenty, feel the curse of total insecurity. I still feel cramped within this cloud of ignorance which has been placed about me

*The author's father's name is Robert Lester Jackson. The author addresses him either as Robert or Lester depending on mood or circumstance.

purposely to make me act against my interests. My bed is just as hard as it was when I went to sleep, my clothing just as coarse and inadequate. Here in the isolation cell the pitifully light breakfasts are just the same. I went supperless to bed the night before. Each morning if I can find or beg a piece of soap I wash myself. This is indeed counted as good fortune. But I mustn't complain. It is un-American to do so. Like the rest of you I should be completely lacking in feeling for myself. I should smile and sing. Perhaps I should thank the lord in spite of the fact that I have had not one moment's mental gratification in all my twenty-three years. I find no relief in baseball and basketball games on the TV. The charges they bring against me now could cost me my life, the last of my possessions, the only thing they have heretofore left me with. But now that I think of it, I have always been forced to fear for my life, so this is nothing new. It merely more direct.

One of you send me twenty-five dollars as soon as you can after reading this. I will get out of isolation next week and be locked up in segregation (slightly better than this because we can draw money or articles from the prison store). I want to buy some envelopes, and books that I will be needing. Important because I have nothing. Have lost everything. If you can get it here soon enough I will be allowed to draw it this month.

Well, I've heard it said that the darkest hour falls just before dawn, so I brace myself to my tasks, never doubting in my ability to struggle on. I feel no defeat could overcome me, and fear no evil but fear itself perhaps. I have removed this emotion from my mind completely, and I languish in misery, waiting. This is a big part of the battle: waiting for the correct moment and then having the courage and wit to move when the time is right. The living condition, though bad, have no effect upon me physically. But how much longer will this last for me in and out of prison, for you in and out of debt, for the others of our kind who suffer jail, mental institutions, and the like. How long will we be forced to live this life, where every

60

meal is an accomplishment, where every movie or pair of shoes is a fulfillment, where circumstance never allows our children to develop past a mental age of sixteen. I've been patient, but where I'm concerned patience has its limits. Take it too far, and it's cowardice.

George

JUNE, 1965
9

Dear Father,

We can spend twenty-five dollars a month here at the canteen for toilet articles, a few dry goods, and food. But we can spend any amount through the mail on such things as books, typewriters, correspondence courses in all the liberal arts. I spend what you have sent me on books. Many that are of interest and value to me cannot be obtained here in the library.

Anything that you send me in the way of finances is a good investment, the returns will be forthcoming after the successful conclusion of the wars.

Mao Tse-tung, leader of the Chinese Communist party, has written many works on politics and war. Please ascertain the exact titles of his works and who they are published by and how much each costs. Also the price of the *Encyclopedia Africana* by William Du Bois. How many volumes are there in the set? Who publishes them? It is very important that I have the publisher's name and address, because if I come by the

61

money to purchase these books I need the exact titles and publishers. To read and study the major works of these two authors would be the climax of my education, and education in itself. Du Bois was a mere fool in his earlier days; but right at the close of his eventful life he gave up this life of toil, deprivation, and tears to join his own kind. He left the United States, went to Ghana, and wrote the *Encyclopedia Africana*.

It is difficult, very difficult to get any facts concerning our history and our way of life. The lies, half-truths, and propaganda have won total sway over the facts. We have no knowledge of our heritage. Our economic status has reduced our minds to a state of complete oblivion. The young black who comes out of college or the university is as ignorant and unlearned as the white laborer. For all practical purposes he is worse off than when he went in, for he has learned only the attitudes and ways of the snake, and a few well-worded lies. The ruling culture refuses to let us know how much we did to advance civilization in our lands long ago. It refuses to recognize and appreciate our craft and strength and allow us some of the fruits of our labor. All this has left an emptiness in our lives, a void, a vacuum that must soon be filled by hostilities. I am most certainly committed, until the day I'm sent to the warrior's rest. By the ruling culture's acts of greed and barbarism the uncommitted will soon learn that compromise with such an enemy is impossible. Our two fortunes move along a collision course. I'm prepared in every aspect, I have nothing, I can lose nothing!

George

JUNE, 1965

Dear Mother,

Even though I have plenty of time now, I don't write more regularly because of my studies. I get involved in some aspect of the subjects that interest me and before I can extract myself the lights are going off and it is twelve o'clock. You know the last thing we discussed just before you people left me when you were up here last, well I've decided to go into it—now.

My life here is slowly becoming one of complete alienation. I talk to fewer convicts every day. Just one lieutenant here has tried to do anything for me. He got me out of segregation twice last year. The die is cast now though, I guess, thumbs down on me. My future is about as sound as a three-dollar bill. I thank whatever forces there are working for me that I'm still able to write you. I'm joking of course, it isn't that serious.

Nothing will help me now though but patience and I have developed plenty. There is nothing left to me now but to await whatever may come. I go back to the board October or is it December. Nine months from March would be December. Yes! Perhaps the fog will lift and I will see some ray of hope by then. You know the thing which they have locked me up for now could mean spending my next few years in confinement here. It would be merely a flight from reality to think that I could get a date this year. I would be happy though to just know how long I will be held, even if it was 10 years. I'd feel better knowing.

Take care of yourself.

Son

JUNE,1965

Dear Father,

One of those tall ultrabright electrical fixtures used to illuminate the walls and surrounding area at night casts a direct beam of light in my cell at night. (I moved to a different cell last week). Consequently I have enough light, even after the usual twelve o'clock lights-out, to read or study by. I don't really have to sleep now if I choose not to. The early hours of morning are the only time of the day that one can find any respite from the pandemonium caused by these the most uncultured of San Quentin inmates. I don't let the noise bother me even in the evenings when it rises to maddening intensity, because I try to understand my surroundings. I've asked myself, as I do about *all* the other aspects of life, why—why do white cons act and react as if they were animals of a lower order than we black men (some blacks get foolish also but we don't refer to them as "men")? Why just because they look like shaved monkeys must they also act like them? It's frayed nerves, caused by the harsh terms that defeat brought when they went against the system, the same system that runs this place. I must ask myself why did they go against the system and why are the terms so harsh? Could it be that a man will most always pursue his interests, system or no? But why should so many people's interests lie outside the system? Why doesn't the system encompass the needs and requirements of all or, to be realistic, the majority. We now come to the part of the question around which the whole contention pivots: Why are the terms so harsh, the price of defeat so high?

64

What is it that causes a man to become power-mad, to deify exploitation and mendacity and vilify the compatible, harmonious things of nature, how many times have you heard that "everyone should help fight the evils of communism," etc.?

George

JULY, 1965

Lester,

I write this letter to inform you that the people who hold me here read that letter sent them. They read it and smiled with satisfaction and triumph. You are under a grave illusion, I must now admit. You didn't think they would inform me of it, did you? But you are in serious error. They let me read it. Apparently every petty official in the prison has read it, all to my embarrassment. For it sounded like something out of Stowe's *Uncle Tom's Cabin*.

It didn't just cause me embarrassment. It also has caused me to be put in a cell that has the lock welded closed. Can it possibly be? Is it within the scope of feasibility that you did not know that to tell these people I was "bent on self-destruction" (to use your reference) would cause me harm? Are you so feeble of mind as to "report," after a visit with me, that I am bent on violent self-destruction and think it would cause me no harm!

I have always respected and loved you people, and hated myself, cried bitter tears of remorse, when, because of circumstances and conditions, which I didn't understand, I let you down. Even after I discovered the true cause of my ills, when I found that this social order had created, through its inadequacies and its abandonment of our interest, the basis for my frustrations, I forgave you for not preparing me; for not warning me, for pretending that this was the best of all possible worlds. I forgave you for misleading me. I forgave that catholic school thing. I tried to understand your defeat complex and your loyalty to institutions contrary to the blacks' interest.

I've traveled widely over this country and some in Mexico. I've met and have had exchanges with hundreds of thousands of people. I've read extensively in the fields of social-economic and political theory and development, all of this done against serious resistance from all sides. But because I knew one day that I would find what I'm after, and answer some of the questions that beset my mind with confusion and unrest and fear, I pushed ahead in spite of the foolish conformity that I saw in you people. Now I have arrived at a state of awareness that (because of the education system) few Negroes reach in the U.S. In my concern for you, I try to share the benefits of my experience and my observations, but am rewarded by being called madman. Thank you for the vote of *confidence* you displayed in that letter to the warden. I'll never forget it! All my younger life you betrayed me. Like I said, I could forgive. At first you may not have known any better, but over the last two years I've informed you of many things. I've given you my best and you have rejected me for my enemies. With this last act, you have betrayed my bosom interest, even though I warned you not to say anything at all. I will never forgive you this. Should we live forever I'll never trust you again. Your mind has failed you completely. To take sides against your son! You did it in '58 and now again. There will not be a third time. The cost to me is too great. Father against son, and brother against brother. This is truly detestable. You are a sick man.

George

JULY, 1965

Dear Father,

I am perplexed and hard pressed in finding a solution or reason that will adequately explain why we are so eager to follow Charlie. Why we are so impressed with his apparent know-how. A glance at his history shows that it has been one long continuous war. At no time in European history has there been a period of peace and harmony. Every moment of his past has been spent in the breakdown of civilization by causing war, disruption, disease, and artificial famine. You send me a date from the moment he emerged from his cave-dwelling days and I'll tell you which of his tribes were at war, either on us or on themselves. The whole of the Western European's existence here in the U.S. has been the same one long war with different peoples. This is the only thing they understand, the only thing they respect—the only thing they can do with any dexterity. Do you accept this miscreant as the architect of the patterns that must guide your future life! If so, we must part company, and it is best we do so now, before the trouble begins. But please stop and think so that you can turn yourself around in time, so that the developments to come won't shock you so badly. I have not wasted my time these last three or four years. I speak with some authority and people are listening. People like me are going to be shaping your tomorrows. So just sit back, open your mind, and watch, since you can't marshal the fundamentals to help me.

Yes, my friend, I remember everything, the reason that Delora and I had to spend that summer and winter in

67

Harrisburg is known and remembered by me. I remember the garbage right under the side and back of our place on Racine. Mama having to wash and wring clothes by hand, carrying Penny and Jon while some fat redheaded mama sat on her behind. I remember how strange people looked to me when I finally had to be sent to Skinner School. You never knew why I was almost killed the first day I went, but I do. I remember how the rent and clothes for us children kept you broke and ragged. All of us hungry, if not for food—the other things that make life bearable. After you and Mama settled down you had no recreational outlets whatever. And everyone on Warren Blvd. knows how you would beat me all the way home from our baseball games in the alley. Robert, can you see how absurd you sound to me when you speak on "the good life," or something about being a free adult? I know you have never been free. I know that few blacks over here have ever been free. The forms of slavery merely *changed* at the signing of the Emancipation Proclamation from chattel slavery to economic slavery. If you could see and talk to some of the blacks I meet in here you would immediately understand what I mean, and see that I'm right. They are all average, all with the same backgrounds, and in for the same thing, some form of food getting. About 70 to 80 percent of all crime in the U.S. is perpetrated by blacks, "the sole reason for this is that 98 percent of our number live below the poverty level in bitter and abject misery"! You must take off your rose-colored glasses and stop pretending. We have suffered an unmitigated wrong! How do you think I felt when I saw you come home each day a little more depressed than the day before? How do you think I felt when I looked in your face and saw the clouds forming, when I saw you look around and see your best efforts go for nothing—nothing. I can count the times on my hands that you managed to work up a smile.

George

JULY, 1965

Dear Father,

Well I guess you know that I'm aware that this is not the best of all possible lives. You also know that I thank you for trying to cushion the shocks and strains that history has made it our lot to have to endure. But the make-believe game has ended now. I don't think it necessary for me to burden myself with listing strains we've endured. You are intelligent enough to know. At each phase of this long train of tyrannies, we have conducted ourselves in a very meek and civilized manner, with only polite please for justice and moderation, all to no avail. We have shown a noble indisposition to react with the passion that each new oppression engenders. But any fool should be able to see that this cannot be allowed to continue. Any fool should be able to see that nature allows no such imbalances as this to exist for long. We have petitioned for judicial redress. We have remonstrated, supplicated, demonstrated, and prostrated ourselves before the feet of our self-appointed administrators. We have done all that we can do to circumvent the eruption that now comes on apace. The point of no return in our relationship has long been passed. I know what must and will take place so I follow my ends through to their most glorious conclusion. Don't make me waste my time and energy winning you to a position that you should already support with all your sympathies. The same forces that have made your life miserable, the same forces that have made your life senseless and unrewarding, threaten me and all our posterity. I know the way out. If you cannot help, sit back and listen, watch. You are charged with the responsibility of acknowledging the truth, my friend, and supporting it with whatever means, no matter how humble, are in your power. I am charged to right the wrong, lift the burden from the backs of future generations. I will not shrink from my duties. I will never falter or waver before the task, but we will go forward—to resolve this conflict once and forever. Of all the twenty thousand known years of advanced civilization, the years that are now coming on will be the most momentous.

George

AUGUST, 1965

Dear Father,

Although I'm still between the life-death cycle, I feel a lot better. How is the teeth situation with you?

I know you stay pretty busy and have a very bad memory, but try to remember to answer this question in your next letter. You told me once when I was at home there never to sleep more than six hours a day. You said that four was really enough. Why did you say this? On what authority? Experience or just something you read? What would be the effects of getting too much sleep?

I've been carrying out some very interesting experiments with myself in here. I quite definitely do not believe in a strict regimen. By strict I mean absolute patterns for thinking and living. But I cannot help feeling there is a judicious mean somewhere. I have been forced to seek the judicious mean, due to the circumstances that history has thrown me into

70

here—now. You see it isn't as simple as you implied. "Thinking and reading" won't fill a twenty-four-hour day. I have something real deep running through me, a burning thing of the mind. I have observed myself pass into a state of anger over something that happened as far away as Rhodesia or the Union of South Africa. And I didn't sleep for two days when those children and women were being murdered down there in your part of the world last week. I've told myself uncountable times that anger is an emotion, a degenerative emotion, unnecessary and controllable, but I couldn't control it until a few days ago when I observed myself being consumed by the force of my own weight. So, my friend, I started conducting these experiments with myself. Why can't I rid myself of the sorrow and emotion that awareness has brought me? I get rid of the self-destructive force of error and ignorance only to be torn and miserable by what I discover. It happened that I knew all along that some imbalance did exist, or I'll say a few imbalances existed, that disallowed me from progressing further in my development. I put my head in my hands and wondered why do I make myself sick, why can't I overcome this, maybe I'm just human after all? I believe that is what got it! I am what I am, and that's all I am. I knew this morbid depression must have some human explainable cause, an imbalance somewhere. The mind and body cannot be separated, a physical imbalance can precipitate effects that could eventually lead to some mental imbalance. Too much sleep, too little, the wrong kind of food, too much, too little, too much reading in the wrong position, too much study, or too long an application to one subject, results in imbalances, conflicts, struggles. I was looking for a solution from one direction only, when no event, no effect in nature, has a single cause. It's a collection of causes! So I look at myself and I discover new ways of knowing myself, seeing and placing myself in the vast scheme. The struggle is almost over, my friend, complete and harmonious development can be mine, everyone's. Only one-fourth of the sorrow in each man's life is

71

caused by outside uncontrollable elements, the rest is self-imposed by failing to analyze and act with calmness.

George

AUGUST, 1965

Dear Father,

I've been on five hours sleep a day and one-and-one-half hours exercise. The rest of my time is divided proportionally between my work and what little pleasure I can make for myself in here. This isn't too much to speak of, a little light fiction, or the radio. The experiment seems to be bringing me some benefits; the tenseness that brings about emotional unrest has left.

I hope you are not too uncomfortable with your teeth being worked on. I will have to have mine worked on also when I leave here. The longer I wear these shoes you sent me the more comfortable they become. You should try some. Of course I haven't too far to walk in here, but I make the best of what I have. I do my best thinking on my feet, so I walk this little ten feet I have rather diligently sometimes.

I was just thinking yesterday how far I have fallen from glory, how very much of my "physical" freedom they have taken from me (I still have mental freedom). I realized how few of the pleasures of life I have tasted. Trouble, difficulties, and sorrow have pervaded these twenty-four years. Twenty-four years without one moment's mental gratification. For us it is always tomorrow; tomorrow we'll have enough money to eat better; tomorrow we'll be able to buy this necessary article

72

of clothing, to pay that debt. Tomorrow, it never really gets here. "To every one who has will more be given . . . but from him who has not, even what he has will be taken away." I like this life, I can never reconcile myself to it, or rationalize the fact that I have been basely used, hated, and repressed as if it were the natural order of things. Life is at best a nebulous shadow, a vague contingency, the merest of possibilities to begin with. But men in general (myself most emphatically included), being at best complete and abject fools, have rendered even what small possibilities there were to love and learn null and void! But I refuse to excite myself about my past, or our future. I have simply taken up a task and I am preparing myself for its execution. I absolutely refuse to give way to emotional involvement or any undisciplined or dogmatic beliefs. Life is too uncertain, and dogmas and beliefs are the product of this sick man who now transgresses against us and the world. If I can bend circumstances to my will I succeed. If not—I'm off the cycle.

You know that the U.S. power elite, the 7 percent who own and run this country and influence the policies of the rest of the European world, want to attack and destroy China in the next four or five years. China has become too strong and it is influencing the rest of the Afro-Asian world too heavily with anti-Western philosophy (self-determination and economic independence). All that stands in the way of the power elite is a few dissenting factions which are daily being won over, and having their opinions molded for them by the communications media, and, second, the domestic unrest and near-revolutionary atmosphere in the black slums of all the large U.S. cities. Do you add well? Can you see what may be in the making? They cannot attack China unless the blacks here in the U.S. support their war effort. What if some black voice denounced the war? Many blacks would go for this. What would happen if large numbers of blacks refused to fight or make weapons, or even say attempted to subvert the U.S. war effort? Remember the Jews of Germany! From what I observe

73

in here, where they don't have to hide their contempt, we're moving toward this eventuality.

George

SEPTEMBER, 1965
6

Dear Father,

This is about six letters I've written in two weeks. Did you get my answer to your last one? In the future I will put the exact date on them and double-check with you on them. You say you got none of these recent letters? When they stop them, they usually send them back to me. I can't say exactly what happened, but I guess these things are to be expected.

I mentioned in one of those other letters that I went before one of these committees last month made up of the top officials here. They informed me that I "can forget about the board transfer or the main population facilities here in the prison." These were their words. So, my friend, I'll be in this little cell for a while yet. I hope you note that all this is done without any proof, and without allowing me to face my accuser. But I guess these things are to be expected.

I want you to send me a portable typewriter and of course the carrying case. We can have them here, and I can use one to build my spelling and vocabulary. It will give me something to do in here. Send a lesson book also. A used one will be all right. Although they sell ribbons here you will have to send a couple of rolls because I have no way of buying any. I've had to secure permission to send out for the typewriter, of course. It took over a month to have it approved, so send it as soon as you are able.

They just turned the lights out. It's 12:15 (A.M., Tuesday). Take it easy.

George

SEPTEMBER, 1965
12

Dear Mama,

Robert tells me that you are not well. I'm sorry to hear this, but I guess we're all lucky to have lived as long as we have. The many years you spent without proper clothing for the cold wet weather back East, with improper food, not enough food, and lack of expert medical attention, is enough misfortune to leave the strongest person ill.

You need to see a specialist. If we were not blacks and consequently poor, you would be able to enjoy the benefits of science. But you are probably seeing some disinterested, half-trained parasite who knows no more about your ailment or the curing of it than I do. Robert doesn't make enough in two years to allow you to get the best attention (that is, here in our present surroundings). His scope doesn't extend any farther than the boundaries of the U.S. Those lies and the propaganda he reads in *Life*, *Reader's Digest*, and *Look*, have completely undressed his mind. I feel very sorry for all of you. I'm locked in a cell 24 hours a day, but I still know my potential, I still feel my strength, I still thumb my nose at the caveman. Because my mind is still my own, no one can lie to me anymore. I know where my interest lies.

For now though, I'm going to be a good boy, as Robert and most of the blacks we see around us are all good boys. I'm going to smile, and I'm going to pretend to accept the small compensations they hand out in return for our soul and our freedom. I'm going to be a good boy and eat what is put before me. I'm going to do this so that I'll stay alive long enough to take care of you. You deserve a lot better than you have had and more than you will have. You don't know it but there is a better life, regardless of what the *Reader's Digest* says. Believe me there is a better life.

Take care of yourself.

George

OCTOBER, 1965
3

Dear Robert,

I have the typewriter in my possession here, so all is well. They didn't, however, produce the instruction book or paper. They let me have the two extra ribbons. I can get an instruction book. Paper isn't too much of a problem. All things considered, it turned out very well.

You can take a chance if you care to on the shorthand book. Put it in an envelope like you say, but also write a letter stating right in the front, in the first lines, that it is a shorthand book. Mail the letter and the book together. If they don't think it's some kind of cryptogram we have going, it may be allowed or overlooked, but you can't just leave it up to them to figure out what it is. That would be asking for too much.

Just read in the *Monitor* that ".6 parts of insecticide to one billion parts of water will kill most all marine animals in salt water or fresh"!

Be sure to look into the course on speed reading. It costs sixty cents. I know it is a great help. I would be nice for me to have someone to talk to.

Take care, and keep your eyes open,

George

NOVEMBER, 1965
7

Dear Robert,

      Nothing has changed. I'm still losing. I'm alive though, so there's still the possibility. . . .

How is Georgia? Don't tell her anything about my condition.* It isn't necessary for you to reveal to her all that I tell you. She doesn't need to know. It can only worry her needlessly.

I hope you are well.

George

*The author had been put in isolation after being charged by the prison authorities with assault with a deadly weapon.

NOVEMBER, 1965
13

Dear Mother,

I am alive and well, and am at present working my way through the adjustment center here. It is an overall improvement in my condition. The prospects of getting out or getting a transfer to a more habitable prison are now better.

I will relish the transfer part. All of the officers here have preconceived notions about my patterns of behavior now. Consequently it is somewhat hard for me to avoid falling under suspicion for almost every misdeed perpetrated by a black. But no matter, if I do have to stay here I am determined to circumvent the little traps.

I sincerely hope your health is improving, or at least becoming no worse. I feel awful disconcerted that I am unable to render any assistance. However, I feel this inability is only temporary. I intend to surge back with a tenacity uncontainable in its relentlessness.

Fortune must soon smile on me because sincere effort is always rewarded. Nature allows no such imbalances as this. I am assured and completely self-possessed in the knowledge that all contradictions and conflicts must one day be resolved.

Give my love to all the women there, please take care of yourself.

Love,

George

DECEMBER, 1965
23

Dear Mother,

I got the food you sent me today; it was very nice, and fills a real need. I almost didn't get it though. You see we are supposed to send out a slip to the correspondent when we wish someone to send us something and you are supposed to send the package with this slip you get from me as proof that you are an authorized correspondent. I didn't send a slip out this year because of the trouble it might involve for you, and the money could possibly have been better placed.

I hope your health is improving. I am doing quite well in that respect, all things considered. You may not know me when you next see me. I find a few new gray hairs every time I look in the mirror. If I live to be thirty, I guess it will be all white.

I'll start writing Jon a couple of letters a week. If you would like me to, let me know. I would tell him as much of the truth as is advisable in one of these letters, but if you don't feel that what I represent is correct for him, then I'll refrain. How old is he now?

I guess I'll be getting a transfer, or going out to the main population soon. A couple of months more of this and I think they will let up on me. About parole, I can't say, but I am not alone. I don't feel so distressed when I look around me and see others like myself experiencing the same thing. The uniformity

80

of our condition seems to lend support to each of us. I don't think the administrators fully understand. I have the strangest feeling that they may not understand how this atmosphere they foster nurtures a mindless, hopeless mass. It is suicidal incompetence. The strong can afford to be incompetent or wrong sometimes without loss of face. Even the mightiest and most capable of men are only human. But he who attributes to himself omnipotence must *never* be wrong. For once a weakness is found, no matter how small, in one who claims omnipotence he is completely exposed. The fall from omnipotence ends only with insignificance.

May this New Year coming be your year, our year.

Take care,

Love,

George

DECEMBER, 1965
29

Dear Robert,

The photographs were nice. Penny sent me one of her baby also. I thought him very beautiful. Send me her address, also send Delora's. Delora looks well. Tell her I love her and that the baby looks just like her. She has two babies now hasn't she? I'm an uncle three times.

Jon should be the main concern now. By now you should have seen enough to know how to proceed with his development. He doesn't look too healthy to me. He looks thin, pale,

81

and soft. Those weights would improve his circulation and make his veins stand out. If he works out in the backyard in the sun every evening in a year, he could be a paragon. He needs that and he needs to be told the truth. He can get these things only from you. That school won't teach him anything except possibly a few Latin prayers, but if you haven't caught on yet, nothing I can say in this letter will help. Don't forget I've been over the road he is straining on now. Maybe it is a little different now with him. You can afford to give him bikes and baseball gloves, but the loose-living thing is going to seem awfully exciting to him in a few years when he compares it against the artificial world of those catholics.

I'm doing all right here I guess. You take it easy.

George

JANUARY, 1966
1

Dear Robert,

I received your gratifying letter. Was it an expression of your love, an indication of your gracious sympathy for the position we were both born into, and that I am presently feeling the cramping convulsions of? I got the money. If I feel like a burden to you, it is best that we suspend exchanges until I've struggled on back to my feet. You probably don't feel that you owe me anything, and I guess you don't since you have accepted the values and customs of these people we live among. In that light, I owe to you the unquestionable honor of my struggle within this American dream.

What can I say to you, my friend? I've been wondering if it would be best to lie to you and hide myself, say only what I know so well that you like to hear. I hesitate to do this because you have been lied to so much already. To add to this may be my last and greatest and most unpardonable crime against you. You are the older of the two of us. You are a man in your way and there is much merit in the manner you have conducted yourself these last 25 years. To have lived through the period of your early youth is in itself a qualifier for respect. The following shocks and strains were surely enough to drive the strongest man to distraction. All the honor that you are due I freely give. However, we, the humble representatives of the future generations, have at our disposal all the accumulated knowledge and experiences of all past generations to build our thoughts. I have made no mark as yet to be sure, but why is it that we cannot communicate? What is it that bars our efforts to exchange thoughts and ideas? The fault could lie in my presentation. If so, I will make every effort to correct my deficiency because it is to the interest of us both that we meet on the same level. Can you understand that a meeting of the minds will have to precede any advancement of our combined fortunes? The question is whether we will be able to overcome the macilious efforts and forces that divide us and be able to put group interests before personal petty prejudice and preconceived notions. Or will we all end by turning our backs on each other and going our way in anger?

I'm tired, my friend, real tired. I've got a pain deep in my stomach and I'm tired pretending that the obvious doesn't exist and that this is the best of all possible lives. It is not, and if a concentrated effort isn't made to finally learn and use the lessons set forth in history, unthinkable chaos will result!

I know that it probably will not come true, but may this be your year, our year to realize the promise that being born a man brings.

George

83

FEBRUARY, 1966
23

Dear Mama,

I have been hoping that you would write and acknowledge my last letter. I hope it doesn't worry you too much that I will not be considered for release for some time yet. It worries me enough. I hope your health gets no worse at least. I'll be with you as soon as I can. I've got some clean time in now already and plan to do as well for the rest of this year so that in December they will let me go. They have promised me this anyway. I don't put any confidence whatever in what they say, but the hope remains.

I am in the main population now. I was released from the adjustment center lockup today (because of good conduct) and have a good program set up for me, one conducive to parole consideration. I have learned something by the experience: never again to look for mercy, never again to expect or hope for justice, never to look for quarter without strings being attached. The last illusion has been shattered; I know the way from here; ask no quarter of fate and give none.

That thing you mentioned concerning Frances has had me perturbed for a week. Some just are not going to make it, some of us have just slipped too far to ever get back. This guy, I promise you, will be sorry a long, long time. Right here at this juncture of time we as a people have nothing, absolutely nothing but each other, some fresh air, the blue and gold of day and silver at night, a clean conscience, and the promise of cloudless days to come. But some do not enjoy these things enough, don't understand the nature of our circumstances and commit unpardonable crimes, unnatural crimes that must in the end bar them from partaking in the benefits of the liberation that is planned for tomorrow. In the end a requiem will be sung over the whole vast complex of disorder.

Please inform me of any new developments there. Help Jon to become a man. Fare you well.

George

MARCH, 1966
3

Dear Mama,

Always good to hear from you, though it makes me sad to know that you are not well. Just hold on though and circumstances will take a definite turn for the better, no ifs or ands about this. The way lies open for us. I'm not just talking or hoping. I know there is a better life for us. I know what there is to be had and of all there is to be had I plan to claim for us the lion's share.

You are right of course in what you contend. The black woman has in the past few hundred years been the only force holding us together and holding us up. She has absorbed the biggest part of the many shocks and strains of existence under a slave order. The men can think of nothing more effective than pimping, gambling, or petty theft. I've heard men brag about being pimps of black women and taking money from black women who are on relief. Things like this I find odious, disgusting—you are right, the black men have proven themselves to be utterly detestable and repulsive in the past. Before I would succumb to such subterfuge I would scratch my living from the ground on hands and knees, or die in a hail of bullets! My hat goes off to every one of you, you have my profoundest respect. I have surrendered all hope of happiness for myself in this life to the prospect of effecting some improvement in our circumstances as a whole. I have a plan, I will give, and give, and give of myself until it proves our making or my end. The men of our group have developed as a result of living under a ruthless system a set of mannerisms that numb the soul. We have been made the floor mat of the world, but the world has yet to see what can be done by men of our nature, by men who have walked the path of disparity, of regression, of abortion, and yet come out whole. There will be a special page in the book of life for the men who have crawled back from the grave. This page will tell of utter defeat, ruin, passivity, and subjection in one breath, and in the next, overwhelming victory and fulfillment.

So take care of yourself, and hold on.

Love,

George

20

Dear Mama,

We have to order books from a bookstore owned by one of the staff here. It is contrary to institution policy for someone to send us books from outside. This is the rule, the law, so I guess it cannot be helped. Situations of this type are what this country is built on, the wonderful system that made it great.

I've read as much St, Augustine as I could stomach. If you don't know about him and Jerome, Leibniz, and the rest of that lunatic fringe yet, my love, you are hurting. Why do you say things like that to me? You know how I feel about those people. You know that I am completely aware of all of them. I can never be deceived again by them. I know their awesome capacity for evil, I'm victim of it now. That Pope Pius XII, the guy you let us pray for, gave Mussolini his blessing as he was about to embark upon his misadventure in Ethiopia. I could give you thousands of examples of this type. I have explained my feeling to you many, many times, so I won't go any further with this. If children being blown out of this existence while attending church services, men being lynched for a gesture, colonialism, the inquisition, and H-bombs haven't affected you, nothing I say here can help you. If you could live my life one week and see the things I see, feel the pain I feel, and die a little bit each day as I do, all your illusions and apparitions would vanish. You talk to me like I was born yesterday, like I was still a little boy. All my life now you have told me about European gods and European christians who were supposed to be knowledgeable. When do you plan to say something that will help me? You may not know any better. If not, I am wrong in saying what I have, but I find it hard to admit that my mother could be so insensitive to the truth! You disrespect me, Mama, when you talk to me like that. It's like you saying to me, "George, you're a fool. You do not have eyes to see, ears to hear, and a brain to interpret, so I'll tell you any kind of outrageous story." Ordinary people, the mediocre, need to feel or believe in something greater than themselves. It gives them false security and it makes them feel that help may be forthcoming. This is self-delusion in the extreme. I cannot partake in any foolishness. Do you want me to be mediocre like the rest of the herd! When I need strength, Mama, I reach down within myself. I draw out of the reserves I've built—the necessary endurance to face down my opposition. I call on myself, I have faith in myself. This is where it must always come from in the end—yourself. I place no one and nothing above myself. What any man has done before me I can do. If there is a god, Mama, he hates me and I'll have to resist what he or it is doing to us. All my life, Mama, I've had to work things out for myself. I've had help from no quarter. I've been alone now for a long time. This is why I've had so much pain and trouble. Robert gave me nothing. You gave me god and that horrible church. Even god managed to take something away from me. I have nothing left but myself.

Love,

George

APRIL, 1966
17

Dear Mama,

I received, your card, nice of you to think of me on Easter. Getting that card sure made me feel a lot better. You know how important Easter is to me.

Are you any better? Have you resolved the insurance problem? Don't worry too much about these things; solutions cause new and sometimes even worse problems to spring up. All of our difficulties will never be worked out. I guess perhaps this existence is merely a constant choosing of the lesser evil.

Penny came to see me last week; I recall a time when all she wanted was to get away from the family group, but now that she's on her own, she didn't want to talk about anything else but you and the past. She is devoted to you. She is a sweet, well-balanced, and wonderful woman, deserving of much more than this life here offers us.

But the weather is fine here, plenty of sun lately. I exercise in the sun an hour every day, I'm getting very big and very black.

Fare you well,

George

MAY, 1966
8

Dear Mama,

All is well here, I'm going to night school again, and have encountered no trouble of late.

Are you well? They say that today is Mother's Day. I can't make much sense out of it, though. I love mine every day. But these guys around me here seem to like being told when to celebrate this and that, so should you also feel this way, let me acknowledge the custom and wish you as pleasant a Mother's Day as is possible under our circumstances.

Take care of yourself. . . .

Love,

George

SEPTEMBER, 1966
9

Dear Mama,

Hope you are better; the typewriter is being repaired so this comes by hand.

We are in agreement on many things. All is as well as it is possible to be between two who are human and subject to human error. You have done much for me and I am sincerely in your debt; your returns will be soon forthcoming. That which you didn't do I never expected, for you are after all a woman and think as a woman should.

The attitudes and methods that I have developed on my own have no reflection on you, but on the nature of our life circumstances and situational pressures.

Is Jon in health? I have some pictures of you on your trip back East. You surely look well and unchanged.

I go to the board in December and as I have stated before I have met all of their terms. My release is almost assured.

What is Penny's new address? I will send her a letter on her birthday and discuss things as they are said to be, and as they really are. She must be having a pretty bad time; that guy seems to be pretty Anglo-Americanized.

Take care of yourself.

Love,

George

16

Dear Mama,

I wish you many happy returns in the birthday department. It sounds pretty empty I know but that's all I have to offer right now, a wish; I have broad plans for the future though. A large villa for you in the Maldive Islands, with an extra-deep bomb shelter.

All is the same here. Each day that comes and goes is like the one before; being a good boy, going to church, reading about the saints, and getting good ratings on my job for the proper attitudes.

Are you well, are you getting any of the pleasant things that life in these United States offers? That reminds me of a thing I read recently concerning China. One of the top political leaders came to an elementary school to lecture (they take education pretty seriously). He told the children to put their heads on the desk and pray to god for ice cream. After fifteen minutes of serious and sincere effort all the children lost interest and grew restive. He then told them to pray to him and the party for ice cream, whereupon a few minutes later they raised their heads from their desks and found, guess what, ice cream. Isn't that disgusting, Mama, to distort the thinking of children like that. . . . Now how is Jon? How much does he weigh?

You don't say much about the folks in the Midwest, are they well? Take care of yourself.

Love,

George

SEPTEMBER, 1966
25

Dear Robert,

What has happened to Penny? Is she having troubles with her man? You were going to send me her address, have you forgotten?

I have been trimming down my weight some, more exercise and less food, I'm getting ready for December. I don't want to stand out. I must fit in with the rest of the herd and look as ordinary as possible. I want my system to grow accustomed to little or no food at all without it causing me the normal distress that it causes others. You would be surprised how little food an adult really needs. I went for two weeks on nothing but three slices of bread and "one" tumbler of water a day without noticeable loss mentally or physically.

Are you well, my friend? Glad to hear you are becoming interested in things of the mind. The school idea is truly out of the ordinary. Most others of your caste and peer group have given up. There are two or three things that I would like to take, but cannot take them here in prison: language (Chinese and Arabic), electronics, and chemicals. Maybe I'll get out next year and if I still feel the inclination I'll buy a few courses. Take care of yourself.

George

OCTOBER, 1966
20

Dear Robert,

Just received your letter of October 15, good to hear that Jon is well, and that your studies are coming along.

I wanted to exhaust the possibilities of getting that free course in drafting here. I wanted to know if I was going to remain here in this prison at least until board before I asked you to put yourself out in sending it. Well it is conclusive that I will not be able to take it here. The school is carrying the course but there is no room for folks like me, just right now, maybe next year. I have found conclusively that I will not be transferred either. So, my friend, if you will, and whenever you can, send the course from LaSalle. I will be able to finish much sooner than you think. My math is excellent and I have nothing but time. I'll suspend my other endeavors in deference to the speedy and satisfactory completion of this course. Upon closer examination of all the facts involved in my doing something like this in here I also find that plastic tools are not necessary. I can have and use anything necessary for the course. LaSalle sends all of these tools right along with the course, so things are not as complicated as I thought them at first to be.

Very likely I will be given a parole date this year. If so, or perhaps to increase the possibility, I should have a job offer here on record. You could correspond with some machine shops or the like right now and tell them that I have completed or am just about to complete an accredited course in drafting, and I need a statement from them on record here to be released. Don't worry about me not being prepared by then. I have thought everything out. But any offer from almost any area will suffice to get me out. If you are not able to get someone to send me in a job offer then there should be a lengthy statement here on record that you are willing to support me while I go to school. I hope you understand what I am saying. I have to have something on record for the board to gain the impression all is secure financially for my release. It may be less difficult just to state officially that I am going to school and that you plan to pay my way completely through it upon my release. We must decide now what will be said for their benefit upon this matter now. Let me know in your next letter which will be easier for you to do. Get me a job offer or state that our plans include school with your full backing. Send it to the Department of Corrections in Sacramento.

Take care of yourself,

George

DECEMBER, 1966
2

Dear Robert,

The typewriter is being repaired again. Never buy a plastic typewriter. Though good for some things, plastic is too flexible for that type of machinery. It keeps the parts out of trim.

I received your letter and nothing that develops from this mess will surprise me. I have taken all possibilities into account, in advance. I have nothing going for me and any good or favorable turn of event will be only luck, good fortune. You don't really think that I mind not being liked by them, do you? I sincerely feel that it is a tribute to my character that they do not. I said what I did only to help you understand my position, and in turn understand any future action I may undertake. But I don't want you to trouble your mind, or lose any sleep about the seriousness of my position either. When things become too hard for everyone else, that's when I start enjoying myself. Just understand in the light of future events that I am guided by necessity and that my needs are different than yours.

The board meets during the last few days of the month.

Take care of yourself, my friend,

George

DECEMBER, 1966
3

Dear Robert,

I am worried about Penny. Does she still write you? Have you let her know that should she need a refuge or a strong arm she can find them in her father. Women need to know these things. It is tormenting to them to know that they are alone, can look to no quarter for string-free aid. If Penny felt that she had no choice in the matter, no help, she would accept ill treatment forever. But then an offer of help must seem freely and honestly given to be of value.

Are you well, my friend? The climate here is terrible, and I am not talking about the weather, each day is a trial. I stay close to my cell these days, reading, working on my book. Take care of yourself.

George

JANUARY, 1967
3

Dear Mama,

      I have at least another fourteen or eighteen months to do. Of course I could do the rest of my life here, not taking into account a possible change in the system of government and economics, a change of hands, that is.

They gave me no consideration at the board, the same people that gave me their promise last year. I was not surprised, I was completely prepared for this.

Take care of yourself.

George

12

Dear Mama,

Your letter was well received; it left me feeling better than I have felt for years. I have never felt as close to any human as I do to you now. Your thoughts mirror mine exactly. Why have you left me alone to my struggle so long? I know the answer to this must be that we hesitate to reveal or acknowledge the existence of ugliness to the ones we love, even though the knowledge of such may better equip them to resist the effects of evil.

I am going into my seventh year here. I have learned as much as I possibly could in this time; I have studied myself closely, I have studied people, human and inhuman, wanting to know and understand. I am given to understand that it is the strong who rule the weak but, in turn, the wise rule over the strong. So you see that I recognize the value of what you have stated concerning faith and wisdom. What is happening to me here, what has happened, what will happen, can never surprise or upset me again. My nerves have been fractured, my sensibilities outraged, for the last time. It's all a matter of course to me now. My outlook is clear and the future holds no more terrors for me. Just existing, life without joy, without real meaning does not appeal to me at all. I am very tired of waking up each morning wondering if I will be worked for nothing again today, or wondering if I will be insulted, humiliated, injured, or even done to death today. There are a few things that I must be decisive about, a few things that I know to be so, then there are things which my faith tells me could possibly be so. I have faith in the fact that we, the majority of peoples (5 to 1) on earth, can live with and complement each other's existence if we rid the earth of the barbarous influence spread by this inhuman, unnatural minority! My faith in life holds still to the principle that we men of color will soon make a harmonious world out of this chaotic travesty of fact. But first we must destroy the malefactor and root out all of his ideals, moralities, and institutions. It is to this end that I have long since dedicated myself, to extinguish forever the lights of a perverted science in any way that I can, by any and all means. To accomplish this we can no longer woo false gods or invoke half measures. Please understand that though I would miss you and all the others, though I love you dearly, I do not want to live in this world as it is. I do not think of myself as one small person among so many. I know what I can do, I know I can build and can cause things to happen, but I also can be hurt.

L. is my closest consort, a true friend, the most trustworthy man I have ever met. This is saying a lot, believe me, trust is a difficult thing to build between men brought up under Anglo-American or Western cultures. I learned much from him. He is also tired of seeing himself through the eyes of others on *Amos 'n' Andy* and *I Spy*. This individual comes to you with my highest recommendation. He will help me. You help him to help me. His intelligence and character are unquestionable.

George

100

JANUARY, 1967
23

Dear Robert,

I tried to write several times these last couple of weeks but my letters all came back with a note attached explaining what I can and cannot say.

Have you been well? How old are you now, pop? Where were you and what were you doing when you were my age, twenty-five? I'll bet you were not doing too much better than I am now. You probably were not in prison. Well, I know you were not, but was your standing socially and economically speaking any better than mine? I guess it was, since you at least had limited freedom of movement. I have none here.

Although I would very much like to get out of here in order to develop a few ideas that have occurred to me—although I would not like to leave my bones here on the hill if it is a choice between that and surrendering the things that make me a man, the things that allow me to hold my head erect and unbowed, then the hill can have my bones. Many times in the history of our past—I speak of the African here in the U.S.—many times we were presented with this choice, too many times, too many of us choose to live the crippled existence of the near-man, the half-man. Well, I don't care how long I live. Over this I have no control, but I do care about what kind of life I live, and I can control this. I may not live but another five minutes, but it will be five minutes definitely on my terms.

George

JANUARY, 1967
31

Dear Frances,

Sorry to have neglected you for so long; things are very complicated for me here. I stay very busy, all of the time. I never have enough time to do the things that I must.

I have made inroads into political economy, geography, forms of government, anthropology, archaeology and the basics of three languages, and when I can get hold of them some of the works on urban guerrilla warfare.

I can use some assistance on the language aspect, though. Next time you pass a bookstore ask about a book dealing with Swahili, a self-teaching Swahili book. Get the proper title and the publisher's name and also a good self-teaching book on Arabic.

Last year Mama suggested that a lawyer could possibly help me get out of here, by sitting in and representing me at the board. I wish I had gone along with it. A couple of people have gotten out like that. There is a lady lawyer up here in San Francisco who specializes in that. She says a grand in her hand, several months before the board, is all that is required to get a date, if a person has his minimum in. My minimum is one year, so I've got seven times more than necessary. Talk to Robert about this. If she doesn't get a client out, she returns his money. If Robert borrowed it and got me out I would of course return it.

If I don't get a new sentence for the stuff I am locked up for now, that is what we must do. Just discuss it with Robert for now. I'll let you know in a few months if you should take definite steps in that direction. First I must ascertain whether or not they plan to fix me with the blame for these recent events.

I must now start doing all that is humanly possible to get out of prison. I can see great ill forecast for me if I don't find some way to extract myself from these people's control. "If we must die let it not be like hogs, hunted and pinned in an inglorious spot, while around us bark the mad and hungry dogs making their mock at our accursed lot; if we must die then let us nobly die, so that our precious blood may not be shed in vain. Then even the monsters we defy shall be constrained to honor us though dead. We kinsmen must meet the common foe, though far outnumbered, let us show us brave, and for their thousand blows, deal one death blow. What though before us lies the open grave, like men we'll face the murderous pack, pressed to the wall, dying, but fighting back." I don't mind dying but I'd like to have the opportunity to fight back. Take care.

George

103

FEBRUARY, 1967

1

Dear Mother,

Things are normal here, the usual turmoil. I hope
you are well. I hope you are doing enough light exercise each
day to work up some perspiration and not eating the wrong
things—pork, sugar, white bread, etc. I'm very careful in this
respect and enjoy almost perfect health and great reserves of
energy and strength in spite of my circumstances. But I do
heavy exercises, maybe two hours worth a day, every day. In
close confinement where I cannot get to any workout
facilities, as now, I work out somewhat differently. I take neat
piles of books and magazines tied together and exercise with
them. For you I imagine some deep knee bends, touch your
toes, and say some push-ups would be fine. You would do five
sets of ten of each exercise. For example, start by doing ten
push-ups, rest a minute or two, do ten more, rest a few
minutes, etc., until you get to five sets, then go to the next
exercise. Stay young and firm that way. Resistance to bodily
disorders stays high, or builds up.

You know when they locked me up this time all my
personal property came up missing. I'll have to replace
everything—two personal chess sets, toilet articles, the black
sweat shirts. I had four of these but saved only the one I had
on. Even the plastic tumblers I used to drink with in the cell,
everything is gone. I'm not sure about the typewriter, I can't

get any information on it. I know that I don't have it here; whether it is safe somewhere else I don't know. Then, too, several of us blacks were locked up at the same time for just about the same thing. They go to the small adjustment center yard each day for two hours; I am forced to remain in my cell, no fresh air, no sun, twenty-four hours a day in here. It doesn't bother me, though. I've trained myself not to be disorganized by any measure they take against me. I exercise in here, and pursue my studies. That fills my day out nicely. Since I know that I am the original man and will soon inherit this earth, I am content to just prepare myself and wait, nothing can stop me now! But I do sometimes wonder just exactly how they got the way they are. I know beyond question the extent of the evil that lurks in their hearts; I see the *insane* passion, inherent in their characters, to dominate all that they come in contact with. What aggressive psychosis impells a man to want his dessert and mine too, to want to feast at every table, to want to cast his shadow over every land? I don't know what they are; some folks call them devils (doers of evil). I don't know if this is an adequate description. It goes much deeper. From their footprints I see that they are descendants of *Pithecanthropus erectus* like ourselves, but here the similarity ends. I refuse to compare myself with a man who for one truth will tell ninety-nine lies; with a vampire who cannot stand in the sun and do a day's work; and with someone who thrives upon the blood, sweat, and tears of any who fall within his power. But doomsday is dawning; on this most awesome day all imbalances and contradictions must be resolved, and it will be some of us who will be left to rebuild this world and people these lands with civil men.

George

MARCH, 1967

Dear Mother,

I guess Robert told you what happened to me here.
My comrades have prevailed upon me to desist for a time, but
I must decide for myself. In any event I won't lose my head.
This is a terrible price to pay just to stay alive, or I should say
just to exist; I have never really lived.

You know I have grown very, very tired of talking, and
listening to talk. King and his kind have betrayed our bosom
interests with their demagogic delirium. The poor fool knows
nothing of the antagonist's true nature and has not the
perception to read and learn by history and past events. In a
nonviolent movement there must be a latent threat of
eruption, a dormant possibility of sudden and violent action if
concessions are to be won, respect gained, and the established
order altered. That nonviolent theory is practicable in civilized
lands among civilized people, the Asians and Africans, but a
look at European history shows that anything of great value
that ever changed hands was taken by force of arms.

I cannot let my feelings become involved. I must not fall
victim to a play of emotions, because it would limit my ability
to act in my defense.

You know the world. The depressed peoples of the world
are very shortly going to grow tired of being wooed and lulled
into passivity and quiet endurance by chromium and neon
lights. The soft music from the many well-placed public-ad-
dress loudspeakers and car radios will no longer serve as balm
to the thwarted hopes, defeated aims, and brutal suppression

106

of needed change. They'll come out of their coma with a bloodlust and justified indignation for social injustice that will sweep the asphalt right from under the empire builders. This is the only reason I hang on. I want to be in the vanguard.

My cell partner puts it this way: "Every sickness ain't death, every good-bye ain't gone, and every big man ain't strong."

I say: "Let Rome in Tiber melt, and the wide arch of the ranged empire fall" and "The jungle is still the jungle be it composed of trees or skyscrapers, and the law of the jungle is bite or be bitten."

Take care.

Son

MARCH, 1967
26

Dear Mama,

Papa* has had the "true release, and at last the clasp of peace." For him to have received this at such a great age and without violence is no small consolation. I loved him dearly and thought of him as one of our most practical and level-headed kin. You probably don't remember the long walks and talks Papa and I used to take, or the long visits when he lived on Lake Street and we lived on Warren. But I remember. He used to say things, probably just thinking aloud, sure that I wasn't listening or would not comprehend. But I did, and I

*George Davis, the author's grandfather.

think I knew him better than most. Do you remember how I used to answer "What" to every question put to me, and how Papa would deride me for this? He later in the course of our exchanges taught me to answer questions with "Why" instead of "What."

Another of our games helped me greatly with my powers of observation. When we would walk, he told me to always look at the large signboards as deeply as possible and after we had passed one, he would make me recite all that was on it. I would never remember as much detail as he, but I did win a kind word or two on occasion. We played this same game at his house with pictures and objects spread out on the table or bed.

I wish he could have survived to see and enjoy the new world we plan to create from this chaos. If I could have gotten out of here last year he would never have gone out on sardines and crackers. I don't know how anyone else views the matter and don't care, but now for me his is one more voice added to the already thunderous chorus that cry from their unmarked and unhallowed graves for vindication.

Don't wait for me to change or modify my attitudes in the least. I *cannot understand*, as you put it, or as you would have me understand. I am a man, you are a woman. Being a woman, you may expect to be and enjoy being tyrannized. Perhaps you actually like walking at the heel of another, or otherwise placing yourself beneath another, but for me this is despicable. I refuse to even attempt to *understand* why I should debase myself or concede or compromise any part, the smallest part, of anything on earth to anyone who is not of my kind in thought and form. I love you, Mama, but I must be frank. Why did Papa die alone and hungry? Why did you think me insane for wanting a new bicycle instead of the old one I stole piece by piece and put together? Why did you allow us to worship at a white altar? Why even now, following tragedy after tragedy, crisis after crisis, do you still send Jon to that school where he is taught to feel inferior, and why do you continue to send me

108

Easter cards? This is the height of disrespect you show me. You never wanted me to be a man nor Jon either. You don't want us to resist and defeat our enemies. What is wrong with you, Mama? No other mama in history has acted the way you act under stress situations.

I won't be a good *boy* ever.

Love,

George

MARCH, 1967
26

Dear Robert,

Why, my friend, did Papa go out alone and hungry. Did Frances and Mama ever talk to you of his condition when they returned from Illinois last year. Was it ever put to him that he could stay with you people and eat when you ate and fast when you fasted, I wonder? "When poverty comes in at the door, love flies out of the window."

Can you see the division among us and its effect? This is our greatest obstacle. I sometimes wonder how this will turn out. Before we can ever effectively face down the foe, we must have had long since learned to share, trust, communicate, and live harmoniously with each other.

Our new state governor has decreed that the daily food

allowance for each convict be cut exactly in half. We get almost no "grade one" protein now.

Stuff like eggs, meat, and milk products is seldom seen now. So my experiments in self-discipline are now paying off. Everyone else is hungry now, while I feel nothing. And this is just the beginning: the reactionary, repressive forces presently at work will bring things to such a crisis soon that Baldwin's warning of "The fire next time" must soon be borne out with all its sinister accompaniments.

Take care of yourself, Pop. Comfort Mom as well as you can and tell her I'm all right, healthy, happy, content. Of course, this is a lie, but she likes to be lied to.

George

MARCH, 1967
27

Dear Mama,

Please don't take what I expressed in my last letter too seriously. I was feeling extremely bad. Try to relax; the mental depression you are presently gripped by comes from a very common cause, particularly among us blacks here in the U.S. As a defense, we look at life through our rose-colored glasses, rationalizing and pretending that things are not so bad after all, but then day after day—tragedy after tragedy strikes and confuses us, and our pretense fails to aid or dispel the nagging feeling that we cannot have security in an insecure society, especially when one belongs to an insecure caste

110

within this larger society. I believe sincerely that you will be a very unhappy and perplexed woman for as long as you try to pretent that you have anything in common with this culture, or better, that this culture has anything in common with you, and as long as you pretend that there is no difference between men, and as long as you try to be more English than the English, while the English ignore your attempts and use your humility to their advantage.

I suggest no action, no physical action that is, for I know you have never been a woman of action, but I do suggest that you purge your mind little by little of some of your Western notions. Direct your nervous animosity at the right people and their system, and stop, for your own sake please stop blaming yourself. If you were, right now, walking toward your kitchen with the whole family's life savings in your hand, let's say, and I sneaked up behind you and pulled the rug from under you and you fell and broke your arm, leg, nose, and the money flew into the burning fireplace, would you *get up* blaming me for pulling the rug, or would you just lay there and blame yourself and pretend that you didn't really fall, or that the whole thing made no difference anyway? The analogy is perfect.

Do you know who I blame for what has happened to me the last 25 years, and before to my ancestors? I would be narrow-minded indeed if I blamed any of you, my folks. I don't blame you for not teaching me how to get what I wanted *without getting put in jail*, nor do I blame myself. I was born knowing nothing and am a product of my total surroundings. I blame the capitalistic dog, the imperialistic, cave-dwelling brute that kidnapped us, pulled the rug from under us, made us a caste within his society with no vertical economic mobility. As soon as all this became clear to me and I developed the nerve to admit it to myself, that we were defeated in war and are now captives, slaves or actually that we inherited a neoslave existence, I immediately became relaxed, always expecting the worst, and started working on

111

the remedy. Can you play chess? It *relaxes*, builds foresight, alertness, concentration, and judgment. Learn, so we can play next year.

George

MAY, 1967

9

Dear Robert,

That's great about the classes. You passed the exams pretty easy, didn't you? It's wonderful to have a pop with brains.

I was approved for a transfer, but it is not official yet. When it is I'll inform you of the details.

I've been getting a lot of work done lately. My mind is fast becoming clear and I am slowly harnessing my emotions, I can go days without speaking a word. With the pursuit of food and shelter relegated to the state, I have been able to channel all my thoughts to important things, significant things, So I attempt to bend this experience to our benefit rather than let them weaken and destroy me, as they would like. You are aware that these places, this one in particular, will either bring out the best in an individual or ruin him entirely.

Wherever they send me, Robert, I will try as hard as my character will allow to avoid all involvement in those situations that lead to trouble. But I can promise nothing, the future holds no surprises for me. I expect anything, including trouble, especially trouble, considering the times. I have adopted, these

112

last several months, a new attitude, however, that will limit the scope of my troubles.

Take care of yourself.

George

MAY, 1967
16

Dear Robert,

That is good reasoning concerning the school issue. It was a wise decision in every way you look at it. The other way (catholic school) you pay more for less education, plus they make emotional pansies of the boys with that sanctimonious dogma. Dear Pop, I'm not just talking for the sake of talking. I am deeply concerned for Jon and you all. Much thought goes into all I attempt to convey. Whenever a man builds an image of himself and of his surroundings that he cannot live up to and that does not conform to the de facto situation, the end result must be confusion and emotional breakdown. If my instructor tells me that the world and its affairs are run as well as they possibly can be, that I am governed by wise and judicious men, that I am free and should be happy, and if when I leave the instructor's presence and encounter the exact opposite, if I actually sense or see confusion, war, inflation, recession, depression, death, and decay, is it not reasonable that I should become perplexed? If my instructor tells me that sex is evil, bad, base, and I happen to like sex, is it not reasonable to assume that I will develop

113

mixed emotions concerning sex? If this instructor relates to me that sex is bad, thinking of it is lustful, and lust is a sign of my moral decay, what opinion will I have of myself? This is what they will do to Jon at that catholic school. But that is just part of it. He will also learn that J.C. was white, which is a lie. That the Egyptians were white, which is a lie. That the people of India are white under their black skin. That Chinese are yellow, when they range from brown to the blackest black. He will get a lot of this misinformation in public school too, but not nearly as much. With a little effort after school from you this can be corrected. Tell him that these men don't always tell the truth. Make him read histories by Ronald Segal, Du Bois, etc. Make him read the pro-Eastern writers, so that he will have a good cross section of all there is to be heard. Show him how to masturbate, and explain to him that making love *with a woman* is the most natural thing on earth. Explain how he can do so without getting the girl pregnant. Tell him that "there is no hell, no heaven, and no immortality, and that *all things* are permissible," as long as the next man's feelings are considered.

None of those at home who contest you in your judgment know nearly as much about life as you. So you must be firm and decisive. None of the Western European cultures know anything about philosophy (love of knowledge). They know nothing of the proper way that men should carry on their relations with other men. Proof of this—who originated the passport laws, tariff laws, atom bomb, competitive enterprise, etc., etc. They only excel in one area, technology. So let Jon learn chemistry at school. You give him his economics, history, and philosophy at home!!

George

114

21

Dear Robert,

Penny was here again last week. She has taught the little guy how to say Uncle George. So "Uncle George" was ringing the length of the visiting hall for a couple of hours. However, I was less than pleased. I tried to get him to change it to "Comrade George," but he didn't seem to understand. Uncle George is too much like Uncle Tom and Uncle Ben (of rice-box fame) for comfort!

I trust you are well. I am holding off the ill effects of the concentration camp as best I can. It seems a losing battle, however. I've had to take to wearing glasses of considerable strength due to failure of my eyesight. Living in this constant half-light, I guess.

When you told me a while back of Frances' serious eye problem, I resolved upon my release to have one of mine transplanted into her head. But this will no longer be any bargain for her.

I have been having trouble with my eyes for a year. When I finally was able to maneuver an eye test, I was surprised at the amount of money they took from my account (money that you have sent me that I have not used yet). I was even more surprised when I finally got the glasses two months later with their strength and how much they improved my vision.

Speaking of money and accounts, Pop, I'm flush for now,

by flush I mean I have stocked up on envelopes and toothpaste, I've come to realize that I don't need much to eat to stay alive and I don't smoke. I can get fat on what the average man may starve on. So the money you have been sending me can be put to use at home there, your books, or perhaps something for Jon, he also needs supplementry reading material. I am sorry that you and Mama don't make each other happy. European-Anglo-American brainwashing is at the bottom of it. Those empty pseudo-middle-class ideas that we have adopted from the opposition make us unhappy in the same way the middle class itself is unhappy. Then too when poverty comes in at the door, loves leaves by the window. We all know who has caused our poverty. I have experienced the same thing with women and men. All the women I've had tried to use me, tried to secure through me a soft spot in this cutthroat system for themselves. All they ever wanted was clothes and money and to be taken out to flash these things. I no longer have time for such small ideas or small people. Blacks that I've met here who exhibit such character- istics I disdain and ignore. The same with any woman I may have when I get out. She must let me retrain her mind or no deal.

George

28

Dear Robert,

I've been a good boy lately, kind, polite, forgiving. Don't know if it will do any good though since people invariably mistake kindness for weakness. I really cannot imagine how anyone can stay detached and complacent for any period of time and still maintain social contacts on any level. It no longer surprises me, but I still find the general acceptance and widespread practice of the more deranged products of Western culture disturbing. Prying, nosy, schizophrenic, domineering, psychoneurotic people press you from all sides. They remain in a continual state of agitation, always on the brink of doing something maniacal! Capitalism, I believe, the capitalizing on the next man's labor, on the next man's weakness, has contributed greatly to the development of the anomalous "Western man"; capitalism, competitive enterprise, man competing against man for the necessary things, for status symbols, for power to repress his competitors and secure his personal well-being to exercise his ego, his fancy. I just cannot get used of the idea of some petty, stereotyped, bureaucratic official, patently suffering from some mental disorder, asking me questions, calling on me to explain myself. It is odd, and ironical, the trickery and turnabout that has gone down these last few generations.

Chew on this a few moments: a colonizer, a usurer, the

original thief, a murderer for personal gain, a kidnapper-slaver, a maker of cannon, bombs, and poison gas, an egocentric parasite, the original fork tongue, the odd man is trying to convey to us that we must adjust ourselves to his warp, that we must learn to be more like him, that because we're not we're backward, underdeveloped, unsophisticated! This is strange and contradictory.

I am deeply sorry that I ever told a lie, stole anything robbed and cheated at anything — mainly because it is so much like conforming to Western ways.

To all appearances they are upset with me for doing these things. That privilege is supposed to be reserved for them I guess. So what do they mean by saying that we must get in with them, be like them, adopt capitalism, clothe ourselves in Western ways? This is a strange and contradictory thing. If we the colored and black of the world adopt capitalism where would we have to seek our colonies, Europe, the U.S.?! Who would we capitalize on if we used their history as a pattern? Them I should say!! Who would we kidnap, murder, lynch, enslave, and then neglect!! So what do they mean by saying, "Do as I do"? I don't think, well I know that they are not serious, not sincere. I think they are employing another trick, a ploy to further confuse us and use us, I think what they mean is not "Do as I do" but "Do as I say"! In the 1770s the Europeans over here wanted to pull away from the Europeans of England. They called it a freedom fight. Now we men of color here in the U.S. want to pull away from these Europeans and they call it subversion, irresponsibility, etc. I don't even speak to them anymore. I go my way and hope to be left alone.

George

13

Dear Robert,

I'm in regular adjustment center—segregation again.
They have let me have my personal property, books, toilet articles, envelopes, that is minus 90 percent of it. It happens every time I transfer from one part of the prison to another or go to isolation, my stuff gets ripped off. I get robbed. I'm sure it wasn't the officials. They are such nice, efficient people, so I won't complain here with my pencil. I'll need a few dollars to replace the necessary things (envelopes, dictionary, etc.), when you can afford it.

Your physical appearance hasn't changed at all over the years, Pop. Clean living has preserved you marvelously. Do you ever drink any alcoholic beverages? I have never known you to, but that doesn't mean that you don't. How much sleep do you average a day? Perhaps I won't live to be as old as you are, but if I do I won't look as good. The loose skin on my face is already starting to wrinkle, and strange as it seems, I tend toward obesity if I eat certain foods. I must have picked that up from Mama.

How is she? Tell her I'm going to be a good boy from now until I can get out of here.

I worry about Penny, does she know that she can come home if the circumstance make it necessary? She respects you for what you have done for us and accepts you as you are. So

119

do I, Pop. I recall that you never had more than one suit or two pairs of shoes all throughout the early years. I never remember you having a moment's personal gratification during those years. No one believes me when I tell them you never went to a nightclub or finger-poppers' party during the twenty years that I remember. I don't think any other man in the U.S. would have reacted as you did concerning that incident with the Hudson car, fixing it with your hands and driving it for five years in that condition. False pride would have forced anyone else into radical and uneconomic acts. I felt real bad about that, but I didn't understand life then as I do now. I'm deeply sorry for the weak, silly transgressions of my past, and I'm sorry that I won't be able to conduct my relations with the world as you would have me conduct them. I see the big picture where you may never have. I think I see the larger historical concept in its full detail. The obligation you felt toward us, I feel toward history. I must follow my call. It is of great importance to me that you understand this and give me your blessings. I don't care about anyone else. I don't feel I must explain myself or be understood by anyone else on earth.

George

JULY, 1967
15

My Friend,

I got your letter of June 5. I have it here before me. I told Les to cooperate with your efforts for me. I sure do need some of the benefits of togetherness now. As I explained I am in adjustment center here for an undefined amount of time.

Les speaks of me coming home with optimism, but I would benefit largely from a transfer. No one, among the officials that is, ever calls me out of my cell anymore to speak with me of my progress or my future. I'm just locked down and forgotten. Can a lawyer do anything about getting me a transfer? He would have to go through Sacramento. The justification for such action is obvious: I cannot adjust here, the officials have preconceived notions about my behavioral patterns and consequently look for the worst in me. The atmosphere here is aggressive, and I'm too far away from home. I cannot get regular visits and thus miss the beneficial influence of you and my parents.

My friend, my thinking has changed somewhat since I saw you last. That fellow who sent pictures of his Cadillac auto up here can explain some of the workings and progress of my thoughts. I hope he doesn't betray himself with that fast living I hear he is doing. Seems he has learned nothing from bitter experience!! I have trained away, pressed out forever the last

121

of my Western habits. You remember I never got intoxicated or spent any money or time on trifles, but in the passing of these last couple of years, I have completely retrained myself and my thinking to the point now that I think and dream of one thing only, 24 hours of each day. I have no habits, no ego, no name, no face. I feel no love, no tenderness, for anyone who does not think as I do. There can be no ties of blood or kinship strong enough to move me from my course. I'll never, never trade my self-determination for a car, cheap mass-produced clothes, clapboard house, or a couple of nights a week at the go-go. Control over the circumstances that surround my existence is of the first importance to me. Without this control, or with control in someone else's hands, I am forever insecure, subject at all times to the whim and caprice of the man in control, and you and I know how whimiscal some men can be. Well, Pop, I'll be going outside to court the seventh of August to testify for a friend. I'll get a glimpse of the world at large, if you can call San Rafael the world at large.

I hope you are doing well. I would have written before now but I was in isolation up until the eleventh of this month, as you know.

Do you have time to read? I'll suggest some books if so, next letter. Take care.

George

JULY, 1967
19

Dear Robert,

I wrote you a letter about two weeks ago. It was returned to me today. It never got out of the institution.

Received your letter of the 15th today, no change here.

I have that address I asked you for. I got it through other channels. I was spelling and pronouncing the name wrong.

Tell A.A. to get busy and make my woman start writing. A visit every now and then would be nice also. Tell him to send me her new address that I may send her a correspondence form. You don't know her, but he will.

Penny has not been up to see me since you came, no letter either, hope she is all right.

Locked up 24 hours a day now. It's all right, though—gives me plenty of time at my work. My cell faces north, and there is a window in front of it. Plenty of fresh air comes into my cell.

George

23

Dear Robert,

        I feel relieved to know that you are taking Jon out of catholic school. Man, falling under the conservative influence of those admen and fakes was the worst thing that ever happened to me. How could you have ever allowed it. It was Mama's idea but you should never have let her sell it to you.

        I remember Chicago all right, in fact I remember too much. I was very much confused and dissatisfied during those years. They had much to do with the development of my character. I've had to unlearn and reexamine all that I experienced in those years. But what you were really referring to was how it stayed hot all night, with people sleeping on the beaches and such.

        I remember the garage roof where I was virtually held prisoner sometimes, there at North Racine Street. It is criminal to do that to a child. And no parks near enough to go to, no yard front or back to play with the neighbors' kids, no neighbors really except the ones on Lake Street. I remember glimpses of our place over there on Lake also. This is a dog's life, Pop, you had nothing then. You have worked hard, hard, and obeyed the laws of our masters but you still have nothing. Is it idle dreaming for me to want an end to something like this?

        I wrote Mama three letters three months ago. She didn't

124

answer or acknowledge any. I owe her loyalty just for being my mother, but she is adult and I never baby adults. She resents me because I won't accept her views on method and means of getting by in this rat race. She once told me that I had a complex that made me view the world as I do. In so many words she was telling me that I shouldn't be complexed about being of the lowest social class or in our case caste. She was saying that I should be indifferent about being used and abused like a goat or milk cow or something. I understand her and all black women over here. Women like to be dominated, love being strong-armed, need an overseer to supplement their weakness. So how could she really understand my feelings on self-determination. For this reason we should never allow women to express any opinions on the subject, but just to sit, listen to us, and attempt to understand. It is for them to obey and aid us, not to attempt to think.

George

Dear Georgia,

      For me, the word "soul" has yet to be properly defined. I have seen or felt no evidence of its existence. I have heard the word and listened to the theory connected with it, but it is abstract and academic at best.

      The theory of an existing and benevolent god simply doesn't make sense to anyone who is rational. A benevolent and omnipotent god would never allow such imbalances as I see to exist for one second. If by chance I am wrong, however, I must then assume that being born black called for some automatic punishment for sins I know nothing about, and being innocent it behooves me to defy god.

      I seriously fail to understand when someone speaks of my soul, but I do know what my body needs. I know what my mind incessantly craves. Gratification of these is what I must pursue. As a woman I can understand your being naturally disposed to servitude. I can understand *your* feelings but what I can't understand is why you would have me feel the same, considering that I am a man. Why have you always attempted to implant womanly ideas into my character. Of course it is your option to do as you please, but please don't feel that I love you less simply because I fail to respond, or feel that I love you any less because I do not have time to explain myself.

      Love has never turned aside the boot, blade, or bullet.

126

Neither has it ever satisfied my hunger of body or mind. The author of my hunger, the architect of the circumstantial pressures which are the sole cause of my ills will find no peace, in this existence or the next, or the one following that; never, never. I'll dog his trail to infinity. I hope I never will feel I've love for the thing that causes insufferable pain. What I do feel is the urge to resist, resist, and never stop resisting or even think of stopping my resistance until victory falls to me.

Extreme, perhaps, but involved is my self-determination, and control of the environment upon which my existence depends, and the existence of my father, mother, Delora's and Penny's sons, and all that I feel tied to. We are in an extreme situation.

I didn't create this impasse. I had nothing to do with the arrival of matters at this destructive end, as you infer. Did I colonize, kidnap, make war on myself, destroy my own institutions, enslave myself, use myself, and neglect myself, steal my identity and then, being reduced to nothing, invent a competitive economy knowing that I cannot compete? Sounds very foolish, but this is what you propose when you place the blame on me or on "us." It was a fool who created this monster, one unaccustomed to power and its use, a foolish man grown heady with power and made drunk, dizzy drunk from the hot air that inflates his ego. I am his victim, born innocent, a *total* product of my surroundings. Everything that I am, I *developed* into because of circumstantial and situational pressures. I was born knowing nothing; necessity and environment formed me, and everyone like me. Please accord me at least the social morality that springs from its contorted brain center. I'm through with weakness and cowardice. I've trained it out. Let come what comes. I can never delude myself into thinking that I love my enemies. I can hardly do any worse than I am doing now; if worst comes to worst that's all right, I'll just continue the fight in hell.

George

127

10

Dear Robert,

Things are looking up, I have a promise on my injured leg, should be seeing about it anytime now. I'm in pretty good shape and it won't kill me. Good move you made on your way out. I could never say anything like that for myself. No one would believe me.

Doing good, minding my business, won't let you down.

Delora is quite handsome, you know that was the first time I'd seen her in seven years.

There are three ways to enforce and build discipline in a child: through terror, through guilt, and through shame. The first principle is the worst and involves keeping the child in constant fear of beating or harsh reprimand. This is not conducive to all-round adjustment. Either the child becomes a confirmed coward or at best unstable and erratic. A child with feelings of insecurity (lack of confidence) may later on try to prove himself by deliberately doing things against what he has been taught is right. Think on that a moment!

Then the guilt concept: it finds expression in convincing the child that he will suffer god's wrath (religion) or be looked upon as a fool, knucklehead, buffoon, or evil and maligned person by the rest of mankind. This is not good in that it causes the child to be too dependent. He cannot develop or become *creative* for fear of disapproval from on high. Then,

128

what man can live up to the expectations of god. Then there are those among us who cannot live up to the expectations of other men, society. What happens to the child who cannot live up to god's or man's expectations, the child trained or disciplined through guilt feelings. His confidence is forever destroyed and he becomes the ubiquitous temporizer, the listless apathetic.

The last principle is the only one worthy of intelligent parents: shame. If a child does not react in the proper way and carry out his duties toward parents and peers he should be taught to feel shame or lose face as the Eastern people call it. The child feels that he has let *himself* down when he fails to do the proper thing. Only constant and calm, rational reproof can cause this feeling in a kid. In other words, it takes brains and persistence on the part of the parent to shape the child's thinking. It should be clear that becoming frantic and beside onself, beating and cussing is going to give the child a new experience and leave an impression that may not be wholesome. Felix Greene wrote that in all the time he spent in a certain country in the East he never saw a child throw a tantrum. He asked one of the social workers there about it, describing the features of a childish tantrum. The Eastern social worker's shocked expression and complete ignorance of any such things happening to the children caused Greene to investigate further and deduce that they don't go through emotional breakdowns "because they have no precedents from their parents." Take care.

George

Dear Robert,

The paper started one week ago, Saturday. Everything is all right. I'll do as you say about the patience. Perhaps I expect too much from people. Hospital and X rays any day now.

I expect help from certain people only, but I'll take your advice and look no more. Of course this doesn't mean that I am going to stop helping others as much as I can. I'll continue to give as good an example of how we should treat each other as I can, but as you indicate I shouldn't expect this to influence anyone else to treat me similarly.

Take care of yourself.

George

SEPTEMBER, 1967

1

Dear Robert,

Jon is about the same age as I was when we first moved out here. I remember well my attitudes and confusion at that time. He can't be too much different since our development was forced along similar lines. Of course he has had a slightly better chance or atmosphere to build the things necessary for the changeover from man-child to man. That school Mama was sending him to did him great harm but not irreparable harm since in his case you were on the job after school sowing pride and knowledge of self and kind, and explaining the promise and problems in acquiring self-determination and control over all the circumstances surrounding our existence. Of course you have been explaining that this control must never be allowed to remain in the hands of strangers or incompetents, etc. So I hope he is not as awed and confused as I was then. Give him my regards. Tell him I said he is charged to take good care of his mother and sisters, that since he has grown so big and strong so soon, he should brace himself to his duties early. Tell him that I said that life is serious and we must be careful, one misstep can cause us "years of regret and grief, and sorrow without relief."

Take care of yourself.

George

SEPTEMBER, 1967
12

Dear Robert,

I am doing well, no new problems. Please say nothing else about the leg to anyone. You could cause me trouble. I'll live. I stay in reasonably good condition just for occasions like this. I can see about it if I get out next year. You should know about protesting with the mouth. It never avails us anything but grief. I no longer do so in any form, for it indicates naiveté. It means that subconsciously one may still be looking for justice or humanity from places that we have ample proof of it not existing.

I worry about Penny and I would like to see her there with you. I have not seen or heard from her since you were here last. Perhaps she feels she doesn't need or want any of us. Have you heard from her? Perhaps it's my fault. I push people away by expecting too much of them. I probably used the wrong presentation with her and frightened her. Or she may not care to hear about clean living and high ideals. People tend to run like hell at the mention of sacrifice and responsibility.

Give everyone my regards and take care of yourself.

George

SEPTEMBER, 1967
14

Dear Mama,

    I hope this year's birthday finds you well. I would like to be able to give you things, and take you places, but I've been unfortunate, and slow learning. But I have learned well. Perhaps next year I'll be able to give you a villa in Tanzania.

    I'm fine; my work progresses well. Seems that all I've predicted is now coming true, though, much sooner than I thought, I must admit.

    Take care of yourself.

George

24

Dear Robert,

Received your letter. All is well here. You have everyone back there with you except Delora now. That is good in a way. You have another chance to teach them how to live, arrange their values and attitudes so that they correspond with our situation, our aspirations, our newly reestablished identity.

Penny expressed the thought to me that since you do not have much to say around there, you don't care much about them and their little problems. She expressed the feelings of all those there who do not understand you in saying this. Women and children enjoy and need a strong hand poised above them. They need direction and someone to show concern for them and you may have to make your presence felt there, a little anyway. Of course I'm not talking about being a tyrant, but just some rational, moderate, but persistent pressure to the left.

I imagine I'll really be able to get down to fighting weight now. I told you what happened to the noon meal. I really don't miss it though.

Take care of yourself.

George

SEPTEMBER, 1967
30

Dear Robert,

Getting plenty of work done. How is your scholastic project going? Are you still attending the night classes? I thought that was a wonderful idea.

Speed reading and vocabulary power are foremost in elevating the mind. They can be worked on in spare time, ten or twenty minutes a day. I consistently work on both: especially vocabulary, out of small paperback pocketbooks sold in the canteen and in the prison bookstore. But since I have much more study time than you, I go one hour or so on each daily. There are dozens of these little books published today. Every time I see a different one I try to make it part of my collection.

Are you well, my friend? I am getting thin as a rail, feel all right, however. Give my regards to Jon and Penny.

Take care of yourself.

George

3

Dear Georgia,

A thank-you note for money and letter. I can always use money, but discharge your obligations at home first. I can do without. If I were you, I would treat Pop a little better. He has been pretty good to us all, when one considers the shocks and strains he has had to live with.

As a woman, you just do not (and I guess never will) understand what it means to be a man in this particular situation here in the U.S. Women just don't suffer the mental mortification of defeat and emasculation that we meen do. Robert has lived with it for many years, trying to rationalize it, justify it, pretend that it does not affect him, but it has affected him very deeply. Imagine how he must feel when his woman won't even let him run the house. For you to just outright countermand his wishes on a matter concerning the education of his son must be a bitter dose for him to swallow indeed. After what he must accept from the outside world everyday of his life, to come to his home and also be made to carry water and cut wood and take orders is adding insult to injury.

Though you may not see much evidence of it, Robert still harbors the desire to be a man and assert himself. He is not completely dead inside. The years and years of regret and grief, discomfort, and defeat he has endured since the

136

depression years of his childhood, all the forgetting and pretending and cheekturning he has had to do, cannot be denied. It lives with him, still jammed back in the dark corners of his mind. I've seen it, Georgia, believe me, I've seen it in him and in many others of his generation. One day in the near future these feelings of mass discontent must break their bounds. It's just as natural and predictable as the sunrise. I am ready now. When they are ready, nothing, nothing will be able to countervail our march to victory.

In Jon's case it is simply a matter of what we need most and how can he be best equipped to survive the crisis that now grips us. I think we need tough, well-informed, and loyal additions to the tribe. Can he develop these characteristics at this terrible place you advocate? You have been living in the big city now for 25 years. It is almost unbelievable that you have not discovered that the guys who will be training him there are 90 percent sex deviates (homosexuals, etc.) and 10 percent free-loading incompetents who couldn't get food and shelter any other way. I would never make a charge like this unless I had firsthand evidence. I hope that you were merely ignorant of these things. I hope that you have not intentionally sold out Jon's bosom interests. Robert has sheltered you from the world to some extent. You have not come in contact with things he sees daily, so let him have some say.

George

137

OCTOBER, 1967
11

Dear Robert,

I received the letter with the money in it all right, thank you. I'm going pretty good here, no problems, no new ones anyway.

I went before a formal two-man review committee here recently. They gave me at least four more months to do here in the adjustment center. I guess we can call this improvement of a sort since I'm usually told nothing.

You say Jon is having trouble with math. And that you feel it's just a matter of his settling down to his work. I wondered when you mentioned this just what it was that is keeping him from his studies. How does he spend his time? Is there anyone there to help him with his studies? Of course, you are right that all he has to do is apply himself to his work. At this stage of the schooling structure, nothing is really difficult. Math is never difficult, since its laws are positive. All that needs to be done is take the necessary time and learn the formulas and principles. Of course, if too much time is spent in class on religious matters, the teacher is at fault, not the student. In fact if *any time* is spent on religious matters during the school hours the student is being cheated.

Take care of yourself.

George

138

OCTOBER, 1967
17

Dear Robert,

The time slips away from me. I'm surrounded here by fools, degenerates, and phonies. I suffer a constant bombardment of nonsense from all sides.

There is no rest from it even at night. Twenty-four hours a day all my senses must endure the shock of this attack from the lunatic fringe. So I insert my earplugs, and bury myself in my thoughts and my work. The days, even the weeks lapse one into the other, endlessly into one another. Each day that comes and goes is exactly like the one that went before. If I am lax in my duties toward you, forgive me. I am living under strain.

I am sorry to hear about your friend. The same has happened to some of mine here. I think I know how you feel; however, I try to think of those things as releases.

How was my letter to Jon received? Mama may have torn it up. If Jon wants to go to the trouble of framing those parts that trouble him into a letter, I have a fair understanding of math.

No new problems here. Just waiting it out. Time is on my side. I'm twenty-six now, and I'll be twenty-six when I leave here. Be it 40 years from today.

Take care.

George

139

OCTOBER, 1967

18

Dear Robert,

How is Penny and the little guy? I guess I miss them quite a bit. What a difference their presence makes here.

My language studies are coming along well. I guess if I don't get out before January—and it's not very likely that I will—I'll go into Arabic next. With four languages plus English I'll be able to communicate with three-fourths of the people on earth. I am presently working on Spanish and Swahili. Spanish is spoken by most peoples from Mexico to Chile in what is the fastest-growing population area in the world. Swahili is spoken by all of eastern Africa. I may find communication with these peoples important in my work. All that remains is for me to learn Arabic and Chinese.

Perhaps I'll start on these two next year, I've done well with the Spanish.

I trust you are well. Don't work yourself too hard. You cannot get rich on wages. I have had no response from Jon to my last two letters. What's happening? Has he forgotten his brother; it has been a long time. He was just a baby when first I came here to the concentration camp. It's been seven years, one month now.

Take care of yourself.

George

OCTOBER, 1967
24

Dear Robert,

I'll be considered for transfer again this week, they'll probably approve Folsom for me this time. It is a maximum security prison like this, so there will be no change in my fortunes. One prison is like the other, except perhaps the minimum security places in the southern part of the state where they have a less aggressive atmosphere where if one can get around the local constabulary, the chances for parole are greater. That is part of the reason that the guy who was arrested with me went home four years ago and I am still here. Right before I was forced into that situation in Soledad and sent here, he was sent to Chino. But his folks had money to pass around.

No new problems here, the same old things. I'm getting plenty of work done with my time.

I am not trying to lose weight, I'm not eating as I should, but we discussed that before. You forget things too fast. But maybe that is good. I'm not sure. Perhaps if I could forget, I could have some peace of mind. But I don't forget anything, wounds scar my mind much worse than they scar my body. But I don't let such things as food, warmth, comfort, and lack of material things cause me any great distress. I'm doing as well as I can expect to, because I don't expect anything. Anything good, that is.

Take care of yourself.

George

OCTOBER, 1967
26

Dear Robert,

Jon tells me they have him studying Latin. I find this very depressing. No one has spoken Latin in fifteen hundred years! They are teaching the poor kid a dead language! Wasting his precious time! His precious talent! A great blunder is again being made regarding your offspring, Robert.

People only learn Latin these days so that they can read that thing they call the bible in the Latin and sound mysterious. It's a lot of European ritual, a lot of hocus-pocus from the dark ages of Europe. The time he puts into that totally useless pursuit could be spent on math or science!

Take care.

George

NOVEMBER, 1967
2

Dear Robert,

I received both your letters today dated the twenty-ninth and thirtieth. True I may forget myself sometimes and I'll have to redouble my efforts to control this. I know it is wrong and I know the proper method. It is the application of method that sometimes causes me trouble. But I'll redouble my effort to get over this. Emotion has much to do with it. All of my past life has been victimized by my emotions. I have struggled mightily with myself these last couple of years in an attempt to erase all emotion. The only method that can succeed is the clinical approach, the analytical technique of treating our problems. It is said and with some justification that the greatest battle is with oneself, so if I can gain a victory here the real work shouldn't be too hard.

On the subject of injury, there is the real and the imagined. You have made several references to the subject in the last month or two and I have let them pass. By telling me that Jon has no chip on his shoulder, you attempted to make me feel alone and isolated in my attitudes. But you are wrong in trying to second-guess me, because I have no chip on my shoulder. I know the simplest way to handle an injury whether real or fancied is to forget it. I bear no one on earth any ill will. I have felt the sting of the knout and I live in the shadow of the ovens. I am the object of the severest ridicule (coon, monkey, shoe, a shoe is something to be walked on incidentally, buck, savage, and child), but even in the face of all this I have not one chip on my shoulder. Aren't I a truly marvelous and forgiving person? Almost every day I have something to forgive and forget. Perhaps most of this is fanciful and illusionary, but every day I have the opportunity to practice this almost godlike facility I have built into myself. But then to be honest with myself, it is not merely or solely due to strength of character that I am able to call up just a little more forgiveness, I also have this thing going with myself about not wanting to get killed. I don't know about that getting-killed thing. Now it would be a great loss to me, but I feel that I could forgive that too. Now I say this at the risk of seeming immodest but to further illustrate my healthy outlook on the matter in question, let me remind you that in spite of all I am human and I have myself done things that require forgiveness from others—I have transgressed against my fellows in moments of weakness and madness.

It's hard, my friend. Because of my temperament it's even harder. I hope I can make it.

Take care of yourself.

George

NOVEMBER, 1967

6

Dear Robert,

Are you well? The changes are as slow as ever here. No new problems, however, except perhaps with my health. It may be failing. Headaches all the time and a skin condition that started some time back. Look at that picture I sent you of me taken upon my graduation. You may be able to see the discolored spots in my face. Well, the condition is growing worse—it is all over my face now, huge discolored spots. I look like a leper. If you have a connection who is a dermatologist perhaps you could pass me on some information on it. It is only on my face now, but it is progressive. It is spreading. I'd like to know what to do about it and what may be the cause. The cause, however, may be most important. I've been thinking that it is probably the food. Quality and quantity. My knee has gone down some and is not too sore anymore.

I hope everyone there is well. Give my special regards to Penny and Jon.

Take care of yourself.

George

NOVEMBER, 1967

Dear Robert,

This last word from you in Jon's presence convinces me that we can never reconcile our differences. I never realized that I was a source of embarrassment to you, I thought most blacks, especially those of our economic level, understood, vaguely at least, that these places were built with us in mind, just as were the project houses, unemployment offices, and bible schools.

Perhaps later if we both live to see the outcome of all this, I will be able to explain myself better, but for now you surely don't need me and I have never needed anyone. Life has failed me. People I have had a right to expect something of, in the past, have failed me. And I fail myself almost every day. But I suffer no lasting effects from any of this because I derive my force and energy from no outside quarter. Your inability to understand and support me puts me at a loss, but I cannot allow this to influence my course. I must follow my mind. There is no turning back from awareness. If I were to alter my step now I would always hate myself. I would grow old feeling that I had failed in the obligatory duty that is ours once we become aware. I would die as most of us blacks have died over the last few centuries, without having lived.

You have misjudged the depth of my feelings on these matters. They mean everything to me. If we could have found grounds for compatibility within the framework of my ideals the purely mental aspect of my job could have been less difficult. I anticipated failure in this from the start, so I am

146

not shocked or surprised now that the last has been said and we find ourselves poles apart.

I'll be all right from here, Robert. I have the nervous equipment and I'll spend my remaining time here checking my emotions and developing the clinical approach.

You owe me nothing. Anything you may think you owe me I absolve you of entirely.

Because we look a lot alike, because the same blood flows in our veins, I thought we could perhaps pool our resources, plan great things, produce some remarkable changes and conclusions, and write a few pages of history. But I cannot see myself as well as other people see me and perhaps you are justified in feeling ashamed of me. The most important abutment of our relation has disappeared; perhaps it never existed. This is certainly my loss, but I cannot see any reason for us to communicate with each other again from this day until such time as I can demonstrate the usefulness of my ideals and methods.

Please take care of yourself.

Respectfully,

George

DECEMBER, 1967
1

Dear Robert,

I guess there is something to be said for a person who does as he is told, lives by the routine set up by his self-appointed bosses, etc. And of course we must learn to fight our own battles. This way we can die alone, one at a time. This is a very old and proven idea. It has worked wonderfully up to now and that is why 1967 finds us all so secure and well placed.

My trouble is that I have expected too much of you. You're already doing your best: what you feel is right. How can I expect more?

George

DECEMBER, 1967

Dear Robert,

I'm all right; no change here. They gave me a little job in here where I am locked up but took it back right away, I think to get a reaction.

It has started to rain almost every day up here now and it is rather cool. It is strange but I think I prefer cool weather to warm.

Have you heard anything from my friend? I don't trust many people very far but I have very strong feelings that this guy will not abandon me or our ideas.

Things must be very difficult for him or he would have had a lawyer up here for me by now, or done something along that line. Of course, we never really get to know anyone to an absolute degree, but I saw this guy in many different situations and he never showed the slightest weakness or reservation or self-interest. We need people like that. When we cannot even put confidence in them we're through.

Take care of yourself.

George

DECEMBER, 1967
13

Dear Robert,

Hope you are well. I received your note and all is normal here.

No new problems. I've got six months clean now, since June 8. That is not much and surely not enough to satisfy my warders but by June of next year it will be twelve months clean. True!

How is Penny doing on the job? Post office isn't it? Tell her I miss her and the child. Is that guy she married honoring his financial commitment.

And Frances, are you keeping up with the movements of the guy she tied up with. I'll be wanting to see him first thing upon my arrival there.

It's cold up here this year but since I don't go out directly in it too very often it doesn't bother me much.

Frances is supposed to be angry with me because I wouldn't let her get in any of her silly clichés last time you brought her up here. I didn't make things any better either when she wrote two months later decrying my supposed rudeness. When I explained to her that she was not supposed to hold any opinions other than those of her menfolk, she stopped writing. Tell her that I feel no ill will toward her, but when she hears us debating method and policy, she is supposed to be silent, listen, and try to learn something. Penny will sit

150

and listen and try to understand. When she doesn't understand she asks intelligent questions. I've bummed across this country three times, seen everything eight times, now what am I going to do with some advice from a twenty-three-year-old girl who has been sheltered from the real world all her life.

It is terrible that we have all been so divided. The social order is set up so as to encourage this, the powers that be don't want any loyal loving groups forming up. So they discourage it in a thousand subtle ways. And as it is said, when poverty comes in the door, love leaves by the window! Too bad! I give up! Blood is not thicker than water. I was wrong ever to let my thoughts pass my lips. From now on you people's reactionary ideals are your own. I never want to discuss anything serious with you again, and if you don't hear from me here too regularly it is because I have nothing to say.

Take care of yourself.

George

Dear Robert,

I went to the board yesterday; they told me that if I kept this next year clean and clear of disciplinary infractions I would have eighteen months clean next time I saw them. Of course I have not seen the official results yet (maybe Friday I will) but it was pretty clear that I got another year to do. I'll write again when I get the final word.

Penelope wrote me a letter last week stating that you and Mama sent a box of stuff up here to me after all, in spite of my asking you not to bother. I appreciate the sentiment but you should not have done it. I probably will not be allowed to have it. You should know that I have to send a formal request from here, etc. They won't send it back either—they will keep it. Things will be much better between us when you start taking me seriously.

Take care of yourself. You'll be able to retire when I get out in '69.

George

DECEMBER, 1967
23

Dear Robert,

      This is Saturday: there is so much noise on the tier that even my earplugs are useless. Grown men are acting like high-school girls. The guards have some kind of sports on the radio. Everyone is happy, emotion-filled cries of joy come from every cell. They're trying to forget their problems or pretend that they have none. It is easier that way, easier than grabbing the bull by the horns. Music and sports. Their whole life, perhaps a little pimping or gambling. I got my official notice on the board meeting.

      They denied me another year, I go back next December. It will be eight years then.

      Take care of yourself.

George

JANUARY, 1968

1

Dear Robert,

It's 5:40 A.M. All the noisemakers are asleep; they've worn themselves out through the night making merry, laughing, singing, pretending. It is strange indeed that a man can find anything to laugh about in here. But everyone in here is locked up 24 hours a day. They have no past, no future, no goal other than the next meal. They're afraid, confused and confounded by a world they know that they did not make, that they feel they cannot change, so they make these loud noises so they won't hear what their mind is trying to tell them. They laugh to assure themselves and those around them that they are not afraid, sort of like the superstitious individual who will whistle or sing a happy number as he passes the graveyard.

Confinement in this small area all day causes a buildup of tension. The unavoidable consequence is stupidity, a return to childish behavior, overreaction.

I refuse to let myself be punished with stuff like this. Locked in jail, within a jail, my mind is still free. I refuse ever to allow myself to be forced by living conditions into a response that is not commensurate with intelligence and my final objective.

This will apply even more on the other side of the wall, out there where you are. What if there was nothing on earth that

154

could be taken from me which would result in my discomfort. What if a person was so oriented that the loss of no material thing could cause him mental disorganization? This is the free agent. He is nameless, faceless, emotionless, loveless. He is without habit, without the weaknesses of the flesh. He travels light and only in the company of those who like himself prize self-determination above baseball and beer. Only the free agent can win for us the necessary control over the direction of our unrewarding lives.

You should know that I only do what I think is best, and most appropriate. I'm a man with few alternatives.

George

JANUARY, 1968
6

Dear Robert,

I hope you are in health. Have you been bothered by the sickness, flu, Asian flu they call it. Everyone on the tier, everyone in the building really, has had it, or still has it, except me. I have been lucky. I hope I do not catch it. We have no medicines.

I have both of your letters here; I did not send the forms requesting a package because I didn't want you spending any money on unnecessary things. If I had money I would never

155

buy anything like that for myself. I am completely indifferent about pleasure, temporary amenities: "a crust of bread and a corner to sleep in, a *moment* to laugh and an hour to weep in"—well, I don't even want the moment. If that is all that I have coming I don't want it.

I don't know who you have been talking to about my condition here. Whoever they are, stop wasting your time. They are only leading you on. I hope you have lost no money, but I warned you about this before. It is clear that I must handle this thing myself the best way that I can.

Take care of yourself.

George

JANUARY, 1968
16

Dear Robert,

Nothing new to report, same situation here. No progress. Went before a couple of persons responsible for the administration of this unit last week. They changed the rules to justify keeping me locked up another six months until June at least.

There is a rule that reads: "If an inmate is involved in an assault upon another inmate and a weapon is associated in the incident the inmate responsible must do at least one year locked up in close confinement." Well, I've done my year for the thing that happened in January '67. Now I must do another for the affair in June '67 where the only weapons involved were those used against me!

I think perhaps the time has come to get legal help for me. We can discuss it when you come up next time. These things are not being handled properly. Or fairly. I am the only one still suffering the effects of those two occurrences. Everyone else has been transferred to other institutions and is in the main population there. And I'm the only one who didn't write a writ at the time the thing took place. I tried to just shrug it off, but I see that that does not work. They have accused me of leading something when all the evidence points to the contrary. I was the only one to cross the picket line during the strike or one of the few. In June I never raised my hand against an official. In fact, in all the seven years I've been in the prison here I have never attacked an official. I have difficulty leading myself, directing my own affairs. At the very least I need a transfer. I cannot get fair treatment otherwise.

Take care of yourself.

George

JANUARY, 1968
31

Dear Robert,

I seriously believe that you have incurable middle-class attitudes, but nonetheless you may be right. Regarding the blacks "not letting me, that is," I'll have to wait and take the situation in for myself, though.

If you happen to be correct about that, I'm buying me a little sailboat and heading for the Indian Ocean area; be a bum, no wife, no kids, no competition, bananas, coconuts, pineapples, fish, and sunshine. I could never bear what you have borne.

I hope you arrived home without incident. I heard the weather was pretty bad.

I almost got sucked into some more foolishness yesterday. All the blacks tilting at windmills again. Mindless, emotional, childish abandon, without a thought of winning. Just an attempt to prove their manhood to themselves, to any who may be watching. The result, further humiliation and a month in a dark hole. I'm still in my cell. I had to turn my back on them when they wouldn't listen. Never, never will I take part in any foolishness. They have me locked up with a bunch of 20-year-old cretins who don't know anything about the ways of the world, hate books, can't think, and won't listen. Things are not getting any better. They are, if anything, getting worse.

158

Bitter experience seems to be bringing out the worst in us instead of our best. Instead of growing thoughtful and determined, they get more emotional and mindless. You swallow a camel and gag on a nut; you accept a certain condition and treatment with apparent ease, but balk at the suggestion of returning the same.

It doesn't matter a great deal to me either way. On an individual basis, I will always make out. I see this world just as it is, the whole thing, and most important I see myself in relation to it. So I will be able to spring in any direction in which my mind tells me the rewards are greater.

I'm going to frame a letter soon to you discussing the social contract, and where the individual stands in relation to the state. None of it will be original. It will be the accepted dialectics of all those past and present who are in a position to know. You don't seem to know why you pay taxes and what you should expect in the way of returns. It should be clear that when one contributes to any enterprise, he has a return coming, and it is equally clear that when I place or allow an individual or group of individuals to administrate and regulate affairs that involve my bosom interest, these affairs must be handled in a judicious manner. When they are not, it is my right to replace these individuals any way that I can.

Take care of yourself.

George

FEBRUARY, 1968

8

Dear Robert,

I think you have gotten stuck in the mud somewhere down the road. There has never been any question as to whether or not we will be allowed to work. There has never been any question in my mind about the folly of one of us attempting to make himself acceptable to the established standard so that he will be tolerated.

Am I for sale and at such a price? Can true self-determination be won working for wages and salaries? What are the chances of the employee one day owning the manufacturing plant?!! What do I lose by allowing myself to be programmed, regimented, and assimilated. Has any people ever been independent that owned neither land nor tool? Isn't what you are calling for, you and the people who wrote the article, more of the same, the hewing of wood and the carrying of water?! Do I want to identify with a loser and a fool? Can I help myself by helping one who is looked upon as the wretched of the earth? This is the question. Don't get sidetracked by specious argument.

I know the answer to all the above questions, but I plan to keep it to myself for now. And of course we are talking about groups of people, our masses (not to be confused in any way

160

with my personal chances for success. I know how to look out for me as an individual).

I agree with what you say about brains, nothing could be clearer. Every mass movement in history has been led by one person or a small group of people. Although everyone is born with a brain only a few choose to use it. The difference between successful and unsuccessful mass movements is in the people who lead them. Successful ones are led by persons gifted with a *delicate balance* of both mental and physical forcefulness. Brains are *useless* without the nervous equipment and the muscle required to execute their orders.

I also agree with what you say about the Chinese. They are poor. They went through the same thing we went through for the same reason (a skin problem), and they suffered it at the hands of the same wretched force. It may be a while yet before they get over the last hundred years, but, and I know you agree, they are wonderful and aggressive, industrious people. They will make out. What I like most about them is their willingness to always help their brothers in Africa and Asia. They understand the need and power of *ethnic solidarity*. When they look in the mirror they see themselves, when they look at us they see their fathers and brothers. Brother, brother, is the way we'll call it.

Jon is well, I hope. Can you imagine how foolish a stranger would be trying to turn me against Jon? I have no love for strangers, regardless of the fact that they own the sweatshop I am forced to labor in.

George

12

Dear Robert,

Congratulations on the birthday. I may not be so lucky, but my values are a little different from yours. I am concerned with living fully, living well, rather than living long. And since I have a measure of control over the former, and none whatever over the latter, this makes sense to me.

I've been to Mexico. I have also been all over the U.S. I've spent several days in the neighborhood where you were born . . . . That neighborhood is far poorer than anything I saw in Mexico. But since Mexico is a colony of the U.S. also (just as our communities are), all I can make of this fact that blacks here are worse off than Mexican nationals in that the U.S. colonial masters think more of Mexicans.

So your taxes do all the things you say including some you omitted, such as school-educational matters, prisons, police wages, armies, H-bombs, spy ships, gas chambers, Tucker's farms, etc. But it is very curious to note who benefits by it all. Which streets get lighted best? Which child goes to school half a day in a trailer, or to a school that is so crowded and understaffed that he might as well not go for all the attention he gets? The police stopped me 5 times (5 different cars) in

162

the space of 3 blocks in Los Angeles once. All the brush wars the U.S. has fought in the last 20 years were against men of color around the world!! I could go on all week about how your tax money is being used, but let it suffice for me to say it is not being used to help you or yours. You are getting no return on your investment. This is what taxes are supposed to be all about, an investment in the community, the society, a pooling of each individual's resources so that the administration can be financed, so that the administration can perform the jobs which must be done to ensure public welfare, and the jobs which no individual can do well alone. Now it follows that if everyone pays, everyone should get proper returns. The streetlights should be the same in Watts and Bel Air. It seems that some dereliction of duty has indeed taken place.

George

FEBRUARY, 1968
19

Dear Robert,

Too bad about Jon; I suggested upon your last visit that he may be getting too much TV. Anyway, you are absolutely correct in that these are his crisis years. You had better give him something good in the way of *purpose*, *identity*, and *method*. It should be taken for granted that he is

163

getting nothing along this line in school; if anything, these things are being trained out . . . so that he will be a good Negro, an individual, a nonperson, an intellectual dependent. If you do not know the definition of "purpose," "identity," and "method," it is already too late for Jon.

I do not want to be addressed as George any longer. You will please respect my wishes enough to use my middle name from this day on. I won't respond to any other.

My work goes well here. I am in health. I hope you are well.

Take care of yourself.

Lester

MARCH, 1968

6

Dear Robert,

I received the money today. Thanks. I got the forms off too. I hope you told them about the life thing. If not, please do it right away. I hope also my age was passed along as a reminder. People would look at you and think that I would have to be in my teens.

Africa is a most wonderful continent. They have everything in the way of human and natural resources. Oil in Egypt, Libya, Tunisia, Algeria, and Nigeria. Copper, diamonds, cobalt, and gold in Zambia. There are large deposits of iron ore in Liberia, a whole mountain of it in fact. You name it, and it is found in some part of Africa. In the savanna area south of the Sahara Desert and all the way south to the Cape, you find the most fertile farmland in the world. Uganda, Kenya, and Tanzania are all just like a big park. The temperature never fluctuates more than 5 degrees the whole year around. Every evening during the winter months there is a light rain to settle the dust. Eighty to 85 the whole year. The five oldest cities in the world are located in Africa. The oldest language is one spoken in Africa: Mande. The oldest relic of man's prehistoric existence was found in Africa, 25 million years old. You find all kinds of black types: with wide noses, thin noses, aquiline noses; all types of hair; all shades of skin from the lightest ivory to blue black. You should be more specific about what you want to know because it would take a month, and a letter the size of a telephone book, to delineate all the resources of Africa.

Speaking just for me I would like Tanzania on the East coast if I had to choose a spot to settle. Julius Nyerere is an enlightened and intelligent leader who identifies with the Eastern world. The country is developing fast, and has unlimited potential in mining, agriculture, and light industry. Its problem, as with all the African states, is the absence of capital to expand the economy at a rate which will realize the rising expectations of the people and close the gap with the Western world. Tanzania has invited the Eastern societies to help them instead of the U.S. and Western Europe, so they will be better off. China charges no interest on loans. When the Chinese set up a factory, they hire Africans and train African managers and leave. The U.S. is motivated by the profit-and-loss thing. They leave U.S. managers and claim 90 percent of the gross as their just share of the profits. They say it's their reward for helping to develop the country. Some African leaders go for this; Julius does not. Does it seem stupid of China to lend without interest, and build without taking over or capitalizing? Must be love.

Lester

28

Dear Robert,

I stay very busy these days. I have accepted a job on the tier (our floor) passing out food and cleaning up. Good for my record and keeps me active.

What do you think of Jomo? He was on his job during those years. He ranks among the top three or four guerrilla tacticians in the world. I speak of this new face that war has taken on, the war of the poor man. He was in the vanguard of the Afro-Asian liberation effort once. It is regrettable, however, that today we have to report that he no longer cooperates with the general movement to which he owes his success. He has gone on record as saying he wants no part of any more revolutions. What can we think of a man who withdraws before the battle is fully won? This man has abandoned his old comrades and left the less fortunate to fend for themselves. The peoples of southern Africa, Southeast Asia, and Latin America could use his cooperation, his support, just as he once was in need of support. Faint hearts never win decisive battles. Take care of yourself.

Lester

166

APRIL, 1968
11

Dear Robert,

M.L.K. organized his thoughts much in the same manner as you have organized yours. If you really knew and fully understood his platform you would never have expressed such sentiments as you did in your last letter. I am sure you are acquainted with the fact that he was opposed to violence and war; he was indeed a devout pacifist. It is very odd, almost unbelievable, that so violent and tumultuous a setting as this can still produce such men. He was out of place, out of season, too naive, too innocent, too cultured, too civil for these times. That is why his end was so predictable.

Violence in its various forms he opposed, but this does not mean that he was passive. He knew that nature allows no such imbalances to exist for long. He was perceptive enough to see that the men of color across the world were on the march and their example would soon influence those in the U.S. to also stand up and stop trembling. So he attempted to direct the emotions and the movement in general along lines that he thought best suited to our unique situation: nonviolent civil disobedience, political and economic in character. I was beginning to warm somewhat to him because of his new ideas

167

concerning U.S. foreign wars against colored peoples. I am certain that he was sincere in his stated purpose to "feed the hungry, clothe the naked, comfort those in prisons, and trying to love somebody." I really never disliked him as a man. As a man I accorded him the respect that his sincerity deserved.

It is just as a leader of black thought that I disagreed with him. The concept of nonviolence is a false ideal. It presupposes the existence of compassion and a sense of justice on the part of one's adversary. When this adversary has everything to lose and nothing to gain by exercising justice and compassion, his reaction can only be negative.

The symbol of the male here in North America has always been the gun, the knife, the club. Violence is extolled at every exchange: the TV, the motion pictures, the best-seller lists. The newspapers that sell best are those that carry the boldest, bloodiest headlines and most sports coverage. To die for king and country is to die a hero.

The Kings, Wilkinses, and Youngs exhort us in King's words to "put away your knives, put away your arms and clothe yourselves in the breastplate of righteousness" and "turn the other cheek to prove our capacity to endure, to love." Well, that is good for them perhaps but I most certainly need both sides of my head.

George

APRIL, 1968
22

Dear Robert,

It was good seeing you, a bit exasperating, but still good to see you.

Reexamine this point: if a government truly reflected the wishes of the people, if it truly represented a fair cross section of the populace, it would follow that if the means of production and distribution were placed in the hands of the government they would be controlled by the people. The central point is that the government must be truly representative. All important positions must be elective, and a man's position within the governing body must be solely dependent upon meritorious conduct of the state's business.

Nationalization is the only answer to the problems of the modern industrial state.

Take care of yourself.

George

APRIL, 1968
26

Dear Mother,

I was looking for you last weekend; Robert had
said he was going to bring you. I hope you are well.

Robert indicates that you two very seldom see anything in
the same light anymore. He also indicates that he doesn't
understand why.

He comes here thinking to give me solace and purpose
(purpose I have, solace I don't require), but appears to be
more upset with the state of his domestic affairs than I am
with my problems here. This is not to say that I do not enjoy
his visits—it is good to have a little relief from this cell—but it
seems to me that Robert may be coming apart and I hate to
witness it. He has attempted a breakout recently from long
years of repression and backwardness, but the combination of
noncooperation from you and his daughters, and the plain fact
that he doesn't understand the changes that are taking place
around him, has placed a strain on his nervous equipment that
may soon prove to be too much for him.

He doesn't have much confidence in himself or in us as a
people yet. His whole mentality, all of his attitudes are built
around the transparent little platitudes and trite clichés that

170

one reads and hears on the mass news media and other thought-control facilities.

He stated in the presence of some of his black coworkers that "he was glad that troublemaker King got killed." He almost had to fight the guys. Now what black would say something like that? It sounds like something that one of the white knights of the KKK would say. Years ago Robert would have said nothing and had no opinion whatever to offer. But now that he has broken out and is trying to get into the mainstream with an opinion, he is all mixed up. I can understand that after such an experience on the job with his peers he would certainly not want to get bullied by his women when he got home. I didn't agree with any of King's tactics but he certainly caused no one any trouble, other than a few whites perhaps, and I don't think I mind that too much.

Robert will change, adapt, in time, if we help him along, and are subtle with our criticism and advice and respect his wish to be the dominant male. He has that coming: it's hard working for those folks.

I heard about your work on the kitchen. That's heavy work. Take care that you don't strain or break yourself. Why isn't Jon doing that for you?

Take care of yourself.

George

171

APRIL, 1968
30

Dear Robert,

Everything is normal here, so far. The transfer is off. I'll be here for a while yet. They wanted to send me to Soledad Adjustment Center but I asked them not to. There are more aimless adolescent types there than here.

I wouldn't mind going to California Men's Colony, or someplace like that, but I have never been offered anything that would be an improvement over this place. Well, anything would be an improvement but not enough to matter.

All reading material is coming right on time except *Ramparts* and *Avant Garde*. No *Ramparts* for April yet. I believe the government may have smashed them.

May end up on that little boat after all. I feel myself becoming impatient with people in general.

Take care of yourself.

George

MAY, 1968

4

Dear Mother,

You are correct in all that you say about the problem of men and responsibility, and about the hangers-on, and the foot draggers, the failures and the failing, the myopic tendencies to squander time and energy in counterproductive efforts. At times I become so depressed seeing it that I feel justified deciding to release myself from my responsibility and just take off (when I get home) with you people in tow to some other part of the world where blacks have already come into their own, with an ocean or two between us and this place.

But this feeling never lasts long, mainly because I understand why many of us react as we do, and I said *re*act. Our responses to the social stimuli (and in our case in this country, they assert themselves as a challenge) must necessarily be negative when we consider that blacks in the U.S. have been subjected to the most thorough brainwashing of any people in history. Isolated as we were, or are, from our land, our roots and our institutions, no group of men have been so thoroughly terrorized, dehumanized, and divested of those things that from birth make men strong.

173

Regarding this domestic issue, I must be the first to admit that I see that the black family unit is in ruins. It is our first and basic weakness. This fact may contribute much to our difficulty in uniting as a people. But for every effect there is a cause. If we are to understand and heal these effects we must understand the causes. To say that the black family unit is slowly eroding because of pressures from without (poverty and social injustice), and from within (negative response to crisis situation) is to completely mistake the depth of the issue. There are three historical factors that have produced the present state of chaos on the family level of our black society. First, the family unit was destroyed during chattel slavery. Men had the sense of family responsibility trained out of them. Second, our culture institutions, and customs, upon which unity depends and without which cohesiveness can never exist, were destroyed and never replaced. The best we could do was ape the ofay, and cling to a kind of subculture that manifests itself today in the hideous notion that if we educate ourselves properly, think the right thoughts, read the right books, say the right things, and do exactly that which is expected of us—we can then be as good as white people. Third, our change in status from an article of movable property to untrained misfits on the labor market was not as most think a change to freedom from slavery but merely to a *different kind of slavery*.

Take care of yourself.

George

MAY, 1968
15

Dear Robert,

It is good that you can afford a new car. Since you have taken up the responsibility of managing the household expenditures, I see you have a little more to spend on what yankees call "discretionary spending," money above what is needed to provide the basic survival materials.

I am doing well and wish the same for you.

You sound like a high-school civics textbook with that thing about free speech and free press. You couldn't believe stuff like that. "Freedom of the press is for *those who own one*." Even they are kept in line by economic pressure from above. Very little of the repression is done overtly, my friend. You cannot see a tree's roots all the time, but because one cannot see them does not mean that they do not exist. The tree couldn't stand without them. Take care of yourself.

George

MAY, 1968
16

Dear Robert,

The silent treatment is counterproductive. Guile, craft, and gentle persuasion are what's happening. When guile fails, then force must be used. Guile only fails when the person one is dealing with is smarter. Men must either be cajoled or crushed depending on the circumstances. But with women I can't see any reason why craft shouldn't always suffice.

These institutional committees are strictly local and inconsequential. They have no fixed number of seats, no fixed personnel. They are governed by caprice, all decisions are arbitrary. I have never received the benefit of the doubt. I never get a break as you well know from the fact of these 8 years. But don't let me start complaining. As a defense I never expect anything, never form attachments for material things, and refuse to be punished or allow my thoughts to be disorganized by anything that happens to me here. So you can uncross your fingers and put your fears for me on that score to rest. Nothing can upset the logical processes of my mind, no amount of hunger, neglect, cold, pain, discomfort, or terrorism.

Well, take care of yourself.

George

JUNE, 1968

6

Dear Robert,

It was good to see you folks. I hope you got back safely. You know they cut our visiting time short...I snapped to it when I got back to my cellblock and noted how early it was. It was not crowded in there either, from what I can recall.

It seems at first sight that Georgia has adjusted her attitudes to conform somewhat more closely with reality; that is wonderful. It is surely past time for all of us to stand up and stop trembling, grab the bull by the horns, and ride him till his neck snaps. The events of the last two days have left me in a most exuberant frame of mind. I haven't felt so good since the first of the year, and the time of the Tet offensive.

Jon is an admirable man-child. You sired a man without question. I just know that you are training him to be a benefit and a credit to his kind, and to act out his historical, obligatory duty. I know you are teaching him to love just us, and protecting him from this alien ideology. I am certain that you are doing this since you remember clearly the failure of your father, and his father, and so on as far back as it goes. Take care of yourself.

George

JUNE, 1968
14

Dear Mother,

Try to remember how you felt at the most depressing moment of your life, the moment of your deepest dejection. You no doubt have had many. That is how I feel all the time, no matter what my level of consciousness may be, asleep, awake, in between. The thing is there and it keeps me moving, pins my eye to the ball, up tight twenty-four hours a day. Our general situation and mine at present especially the inadequate response, the absence of genuine remedial thought and action, these are why I am as I am.

I had a letter from Robert this morning professing a heartfelt sorrow at the passing of one of our strongest enemies, a slick-tongued, opportunistic, demagogic falsifier. What a prodigal waste of affection! Especially when we consider that Robert felt only relief at the time of the last political kill (M.L. King). I can't reach Robert, he has a natural slave mentality like so many other black men of his generation. I understand why the mindless pursue the favor and affection of an insensitive and implacable opponent, but I cannot understand why they insist on planting those ideals in the minds of their sons. They go through life discovering that this enemy cannot be appeased, that he is relentless, calloused beyond repair, dedicated to personal financial success, heedless to its cost in human suffering. Yet when the son comes along, instead of acting upon these discoveries in a positive way, they lie, pretend, defend their inaction and collaboration, head down, shoulders bent, nose stained brown. I tolerate Robert because he stuck with us or you pretty faithfully (no small qualifier when one looks around at other families in the black community), but he has to go through many a change before I can really accept him. It may be too late for us to establish a relationship conducive to the remedying of our physical and material problems. I hope not. As I have stated before you can help us both. Just as those regressive ideals were sneaked into his consciousness so we can sneak some progressive ones in. Propaganda works both ways, but one must be subtle. He is sensitive about being bossed (by blacks anyway).

I have wanted to write this letter for two weeks now, but I have been preoccupied. I wanted to enlarge upon some of the things we discussed when you were here. First, all men want to own things, to possess material goods to make themselves comfortable today, and to secure themselves against the unpredictable tomorrows. This is self-preservation, a natural thing found in all animals. It is only latent in some men but it is still there all the same. When this instinct works on a man without his full understanding, he does radical things. Now read carefully, Georgia. When the peasant revolts, the student demonstrates, the slum dweller riots, the robber robs, he is reacting to a feeling of insecurity, an atavistic throwback to the territorial imperative, a *reaction* to the fact that he has lost control of the circumstances surrounding his life. Whether he knows it or not, it is all the same. This system, its economics, its politics, was formed around an age that is past. It was inadequate even then. Men can no longer stake out land or section off a part of the earth and say to themselves, "I will use this as a guarantee," mainly because of the monopolistic stranglehold of those who have already established themselves

179

and who pretend to know what is best for the rest of the world. Wealth *is* land. By having only labor without land and its potential products, we lose independence. We must sell our labor. Then because of today's specialization and complicated division of labor, it follows that the only way man's natural urges and the modern industrial society can be brought into agreement is by all people possessing everything in common through a representative government. Only in this way can all men satisfy the ungovernable urge to secure things and control their existence.

George

JUNE, 1968
29

Dear Georgia,

I'll be out of here soon, perhaps in eight or nine months. I'll have eighteen months clean when I go to the board in December. You know that I have my time in. That's what they want, time and clean conduct.

It is always a job getting along with our friends and relatives. Establishing lasting and mutually rewarding relationships always calls for delicacy, sensitivity, and, mainly, suppression of the ego. One simply cannot say the first thing that comes to mind with no regard for the next person's ego

180

problem. If I constantly say or do things that make the next person feel as if I am challenging his person, his capacity to reason, his standing as an individual, how can I ever hope to relate to him.

People the world over are not the same but those that we meet here in the U.S. are generally of a single type. By and large they are all fools, intellectual nonpersons, emotional half-wits. Status symbols, supervisory positions, and petty power motivate their every act. Personal, individual, financial success at any price is their social ethic, the only real standard upon which their conduct is built.

For us blacks in particular this is a nightmare proposition. When this standard, this criterion for the measurement of individual merit and worth in this society is applied to us, measured against our standing or holdings, we cannot help but come out with a very low opinion of ourselves. From the womb to the tomb this plays in our minds. *We are not worth more than the amount of capital we can raise.* That is why you see blacks pretending to be doing all right. That is why a black man will buy a new car (status symbol) before he will buy food for his child or clothes for his wife.

And again with blacks this whole thing goes even deeper. No man or group of men have been more denuded of their self-respect, none in history have been more terrorized, suppressed, repressed, and denied male expression than the U.S. black. This is what you are up against in relating to Robert. As I said before, he is going through a breakout. He is trying to get back. He wants to express himself after years of being a vegetable. As with most of the men of our community, he is just starting to feel his strength now. But soon this will build into a rage, " and when I rage I rage unbounding." Don't interfere with that thing. You should have never objected to the social club! You caused him to transfer just a bit more of the subconscious disregard he has for our enemies onto you.

Jon's *real* problems can be solved only through community action: a massive, total, mutual affort. We are not surviving and cannot survive as individuals or as family units; we must get together. And then too, what can Robert give Jon in his present state of mental development? He can only benefit from contact with people he might learn from. He must first learn *what to give and how to give it* to Jon before he can help him. Just spending some time with him is nothing. I don't think you handled that right, you should have offered to help his organization, perhaps even participate to some extent. Don't be backward.

George

AUGUST, 1968

9

Dear Mother,

It was good for me to see you again. I also have your letter here before me. I commented to Robert last week that you seem to have gone through many changes these last few years. That's what life is all about, growth and change. You will at least listen. Few people are so endowed.

I feel much better as the result of your visit. Please try to come more often, or at least when Robert comes. I understand that you people have never had any exposure to these things that interest me and I know that everyone cannot be alike, but I also know that if we are to relate to each other, work together, build together on the basic things we must agree. I agree with many of the things you say. I concur with any rational and constructive judgment or assessment you may make, as long as it is intended to forward "our thing."

No transfer for me; they turned it down. No relief in my ordeal, 24 hours a day in this cell. I've been in here for over 18 months now; in prison 8 years next month. I've forgotten what it was that earned me this.

George

AUGUST, 1968
17

Dear Mother,

It can all be reduced to the simple fact that we want you to be yourself, secure within your *reality*. Why should my woman have to follow someone else's criterion of right and wrong, beauty and ugliness? Please believe me, Mama, the truly ugly thing is the pretending, faking it, imitating—monkey see, monkey do—adoration of the repulsive.

On close examination, what you are saying is that black women standing naked and natural are ugly or less than beautiful. From this nakedness and natural posture the *only* way for her to remotely resemble anything beautiful is to bleach and straighten her hair, and hang her limbs with clothing designed in Paris, London, the U.S., and other parts of the barbarian world. For you there is only this one standard of beauty, the Western standard. I revolt against this absurdity. I understand that this is all you have ever known, I allow for this, but you must be able to see by now that this model of perfection you have subscribed to in the past is no longer the fad. Black is back. I'm going to fulfill my role as the man, even if it kills me. I will provide the material goods and protect my family with every ounce of energy and resource that I can call up. The woman's role though will go unfulfilled because you folks don't seem to be able to change, or reestablish the values and cultural entities of our antecedents.

Reality is the key. In order for you to be intelligent, as you state it, you must like Western music, clothes, food, architecture, Western education, religious superstition, pseudophilosophy, and Western ideals. St. Augustine!! What kind of example is that?

The reality is that we are a caste at the bottom of a class society, the only group that has built-in factors (physical characteristics) that prohibit any form of socioeconomic mobility. We are the totally disenfranchised, the whipping boy, the scapegoat, the floor mat of the nation. I am not so foolish that I cannot detect the fact that I am hated, especially when it is obvious. At least the obvious does not escape me.

To clarify, however, let me state that some blacks are liked. I see that every day, but I am not of this kith. They hate me. I don't find this at all uncomfortable because I have some prerogatives. I would be doing something wrong if they liked me. Do you understand? I don't want anyone to accept me. As an individual, I don't worry about my future. I know my ideals will prevail, so I don't worry about that. They can't harm me, because the reality is that I have nothing to lose but my chains!

It is clear that they are not going to give me a chance. You were right, that is exactly what they fear. Just because I want to be my black self, mentally healthy, and because I look anyone who addresses me in the eye, they feel that I may start a riot anytime. I've stopped more trouble here than any other black in the system.

George

DECEMBER, 1968
3

Dear Mother,

I'm supposed to be going to Soledad again anytime now. It is a much better place than this. Remember when you came to see me while I was there before; we sat around a table in easy chairs by ourselves.

How have you been? Healthy and wise, I hope.

No noticeable change here, except for the prospect of my transfer and a cold that has me doubled over all day coughing.

Penelope *asked me* to send her my package approval form so she could take care of me. I sent it and told her that she must send the stuff right away so that I will get it on the very first day packages are allowed, to avoid any possible mix-up due to the transfer. Remember in 1962 when I transferred here in December? There was such a mix-up that I got nothing you sent.

I can't say just what the problem is. We all seem to be in the grip of some terrible quandary. Our enemies have so confused us that we seem to have been rendered incapable of the smallest responsibility. I see this same irresponsibility in every exchange with my kinsmen here, irresponsibility, or mediocrity at best, disloyalty, self-hatred, cowardice, competition between themselves, resentment of any who may have excelled in anything, heads bowed, knees bent to some man or some stupid idea of a god. I've stopped saying anything at all. I haven't uttered a word in two months, refuse to even acknowledge a greeting with anything larger or longer than a raising of the head. One step forward and three backward. Where are we going?

George

DECEMBER, 1968
22

Dear Mother,

I probably won't leave here until next month. They are sending me to the board here. It meets the thirtieth and thirty-first of December and the third of January.

I'm doing all right, and have some very efficient earplugs to help me preserve my sanity. Have you any theories why blacks talk so much and so loud? A Chinaman told me once that blacks were the oldest and finest people on earth "but one thing wrong, talkie-talkie-talkie. . . . "

Wish the best for you, the best of everything this year. May be in a position to help work something out before this one's gone.

Take care.

George

APRIL, 1969
14

Dear Jon,

Black culture is a monumental subject that covers countless years. The first man and consequently the first culture was black. You can't expect much coverage of so large a subject in nine thousand words. I will however write an essay that starts with the beginnings and touches on all that is important, with a brief resumé on the black subculture of the present-day United States.

You can make your own bench cheap. Buy or find or take from someone a 6' x 15" board, rather thick and heavy, say 2" at least. Tack on some old surplus army blankets and that's it. You then simply lay your board on top of three wooden horses, old wooden milk crates, or any strong or reinforced wood boxes, or stretch it between two chairs. Leave it unattached, however, because that way you can use it for incline presses by leaning it against the wall, or letting it rest one end on the ground, one on your box or chair.

I'll get started on the other thing now. Why did Georgia take your books? Sounds pretty bad for her. I gather she wasn't serious about the things she said when she was here last.

George

JUNE, 1969
12

Dear Mother,

Final results: Denied, one year, go back to board next June 1970.

George

JUNE, 1969
28

Dear Jon,

It's good in many ways that you will now be able
to drive. Perhaps you'll be able to get up here to see me more
often.

I am well, and working hard; four hours a day on exercises.

Mix your theoretical reading with some practical technology. That aspect of chemistry that will be useful to us. Perhaps
electronics as well.

Be careful and learn fast, how to handle the automobile.
Robert is most impressed if you remain calm. If you don't let
him think you are excitable under the strain of heavy traffic
you will be able to convince him that you are ready to go out
on your own sooner. Driving that '69 should be easy.

Take it easy.

George

AUGUST, 1969

17

Dear Jon,

The usual here. Each day comes and goes like the one before. This little joke isn't funny any longer.

I add five words to my vocabulary each day, five new ones, right after breakfast each morning when I have forty-five minutes to kill. It's not enough time for anything else and since I don't want to waste any time, I work on words. It is by words that we convey our thoughts, and bend people to our will.

If you must have a job, though I can't see why you want to work for someone if you don't absolutely have to, try this. Go to some business concern where the guy who runs it doesn't employ too many people and watches all of them closely. Then just start working for nothing. Don't say anything to anyone but the boss. Tell him what your name is and that you need a job. Then start working in spite of his reply. Of course you work hard. Do you get it? In two days, three at the most, you'll have bent him to your will. You may have to work for nothing the first day or two. In fact, it is best to refuse the first day's offering if he breaks that soon. You have to be sure, sure of yourself I mean. In order to pressure a man you must be a better man that he. You can't let embarrassment or shyness stand in your way. These two things must be thoroughly and completely removed from your character. Loading trucks in a junkyard where the work is hard, garages, warehouses, etc.—these are places to consider. Don't try anything that requires skilled labor. You'll mess up someone's stock.

How are your eyes? Have you had them checked? We all have bad eyes . . . mine seem to be getting worse. I hope not. I can see very well at a distance, but cannot focus well on close objects without the glasses.

Find out for me if Georgia sent the shoes and other stuff. If she did I didn't get them for some reason and will investigate. Give her my love.

Send me a sexy picture of the lady that you met like I told you last week. Let her oldest kid take the picture with you and her in it. I want visual proof that you did take care of business. When I was sixteen I had one that was twenty-eight and a mother four times. I was good to her; no beatings like her other men had done. I wouldn't accept any money from her or eat her kid's food. I took her to places where she could show me off, most of the time to places that cost nothing. I had money but I looked so young that I couldn't get into places that adults went into.

Take care of yourself.

George

SEPTEMBER, 1969

9

Dear Jon,

Doing no good here. It is looking no better, but at least I have developed no new problems.

What do you think of your old man? Were you listening when he told me that the guys (those guys) on his job call him everything under the sun! He *pretends* that he is proud of his self-control. I believe he actually has twisted his thinking to consider himself a better man, "Now that he can take it." A lot of us colored folk are like that, in fact he is the majority. That is why we are the floor mat of the world, because we can take it.

Robert is a good brother on an individual, personal, brother-to-brother basis, but you must reject his philosophy: the credo of the slave, the self-destructive, self-perpetuating doctrine of the menial, the wooductter, the waterboy, the groom, the employee, the flunky's flunky, the abased.

However, the rejection should be a silent one. There is no chance of changing Robert, so he must be accepted as is, and protected as much as is possible. There are those among us, we must admit, who cannot take any sizable amount of freedom. They are in the majority! You cannot relate to them with

192

ideals. They have fallen beyond caring about ideals. The only thing that will make them move is a push, no explanation, just a shove.

You are concerned about working, having money, living better, etc. I have given you several leads but it seems that none fit your character and disposition. I hope that you at least tried. That last thing I mentioned to you last Monday may be just the ticket. See a brother named E. He can help you get that kind of work. You have your driver's license now, so there should be no problems. But if there are you should be old enough and prepared to handle them now. If I am wrong then you will never be ready.

Well take care of yourself, and write me like I asked you to.

George

SEPTEMBER, 1969
15

Dear Jon,

Got your letter today.

On the job thing, it is up to you. I think you made a wise choice, however, if you can stick with it. There will be plenty of lures at the school, soft, warm, smooth lures. When do you start back, and what year are you in? This should be your last year, isn't it?

I'm just drifting now, doing a lot of reading, waiting for my shoulder to get together. It is a little better.

Things are awful tight here, everyone tense, I'm just watching them and waiting.

Take care.

George

SEPTEMBER, 1969
25

Dear Jon,

Robert told me that you were driving the new automobile to school. If that's right, you're not doing too bad. Do you use it at school and drive home too? But he also mentioned that if you didn't show improvements in things of a scholastic nature, he would be very disappointed.

I am thinking that he feels a lot for you. He really does, I know. He simply doesn't know how to relate to you. When I was young, I felt that Robert didn't care for me very much because he wouldn't take me anywhere or even talk to me in anything less than a shout. Mama used to talk him into beating me up just for leaving the house to play ball or talk with my peers. I mean real beating, belts, table legs, fists, etc. But what I didn't notice was that he was feeding me and that whenever I got into a bind with the local representatives of the oppressors (police), he would always be there to help me. *Always,* no matter what I had done or how much he hated what I'd done.

Life has been one long string of disappointments for Robert. It wouldn't be good to just take lightly his wishes to see you become more aggressive in your development. It isn't necessary to disappoint him. You can satisfy him, help yourself, and serve the cause of black self-determination by picking yourself up and taking Chairman Mao's Great Leap Forward.

I hope you are involved in the academic program at your school, but knowing what I know about this country's schooling methods, they are not really directing you to any specialized line of study. They have not tried to ascertain what fits your character and disposition and to direct you accordingly. So you must do this yourself. Decide now what you would like to specialize in, *one thing* that you will drive at. Do you get it? *Decide now.* There are several things that we as a group, a revolutionary group, need badly: chemists, electronic engineers, surgeons, etc. Choose one and give it special attention at a certain time each day. Establish a certain time to give over to your specialty and let Robert know indirectly what you are doing. Then it only remains for you to get your A's on the little simple unnecessary subjects that the school requires. This is no real problem. It can be accomplished with just a little attention and study. But you must now start on your specialty, the thing that you plan to carry through this war of life. You must specialize in something. Just let it be something that will help the war effort.

George

OCTOBER, 1969

17

Dear Mother,

I hope that all is normal there with you. Jon told me about the h—— deal. I didn't know it was that bad. How will we ever make it back from here? We all seem to have fallen from glory in the uttermost way. I'm sure we will simply have to redouble our efforts to forgive, understand, to rebuild the bridges between us; we must attempt to comprehend fully just how these bridges came to be destroyed. There is no other recourse. We must, of ourselves, by ourselves, recognize the roots of our illness, and do all that we can to extricate ourselves from this mess.

Tell Penny that I love her no matter what. We'll agree on the essentials anyway. Tell her that I may not be able to write for a while. Explain this to Robert too. A little trouble here for me, and this may be the last envelope and the last time that I'll be able to borrow a pencil, for a while anyway. But I'll attempt to stay in touch. I've done nothing. It may work out all right but then I have no way of knowing for sure. They sweep in and sweep me away to a little closed cell in a closed wing of the prison without any explanation. I don't have any of my personal property.

196

Forget the phonograph and records. I won't be allowed to have them. I didn't really want them anyway. I'm going to send the typewriter home first chance I get also.

What's happening now is what I tried to explain to you several months ago. They know that in a year, the year between board appearances, anything can be made to happen.

But at least I am alone in here. I don't have to be bothered with anyone, and someone who knew me before somewhere else has sent me something to read. I have books and toilet paper, I'll be all right.

I'll write again when I can. Relay to Penny that no effort toward self-determination is futile: it is one of the things that men just cannot do without. Without it life loses its value.

Love,

George

NOVEMBER, 1969
7

Dear Jon,

I know what happened concerning your letter. It was too thick. You sent too much. That is all right, however. I get what I want one way or the other and do what I want in the end. The fools are awfully presumptuous to think they can dictate my every action.

That is good about the chemistry. I can't report too much progress. I'm holding on, however.

How are the honeymooners getting along these days? You know that they are much too old to relate the way they do.

Take care.

George

NOVEMBER, 1969
13

Dear Jon,

I'm sending you these two package slips because you can explain to the folks there and see that it is taken care of better than anyone else.

First I want them sent the very first day of December. They are special Christmas packages, the only kind I can receive, and I don't want to wait for them until Christmas. You understand.

So that means that you must explain to them to get the stuff together now and put it into two packages and use the reverse side of the slip as an address form. It should be glued to the outside of the package and addressed to me here, as soon as December 1 gets here.

The important items are: cigarettes—I want three cartons in each box; four pounds of nuts in each box, walnuts and Brazil

198

nuts only; the full quota of cigars—150 in each box; and finally the salami—two pounds, one in each box. It must be the type that will keep without refrigeration for a while, the rest of that stuff is unimportant.

Impress upon them now not to delay past Demember 1. It should be mailed; you understand, I hope.

Give everyone my regards, take care.

George

NOVEMBER, 1969
27

Dear Jon,

I'm doing all right here, I guess, hanging on.

Heard you were going to medical school. What happened to the chemistry? They called me up to classification last week. Said they were considering sending me back to San Quentin. They are supposed to need the space here for something, and I wasn't doing well enough. They said if I improved a great deal, it is possible that in four or five years I might be considered for Chino—the prison for honor inmates.

Let me know now and then how you are. Take care.

George

DECEMBER, 1969
5

Dear Mother,

The packages came in all right. They were opened in my presence so there was no chance for foul play. Thanks, you're a good girl, couldn't possibly get along without you folks. I hope I can justify your faith in me in some big way before long.

Jon is a wonderful man-child, you should be quite content with him. The apathy is not permanent. I love him, love him, love him. He is a great deal ahead of the average black his age, a lot smarter than I was. I hope he can avoid the many traps they have set up for him.

Send me some photos of everyone—you know, when you get together over the holidays.

Take care.

Love,

George

DECEMBER, 1969
21

Dear Jon,

Marcia is a sweet sensitive sister. I want you to see her and represent me in my absence.

You know what that means: show no weakness of any kind, present the strong, unapproachable, serious, intelligent, big-brother side of your character, the new black man, in his highest revolutionary form.

You know, look out for her. Try to stabilize her. She is confused. She is the sister of one of my best friends. So bust your heart for her. If she has personal enemies, smash them. Call her in the evening and read to her from Mao or Fanon.

George

DECEMBER, 1969
21

Dear Jon,

Just got your letter. Good to hear from you, and hope you are still alive. For the 357th time let me advise you to take all threats seriously. If you would firmly grasp the depth of the sickness caused in some men's minds by this environment, I would never have to relate this to you but once. When a sucker gets so foolish as to warn you in advance that he is going to kill you, the next sound he utters should come through swollen lips.

Two people I want you to see for me. It is important. See Guy and find out if he got a regular institution correspondence form to fill out and return with the letter I sent him. I have reason to believe that these people did not send him the form so that he can become a *regular* on my mailing list. Also dress yourself up and see Marcia, one evening or weekend. She works in the daytime. Also ask her if she got the form to fill out and return when she got my letter. Ask her if she returned it yet, and explain that we will not be allowed to exchange letters if she has not returned the form. I think these people neglected to even send one, since they want to keep me isolated. Tell Marcia that I got her letter of December 15 and I will try to answer. If she doesn't hear from me, it will be due to the hang-up in getting those forms out of here to her and back from her. Tell her that Tony is doing well. You can phone first to tell her you are coming or make an appointment, but I'd rather you see her in person to relate the messages. Do this right away and let me know what's happening.

I don't know what to tell you about that school thing. I know it is boring, listening to those idiots and falsifiers seven or eight hours a day, but it's best to stay with it until you are ready to revolt. Just don't mistake any of the lies for the truth. Robert will lie to you if he thinks it will help you to survive. He has been surviving on one for half a century.

Take care.

George

DECEMBER, 1969
25

Dear Mother,

I'm well, warm, fed, get plenty of rest, plenty of exercise. I really can't complain, especially since I don't expect any more.

Everyone got packages from home and we shared everything. It was just like down on the commune. I have gained ten pounds at least.

Hope you are feeling better, and I hope also that this next year will bring you some solace. I wish you the best, Mama. Take care of yourself.

George

DECEMBER, 1969
28

Dear Jon,

Received your letter. You said nothing about Marcia. See if you can do anything for her—when I was your age, boy, I had a couple of women her age, and with two and three children each. But you treat her good. You're supposed to be representing me, meaning that you are to be strong, intellectual, watchful, serious, unapproachable.

I like her and she is the sister of one of my best friends. I'm supposed to be getting out anytime now, she thinks.

I wanted her to see you, the man-child, so that she would have a better idea of what the "man" is like.

Forget that Westernized backward stuff about god. I curse god, the whole idea of a benevolent supreme being is the product of a tortured, demented mind. It is a labored, mindless attempt to explain away ignorance, a tool to keep people of low mentality and no means of production in line. How could there be a *benevolent* superman controlling a world like this. He would have to be malevolent, not benevolent. Look around you, evil rules supreme. God would be my enemy. The theory of a good, just god is a false idea, a thing for imbeciles and old women and, of course, Negroes. It's a relic of the past when men made words and mindless defenses for such things as sea serpents, magic, and flat earths.

Strength comes from knowledge, knowing who you are, where you want to go, what you want, knowing and accepting that you are alone on this spinning, tumbling world. No one can crawl into your mind and help you out. I'm your brother and I'm with you, come what may, and against anything or anybody in the universe that is against you. You'll meet women and they will say they are with you, but you'll still be alone, with your pain, discomfort, illness, elation, courage, pride, death. You don't want anyone to crawl into your head with you, do you? If there were a god or anyone else reading some of my thoughts I would be uncomfortable in the extreme.

Strength is being able to control yourself and your total environment—yourself first, however.

Take care of yourself.

George

FEBRUARY, 1970
13

Mrs. Fay Stender
Attorney at Law

Dear Mrs. Stender,

This is to confirm your letter of February 11. I had just heard of Judge Wollenberg's move. The next time you come to see me, push the idea of removing my restraints. It will be interesting to note their reaction. You know those things are placed upon me whenever I leave my cell area. He reaches through the bars to place them upon me. The animal farm effect is complete.

Sunday, the day after tomorrow, I am supposed to be released from isolation. No one is supposed to do more than twenty-nine days down here. I'll then be able to read my newspapers and weekly periodicals, smoke, and sleep in a bed. However I will remain separated from the general population (in jail, within the jail), probably on maximum security. This does not bother me any longer. Of the ten years I have done, seven of them have been in close confinement; I read, exercise, and write. Sometimes I'll daydream.

I said that it doesn't bother me any longer—but what I

206

meant is that since I am in jail, which part of the jail I'm in doesn't matter. Your wishes of cheer and hope are well received. Hope and I are old friends. Thanks, and let me know if you can do anything with the novel idea.

Sincerely,

George L. Jackson

FEBRUARY, 1970
26

Dear Fay,

You are aware that I want to read the transcript of grand-jury testimony. All three of us would like to go over it. Since we are living so close together down here, one copy would be enough for all three of us. I had a chance to read only parts of it on the twenty-fourth.

Do you have any trouble reading my writing? It is the best I can do. If you are having trouble, however, I'll print.

I'm warm, I never have liked to eat too much, so all is well with me here. I won't complain. I've never had much of a problem with the purely physical things, the weaknesses of the flesh. I get fat on what the average individual would starve on.

Clothing? I prefer something dry and clean if it is readily available. I feel guilty when I sleep more than three hours a day. Where I am presently the night-light in front of my cell allows me to read or write as late as I wish.

The cruelest aspect in the loss of one's freedom of movement is of course the necessity to repress the sex urge, but after ten years I have even learned to control my response to that stimulus (one thousand fingertip push-ups a day). I probably have the world's record on push-ups completed. So, if they would reach me now, across my many barricades, it must be with a bullet and it must be final.

The lash affects me for sure. If it failed to affect me at all I would be guilty of using the tortured logic of my father's twisted mind, i.e., that this is the best of all possible worlds, or that this is the only country that provides flush toilets for all. It affects me, but not my physical parts. It shocks me somewhere behind the eyes, strains my instinct to survive. . . .

I know you are a busy woman and it probably isn't proper for me to steal your attention with my ramblings. Take care, You have my regard.

Sincerely,

George L. Jackson

MARCH, 1970

2

Dear Fay,

We received a copy of the transcipt today through the mail. It was John Clutchette who actually received it.

I also had a letter from my father. It was a long letter, considering that he normally writes only a few lines. It seems that he is now prepared to accept the validity of the many charges I have long made against certain forms of organization and specifically certain elements within the forms. I suspect that Georgia may have had something to do with it. Just to make me feel better. Either way, it denotes the effects that trauma has on people, especially people who are affected by little else. I am convinced that black people can never be influenced by ideology alone. The men have been too conditioned against it by violence and they are afraid. The women think of themselves as too practical, they can be moved by one thing only: "Money honey." However, I love them all just the same. I reason that with a continuous stream of shocks and the promise of spoils they can eventually be induced to reach beyond their immediate surroundings. A guard said something nasty to one of my sisters last Tuesday, this may have been the catalyst with my father. He's a stranger to me, almost.

I just got the letter and the book you want me to read. I see that you posted it on the twenty-sixth. Thanks, I'll get right on it.

You have my regard, please give my further regards to our friends.

Sincerely,

George L. Jackson

MARCH, 1970
5

Dear Friend, Fay,

I have started this three times. This first is in the way of an apology. For I feel one is due you. At the close of today's proceedings, I left without as much as a look in your and John's direction. I am afraid that you may mistake such behavior as the unfeeling and calloused disregard of the slave. I hope I have trained all of the slave out of me. Neither would I have you feel for even a second that I could make any (any at all) mental associations between you and your people, and those who stand in my way, simply because of the external resemblance or let me say any external resemblance. I never have, even in the really bad moments, lost the ability to evaluate people one at a time and never will. The only way I

210

can explain the little thing that occurred this evening is with an explanation of that pain or shock that strikes me at times just behind the eyes. I don't understand it entirely myself. From early this morning I carry the metal around. That vehicle they transport us in and in which we ate lunch (hands to side) is very cramped, and then and most important the attitude of the pig in the jury room when he came to take me back. I believe it first started bothering me then, the thing in my head, Campbell* again, ruling on . . . You see, someone failed before me, trembled and failed, my father, his father, leaving Campbell in a position to rule me out. I have very bad moments when I think of that, and of course it follows that I must think of my own failings—can you understand that being a helpless type affects me deeply. You are a very intelligent, sensitive, and wonderful person and the image you form, wedged between me and who knows what fate, elates me in one sense and infuriates me in another. Why should I have to relate and exchange from such a position of weakness. It comes down on me at times. I am tortured by the vision of someone like myself standing at the bars of his cell two hundred years from now cursing *me*—dereliction!! So let me apologize for today, because it bothers me. Let me take this occasion to apologize in advance for the seemingly crude responses you may detect from time to time. My sensibilities may be somewhat damaged. You can help me with this over the years to come. The tape† left me feeling better than I have felt for ten, perhaps fifteen years.

I got the transcript and your letter upon my return this evening. When will I see you again?

George

---

*The first judge assigned to the case. He later withdrew after the defense accused him of blatant expressions of racial prejudice.

†A personal message from Huey P. Newton.

MARCH, 1970
9

Dear Fay,

Just heard something of Campbell's imminent retirement. It could occur at any time. Did you, by the way, take note of his statement in court the other day to the effect that he "was also once an attorney and had defended—unpopular—causes." His words exactly!

I don't know if it means anything or not but the court reporter stated on his page that he recorded 1–48 pages of testimony, and we have only 1–46 pages.

I guess you have learned by now that my mother loves to talk. She also at times will say what she is thinking without considering the effect it may have on the listener. She gets so carried away at times that I have been led to suspect that she may be affected with—well she may be a mild hysteric, not the sexual type but the simple nervous type. She is, however, a sweet woman with plenty of guts. We have always related well.

I am still among the living, so I guess I'm doing all right. The dentist denied me medical attention for the tenth time today, this morning that is. We may have to discipline him soon. He apparently hasn't heard of my small but mighty mouthpiece.

Please take care of yourself, you have my regard.

George

P.S. I would like to know in advance when I will see you again.

12

Dear Fay,

I received the copies of the motions, I think day before yesterday, the tenth. I have been slow to confirm. Sorry, it may seem strange but I find my time (twenty-one hours awake) inadequate to meet all the needs.

My metabolism is such that I need four hours of exercise to feel normal (relaxed). This may just be the result of years of being in places like this, repressing things. You know we aren't even allowed to get angry. They took away my showering action (the half hour on the tier we were getting each day) on Monday as a result of that contact with the dentist. No problem, however. There is a sink in my cell.

Then I have my vocational work to do. I'll get lost in that for hours sometimes. Old slave trying to deal with his environment. In this connection you may have to help me as you said you did with my friend. They are purposely making it difficult for me to get what I require. We can discuss it when I see you.

Georgia was up to see me yesterday. The three mothers and one aunt all came together on the bus.

I have your letter of the tenth here before me now, thanks. You have my sincere regard.

George

MARCH, 1970
22

My Friend,

The thought just occurred to me that you could challenge that guy B—— on his theory or statements concerning the possibilities of his secret witnesses being done in, if he allows discovery*. You see every time a rat does get put away, the prison authorities always release a different reason for the attack, never that he was an informer. Their purpose for always withholding the truth is that they don't want to discourage other potential rats and the truth would aid the convict in the psychological war—con against cop. For it is their purpose to always keep us divided and fearful of trusting the next con. You are aware that it's always the goal of oppressive authority (those who govern without the consent of the governed) to keep their wards divided. They can maintain their control in no other way.

Divide and rule in its simplest form is standard police procedure. They must always display their rats, boast of

*At the prosecution's request, the judge initially denied the defense the right of discovery on the grounds that it would jeopardize the lives of the inmate witnesses.

214

knowing all that goes on among us. When it's more than one person on some crime, they will be split up and each told that the other has confessed and implicated him, etc. You know the line. Inside the joint it is the same only much more intense. A sense of terror, betrayal and insecurity prevails at all times. It flows outward from the captain's office—divide and rule, divide and rule. An Italian in the Syndicate at one time killed a Mexican in Folsom because the Mex suddenly started telling everyone not to trust someone, who was supposed to be a rat. The pigs wanted to put him out of business (importing dope into the joint) and wanted to get the Mex killed. So they called the Mex into their office and showed him some phony papers indicating that the guy was a rat. The Mex went for it and got killed. The guy was out of business in 4A for four years (4A is Folsom's adjustment center).

Terrible conflict going on all the time. At issue is who will run the joint, cops or cons. So it is never released that a police informer was killed for his mistake. I'm thinking that B. will be at a loss to cite some cases in support of his fears that his witnesses will be harmed. We could state that he is playing on some concept of prison conditions that existed in 1920 but that do not exist today.

Monday, March 23, 1970

I'm looking forward to a good Friday. Never had one.

I don't think Los Angeles is a good place for the trial. Fifteen floors above the ground. One million pigs!!

I was pushing you, rushing you, encircling you—recall—it occasioned the remark from you that "I don't know you that well." Look, I do plead guilty but with this explanation, that I hope you'll accept the past months as, say, the equivalent of five or more years' acquaintance. I encircle the people that I dig, there are only two types of people inhabiting my closet, friends and foes, the ones I accept, the ones I reject. I accepted you from the onset, and in spite of the bitter experience of these years I still find it easy to trust people. I sensed from the

215

start that we were of kindred spirits. I rejected others as you recall, because there was no kinship of spirit there. To me length of acquaintance matters very little. I've been living in the trenches where it's understood that it's us against them, hide and seek. They're always it and getting caught means getting dusted. There never are many of us, so when I've met one in the past it's been my method to encircle and push. But "push" isn't a good term. It implies that I've put someone in front of me and there can never be any room in front of me. Let me say encircle and pull.

You can never fully understand. It is an existential impossibility for you to know how it's been with me. My character and disposition are such that my response to a crisis situation always leads to a situation more desperate than the one which provoked it. But that's the way I like it, and believe me, Fay, I probably wouldn't be alive now if it weren't my habit to overreact, and look forward for the trouble that I know is coming.

It probably didn't have to be this way for me. Other blacks have faced the same situations and have not been hurt too badly. I couldn't take it. I'll never be able to take it, a knife in the back, the nightstick, the gas chamber, death over a slow fire notwithstanding.

And things just keep escalating from one desperate situation to a situation more desperate, and I seize the bull by the horns. I'll ride him till his neck breaks or until he pins me to the wall—conflict, struggle, and preparation for more struggle. You can't understand how it is to have to watch everyone who gets within arm's reach, or when under the gun to have to stay close to something to crawl under. When you came to see me in February my heart was cold as Antarctica.

Tuesday, March 24, 1970 (early morning)

I'm convinced that it is the psychopathic personality that searches out a uniform. There's little doubt of

216

what's going on in that man's head who will voluntarily don any uniform.

Did you know that in these prisons there is a very fierce competition between the pig who wears a uniform and the pig who works in civilian dress? The uniformed pigs call themselves the Custody Department, while the others go under the heading of Care and Treatment.

It is the function of the uniform to hold a man here. This means they do the key work, the searching, beating, killing. The individual with the tie and white shirt (really just another type of uniform) determines what we'll eat, what bullshit academic and make-work programs we'll have. He presides over the silly group therapy games that always end in fights or snitch contests. Oh, and he also makes out board reports.

These two types of cops have been vying for control of the joints ever since the counselor breed came on the grounds.

It was intended of course that these two groups of cops work together against the con, the rationale being, the more cons broken, the fewer will have to be killed, consequently less bad publicity for Department of Corrections political appointees and the political machine that appointed them.

We killed that off by playing them against one another. If a uniform denied some small request, we would take it to the counselor. If he granted it, well you can take it from there, but we would purposely ask the uniform (and in a way that made it certain he would refuse) for things we were sure the counselor would approve. Everyone connected with the power complex has made the outcome reasonably predictable, chaos. You have a picture of them trying to divide us, manage us, denude us of individuality. When this maneuver fails, they arrange for one unmanageable to murder another unmanageable. At the same time they can't agree among themselves on anything. Cretins with guns. You couldn't count the personality conflicts between cop + cop, cop + con, con + con (usually fomented by some cop or some unnecessarily harsh living condition). You couldn't count these conflicts with an

217

IBM. And I mean the ones that transpire openly in, say, one hour's time.

To be certain that you dig what I'm saying, I'll here admit that most of the people who come through these places are genuinely sick in one way or the other, monsters, totally disorganized, twisted, disgusting epitomes of the parent monster. Those who aren't so upon their arrival will surely be so when they leave. No one escapes unscathed. An individual leaves his individuality and any pride he may have had behind these walls. When you first enter Chino you're required to write a confession that will be placed right in the front of your jacket* under your picture and number. Failure to write this confession means you go to the board. It means that you haven't taken the first step toward rehabilitation. All this is carefully explained to you in Chino. "No confession, no parole." No one walks into the board room with his head up. This just isn't done! Guys lie to each other, but if a man gets a parole from these prisons, Fay, it means that he crawled into that room. Plus it means that he adopted the philosophical attitude toward shit in the face several times since his last board. Of the billions of conflicts and negative exchanges that take place in a year, the pigs choose which ones to pass over. The guy who earns a parole surrendered some face in the course of his stay here prior to board. He walked away from some situation to save his body—at the cost of some part of his face (read mind, or pride, or principle). No black will leave this place if he has any violence in his past, until they see that thing in his eyes. And you can't fake it—resignation, defeat—it must be stamped clearly across the face.

I've seen it, eyes in black heads, on the yard in San Quentin, Tracy, here. When I hit the yard in December '62 the brothers were lining up in the rain, outside the protection of the shed that covers half of the upper yard. The Mexicans and

*Convict's record folder, log of all observations made by prison authorities.

218

whites had occupied all the lines under the shed. They would save long stretches of space for friends who never showed. So I had a picture on my first day there of the old slave, wet and trembling while these other people relaxed with plenty of room under the shed. The brothers were mainly concerned with avoiding any trouble, since the pig invaribly will shoot at the black face in a black and white altercation. Then it seems that blacks are much more concerned with establishing records that will lead to parole than whites or browns. I can't understand this, since they have so much less to go home to.

Earlier that same year, right here in Soledad, a white (nameless and faceless now) stabbed a brother with my surname because another brother called Butch beat him in one of those childish hand-to-hand disputes in the third-tier shower (the place for settling all disputes). The white inmate ran to his cell and asked for police protection. Two hundred blacks went after him with the intention of taking him from the police. Before it was over there were only four of us against all the police in the county. A——. A. was there with me then, and two others, all the others—well, it started with a trembling of the lips, then a flaring of the nose, then that thing in the eyes. . . .

They sent us to San Quentin lockup for a month. Then J.C. and I were sent to Tracy, being the youngest of the four. In Tracy I did six months in adjustment center and was released to J Unit, the unit for unmanageables. Actually they put me in this unit so that I would be close to some old enemies. A Mexican got killed in Soledad the year before. J.C. was picked up for it but later released. No one was ever convicted. In an honest case of mistaken identity, the Mexicans were supposed to be out to get me for it.

I don't know where you got the tale of me attempting to integrate a movie area. It is a bit off, but it could have come from the events of that week I spent in J Unit. The blacks had to sit in the rear of the TV room on hard, armless, backless benches while the Mexicans and whites sat up front on

219

cushioned chairs and benches with backrests!!! Now check this, if one of those punks was in his cell or the shower, no one could sit in his seat and certainly no black dared sit there, I'm serious!!! All of this taking place in front of a uniform and a large, bold-print sign in English and Spanish that read "No Saving of Seats Allowed"!!!

The first three nights I went in to catch the news I *stood* in the front, looking down the room at the old slave for some sign of support. Old slave ignored me, eyes darting. He wants to go home, so do I, but I don't want to leave anything behind. Since my father didn't bequeath me much to begin with, any further losses leave me with nothing. I sat right in the front the fourth night but I couldn't watch TV. I had to watch my back. The cop walked up and looked at me like I had lost my mind. The cons tolerated me (215 pounds and apparently a lunatic) for three days. On the fourth (or seventh day out) night of sitting, they attacked me. They *locked me up* afterward, and sent me back to San Quentin to stay. The 115* was so clearly racist that I think they removed it in San Quentin. If you ever get the chance, see what reason they have in my jacket for the 1962 transfer to San Quentin from Tracy.

So most of these inmates are sick, my friend, but who created the monster in them? They all stand right now as products of their environment. But in my humble opinion the inmates of these places are not quite as—well they aren't nearly as psychologically disturbed as the guy who calls himself a guard. They really could change roles without noticeable alteration in the qualitative factor of administrations. Any alteration would be positive.

United States prisons are the last refuge of the brainless. If the inmates are failures, at least they were reaching—most in very small ways, but some reach is certainly prefereable to no reach at all. The cop, as I've stated before, is a guy who can do

*Bad conduct report form.

no other type of work, who can feed himself only by feeding upon this garbage dump.

What am I doing here, Fay? I fell into this garbage can in a narcotic stupor and they just closed the lid for good. Someone is going to be hurt, my friend, when it's over someone's going to be hurting, bad, and it won't be us. It won't be you. Be assured that your safety will always enter any defense move I make, your safety first, always. I was supposed to be gone from this place years ago, free, wrecking worlds, destroying the unrighteous, dying on my feet.

Pigs come here to feed on the garbage heap for two reasons really, the first half because they can do no other work, frustrated men soon to develop sadistic mannerisms; and the second half, sadists out front, suffering under the restraints placed upon them by an equally sadistic-vindictive society. The sadist knows that to practice his religion upon the society at large will bring down upon his head their sadistic reaction. Killing is great fun, but not at the risk of getting killed (note how they squeak and pull out their hair over losing even one).

But the restraints come off when they walk through the compound gates. Their whole posture goes through a total metamorphosis. Inflict pain, satisfy the power complex, and get a check.

How can the sick administer to the sick.

In the well-ordered society prisons would not exist as such. If a man is ill he should be placed in a hospital, staffed by the very best of technicians. Men would never be separated from women. These places would be surfeited with equipment and meaningful programs, even if it meant diverting funds from another, or even from all other sectors of the economy. It's socially self-destructive to create a monster and loose him upon the world.

But we can't cure with diagnoses, Comrade Stender—and I dig speaking with you like this. You can only listen, no back talk.

Breakfast is here. Power to the People.

221

Tuesday, March 24, 1970 (evening)

This monster—the monster they've engendered in me will return to torment its maker, from the grave, the pit, the profoundest pit. Hurl me into the next existence, the descent into hell won't turn me. I'll crawl back to dog his trail forever. They won't defeat my revenge, never, never. I'm part of a righteous people who anger slowly, but rage undammed. We'll gather at his door in such a number that the rumbling of our feet will make the earth tremble. I'm going to charge them for this, twenty-eight years without gratification. I'm going to charge them reparations in blood. I'm going to charge them like a maddened, wounded, rogue male elephant, ears flared, trunk raised, trumpet blaring. I'll do my dance in his chest, and the only thing he'll ever see in my eyes is a dagger to pierce his cruel heart. This is one nigger who is positively displeased. I'll never forgive, I'll never forget, and if I'm guilty of anything at all it's of not leaning on them hard enough. War without terms.

Wednesday, March 25, 1970 (early morning)

I just reread the above paragraph, foul mood last night. It's not light out yet, so I guess I can say tonight, but I've been asleep. There's a Hawaiian on the tier who wants a transfer to Vacaville. He is playing crazy. His dementia takes the form of "nigger baiting," especially when the bull is on the tier (who by the way enjoys the shit out of it)—none of the brothers say a word, however. This little boy blows the whole line. The other little boys laugh, the pig grins. I don't get too upset at the little boy. He is a minnow—the upsetting point is that this Hawaiian has very large purple lips, skin tones darker than mine, and a very large wide nose. His hair is very nearly like my sisters'. This clown is talking about killing all the niggers. The pitiful jackass would die right beside me. I think what may be most bitter in a thing like that is the knowledge

222

that my enemies have turned the entire world against me. The shibboleths that defame me are now universal. Anyone who learns them is in (or out—depending).

How do you deal with the perverted, disease-bearing, voracious bastard who wants to cast his image over all things, eat from every plate at every table, police the world with racist shibboleths and a dying doctrine of marketplaces peopled by monopolies, top-heavy bureaus, and scum-swilling pigs to gun down any who would object?

The concept of nonviolent protest, whatever political forms it may take, presumes two things about the imperialist establishment that are so obviously historically unrealistic, so logically unsound, that the espousal of any purely nonviolent anti-establishment moan reduces one automatically to the absurd, and any strong espousal of the purely nonviolent anti-establishment policy reduces one automatically to a corpse.

The first presumption is mercy. It presumes the possible existence of mercy on the part of a breed whose heart is as cold as the snows. It presumes existence of a restraint mechanism that in other breeds and other animals precludes the harming of one's kind unless placed under the most extreme compulsions of self-preservation. But history shows no justification for so wild a presupposition. I refer you to Leopold II's Congo, the Indian wars of the last century, the Union of South Africa, Sharpsville, the Philippines at the turn of the century. I refer you to Germany during the depression and war years. I refer you to Vietnam! Just a cursory reading of history and just a glance about me now would show—that I could expect more mercy from a pack of Bengal tigers. Any claims that nonviolent, purely nonviolent political agitation has served to force back the legions of capitalist expansion are false. The theory of nonviolence is a false ideal. The Hindus failed *because* of this moral aspect in their characters precluding any large-scale organized violence. The forms of slavery merely changed for them. Of what value is quasi-politi-

223

cal control if the capitalists are allowed to hold on to the people's whole means of subsistence?! And in the case of India and foreign capitalists, have any of the people's needs been met? Do they still have race riots, do they still sleep in the streets? These people were betrayed by false leaders with false ideals. Compare India with China. They were both supposedly liberated at the same time, India may have had a year or more of what is loosely termed "political self-determination". China's problems in the late forties were ten times more severe, but today there is no one hungry in China. For the first time its population is united and organized under a government as decentralized and representative as a huge modern industrial based society can be. China, land of the coolie, slave labor, open-door policies, floor mat of the West—they're vying for first place in every important economic sector today. Remember the 1839 Opium War, the Boxer Rebellion. A trial of combat with China today would be Russian roulette with a fully loaded .45 automatic, self-destruction, suicide.

All of the third world political movements that are forcing the retreat of colonialism have learned to deal with the expeditionary armies of colonialism. There is no case of successful liberation without violence. How could you neutralize an army without violence?

The people of the U.S. are held in the throes of a form of colonialism. Control of their subsistence and nearly every aspect of the circumstances surrounding their existence has passed into the hands of a clearly distinct and alienated oligarchy. If today's young revolutionary vanguard are not merely entertaining themselves with a new kind of "chicken," a political form of bumper tag, if they seriously intend to step out front and take the monster to task, they should understand from the outset that the monster is merciless.

The second presumption contained in the concept of nonviolent political agitation is inherent in the statement of this policy, as it stands alone. The mere utterance of nonviolent policy statements *implies* that it is possible for one

224

to take the opposite course and pursue violence. But in our case this has not been proved. In all cases, there is a contradiction and a dangerous presumption in the statement and pursuit of nonviolent political policy, especially when the opposition is not so committed. The danger derives from the very realistic fact that the statement and pursuit of nonviolent tactics will always be mistaken for *weakness,* as these tactics stand alone. The contradiction is then revealed, in that power is expected to surrender to weakness.

Pure nonviolence as a political ideal, then, is absurd: Politics is violence. It may serve our purpose to claim nonviolence, but we must never delude ourselves into thinking that we can seize power from a position of weakness, with half measures, polite programs, righteous indignation, loud entreaties. If this agitation that we like to term as nonviolent is to have any meaning at all we must force the fascist to taste the bitterness of our wrath. Nonviolence must constantly demonstrate the effects of its implied opposite. The dialectic between Narodnik and Nihilist should never break down. One should not exist without the concomitant existence of the other.—Breakfast is here.—Long live the guerrillas!

Wednesday, March 25, 1970 (late)

I suspect that the pigs have stopped the correspondence form that I sent to your friend.

The four or five people who attacked the pigs last week—recall they had weapons (?), took the keys—they're out of the hole (isolation) already, over here with us. I don't, however, suspect foul play too strongly. The Mexican was beaten pretty badly. Just lit the forty-first cigarette.

The punks throw stuff at us through the bars when they are let out for showers. I mean foul stuff too. We each get a half hour a day, six days of the week, to shower or exercise in the limited space in front of our cells. The walks are segregated. Blacks are never allowed to walk or shower or even to come

225

out of the cells at all when the whites are out of their cells. The more perverse of "Hitler's Little Helpers" save their excretions to throw in our cells as they walk back and forth to their shower and exercise. The shit literally flies at us almost every day. The blacks don't even consider throwing excrement. We retaliate by shooting at them with little, crudely-made zip guns and powerful slingshots fashioned from the elastic on our shorts. If the pigs were interested in stopping this silly shit, they would integrate the shower walks. If they fear they would lose control that way, they could segregate the whole building. No whites or Mexicans on this floor at all.

To seize power for the people and relegate fascism to the history books the vanguard must change the basic patterns of thought. We are going to have to study the principles of people's movements. We are going to have to study them where they took place and interpret them to fit our situation here. We have yet to discover the meaning of people's war, people's army. The righteous people of the world who are struggling with the monster on the only terms that he can be fought must have many reservations concerning us, especially those of us who are black. What are the fierce and wonderful people of Vietnam thinking of us? Where is the real left wing? What has been done to us, that makes us fail to resist?

The successes of China, Cuba, Vietnam, and parts of Africa cannot be attributed to any innate, singular quality in the characters of their people. Men are social creatures, herd animals. We follow leaders. The success or failure of mass movements depends on their leadership and the method of their leaders. We must take our lessons from these people, reorganize our *values,* decide whether it is our personal desire to live long or to chance living right.

People's war, class struggle, war of liberation means *armed* struggle. Men like Hoover, Reagan, Hunt, Agnew, Johnson, Helms, Westmoreland, Abrams, Campbell, Carswell are dangerous men who believe that they are the rightful Führers of all the world's people. They must be dealt with now. Can men

226

like these be converted? Will they allow anyone to maneuver them out of their positions of power while they still live? Would Nixon accept a people's government, a people's economy? How can we deal with these men who have so much at stake, so much to defend. Honesty forces us to the conclusion that the only men who will successfully deal with the Hoovers, Helmses and Abramses will be armed men. It's obvious to me that nothing of any consequence can be achieved while these men rule. Class struggle means the suppression of the opposing class, and suppression of the Amerikan General Staff, and The Corporate Elite. The moment this three-headed monster detects the danger contained in our ideas and ideals, he will react violently against us. Just the whisper of revolt excites in him a swift and terrible reflex, so swift we won't even know how we died.

Thursday, March 26, 1970

So, my friend, the terms have been established. That is the only way I will accept any more time in this life. I don't *want* to live any other way. I *want* my food and drink from the people's stash. I *want* to hide, run, and look over my shoulder. The only woman that I could ever accept is one who would be willing to live out of a flight bag, sleep in a coal car, eat milkweed, bloodroot, wild greens, dandelions, a rabbit, a handful of rice. She would have to be willing to run and work all night and watch all day. She would bathe when we could, change clothes when we could. She would own nothing, not solely because she loved me, but because she loved the principle, the revolution, the people.

I don't think this rotten society has produced any such wonderful creatures. There is a Cuban brother here on the tier. His folks left, but he supports the revolution. He can run some beautiful things about the people of Cuba when he'll talk and when I can understand him. The thing that fixes me best is how the revolution is gauged to operate on the family plan—

227

children with a role, women in the same roles as men, education standardized.

I remembered that those people had been some of the most corrupt in the Western world. Remember when the U.S. was in control, it was just like one of the Mexican border towns. The revolution brought all of those wonderful new people into existence. It will be the same here—right on—to the most beautiful conclusion.

Power to the People.

If they try to read this it will explain my somewhat damaged condition in court tomorrow.

You are my favorite person, Fay Stender, take care of yourself.

George

MARCH, 1970
30

Dear Fay,

I'm well—no new problems. You can, however, when time allows, write Dr. Boone of the medical staff here and tell him to provide me with medication for my sinus condition so that we will not be forced into the imposition of going through the courts for it. Also let it be known that you are aware of the APC and brown-sugar-pill put-off. Do you understand? When I ask for medication, the MTA gives me an APC or two and some candy pills (brown). This doesn't help me. They have better stuff that is reserved for the other cons. They're about to stretch me to my limit with this racist stuff. I'm tired of hearing it, seeing it, and I'm tired of smelling it. I know they read these letters. That's good, because I want them to know that the first time they let one of these punks throw something on me we're going to all blow like a thermonuclear bomb. I'm just not going to understand!!

The blacks on this floor never engage in any form of name-calling, never defy the lockups, never ask the officials for anything other than the state issue. Very seldom do any of the brothers ask the officials to pass things down the tier. We do the passing. When we come out for showers, we never even talk to the other inmates or officials, but still we've been attacked in every way conceivable (considering that there are always a set of bars between us and them). It doesn't have to be this way. Since the officials are segregating anyway, they could do it in such a way that there would never be any contact between blacks and whites. They could give us this side of the first floor and them the other side or the reverse. They could even give people a choice as to whether they want to be segregated. I'm putting you on notice, *Moody,** the first time I get shit thrown at me the whole country will know how it displeases me.

How ridiculous can animals get. The whites get angry with me for just existing. But they seem to get on well with the people who are holding them here, the people responsible for the living conditions that cause their frustration.

For the People's Lieben—

George

*One of the captains at Soledad.

MARCH, 1970

31

Dear Fay,

I've finished the legal book you sent me.* Do you want it back the next time I see you, or am I free to let a couple of other brothers read it?

It pertains to all of us, I believe. I read your section several times. Did you put it together by yourself? It's very heavy! I'm thinking that if the Court of Appeals passes favorably on it, and other attorneys incorporate it into their defenses, we could come up with a detaining or delaying tool at least. It's good! I'd stake my life on you any time.

We have a situation then where dull, heavy-handed, desperate types like myself run afoul of the law from time to time. Then we have the gracious, sensitive, brainy types, of whom you are the quintessence, to hold the legal pigs to the strictest interpretation of the Constitution possible. The cynic in me, although it allows for the short-term benefits, sees another situation building down the road, a situation where they will simply hold court at the scene, there in the street.

Milestiba for the People—

George

*Ann Fagan Ginger, *Minimizing Racism in Jury Trials: The Voir Dire* Conducted by Charles R. Garry in *People of California V. Huey P. Newton* (The National Lawyers Guild, 1969).

APRIL, 1970

Dear Fay,

I just got your letter with the writ article in it. You are positively my favorite person. We must take time to get acquainted. You have mentioned yourself and your other life only once. Please don't misunderstand, I simply wish to know you better. I haven't had much contact with anyone outside my family and the people who have come through these prisons in the last decade or so. And I dig people, righteous people. I always have found it hard to really hate anyone. I loved people. I understood from the beginning that the end purpose of life was simply to live, experience, contribute, connect, to gratify the body and mind. I began to hate when I discovered that the mystification was interjected intentionally. I can't say where it started. I can't trace it, but I believe it goes back to my earliest years, I mean the feeling that what everyone else around me accepted as right wasn't necessarily so. The family, the nuns, the pigs, I resisted them all. I know my mother likes to tell everyone that I was a good boy, but that isn't true, I've been a brigand all my life. It was these years in prison with the time and opportunity available to me for research and thought that motivated a desire to remold my character. I think that if I had been on the street from age eighteen to twenty-four, I would probably be a dope fiend or a small-stakes gambler, or a hump in the ground.

Power to the People,

George

232

APRIL, 1970

4

Dear Fay,

For very obvious reasons it pains me to dwell on the past. As an individual, and as the male of our order I have only the proud flesh* of very recent years to hold up as proof that I did not die in the sickbed in which I lay for so long. I've taken my lesson from the past and attempted to close it off.

I've drunk deeply from the cisterns of gall, swam against the current in Blood Alley, Urban Fascist Amerika, experienced the nose rub in shit, armed myself with a monumental hatred and tried to forget and pretend. A standard black male defense mechanism.

It hasn't worked. It may just be me, but I suspect that it's part of the pitiful black condition that the really bad moments record themselves so clearly and permanently in the mind, while the few brief flashes of gratification are lost immediately, nightmare overhanging darkly.

My recall is nearly perfect, time has faded nothing. I recall the very first kidnap. I've lived through the passage, died on the passage, lain in the unmarked, shallow graves of the millions who fertilized the Amerikan soil with their corpses; cotton and corn growing out of my chest, "unto the third and

*Proud flesh is a medical term for the abnormal growth of flesh that sometimes forms around a healing wound.

233

fourth generation," the tenth, the hundredth. My mind ranges back and forth through the uncounted generations. and I feel all that they ever felt, but double. I can't help it; there are too many things to remind me of the 23½ hours that I'm in this cell. Not ten minutes pass without a reminder. In between, I'm left to specualte on what form the reminder will take.

Down here we hear relaxed, matter-of-fact conversations centering around how best to kill all the nation's niggers and in what order. It's not the fact that they consider killing me that upsets. They've been "killing all the niggers" for nearly half a millennium now, but I am still alive. I might be the most resilient dead man in the universe. The upsetting thing is that they never take into consideration the fact that I am going to resist. No they honestly believe that shit. They do! That's what they think of us. That they have beaten and conditioned all the defense and attack reflexes from us. That the region of the mind that stores the principles upon which men base their rationale to resist is missing in us. Don't they talk of concentration camps?. Don't they state that it couldn't happen in the U.S. because the fascists here are nice fascists. Not because it's impossible to incarcerate 30 million resisters, but because they are humane imperialists, enlightened fascists.

Well, they've made a terrible mistake. I recall the day I was born, the first day of my generation. It was during the second (and most destructive) capitalist world war for colonial privilege, early on a rainy Wednesday morning, late September, Chicago. It happened to me in a little fold-into-the-wall bed, in a little half-flat on Racine and Lake. Dr. Rogers attended. The el train that rattled by within fifteen feet of our front windows (the only two windows) screamed in at me like the banshee, portentous of pain, death, threatening and imminent. The first motion that my eyes focused on was this pink hand swinging in a wide arc in the general direction of my black ass. I stopped that hand, the left downward block, and countered the right needle finger to the eye. I was born with my defense reflexes well developed.

It's going to be "Kill me if you can," fool, not "Kill me if

234

you please."

But let them make their plans on the supposition, "like slave, like son." I'm not going for it, though, and they've made my defense easier. A cop gives the keys to a group of right-wing cons. They're going to open our cells—one at a time—all over the building. They don't want to escape, or deal with the men who hold them here. They can solve their problems only if they kill all of us—think about that—these guys live a few cells from me. None of them have ever lived, most are state-raised in institutions like this one. They have nothing coming, nothing at all, they have nothing at stake in this order of things. In defending right-wing ideals and the status quo they're saying in effect that ninety-nine years and a dark day in prison is their idea of fun. Most are in and out, and mostly in, all of their life. The periods that they pass on the outside are considered runs. Simply stated, they consider the periods spent in the joint more natural, more in keeping with their tastes. Well, I understand their condition, and I know how they got that way. I could honestly sympathize with them if they were not so wrong, so stupid as to let the pigs use them. Sounds like Germany of the thirties and forties to me. It's the same on the outside there. I'll venture to say that there's not one piece of stock, not one bond owned by anyone in any of the families of the pigs who murdered Fred Hampton. They organize marches around the country, marches and demonstrations in support of total immediate destruction of Vietnam, and afterward no one is able to pick up the tab. The fascists, it seems, have a standard M.O. for dealing with the lower classes. Actually oppressive power throughout history has used it. They turn a man against himself—think of all the innocent things that make us feel good, but that make some of us also feel guilty. Think of how the people of the lower classes weigh themselves against the men who rule. Consider the con going through the courts on a capital offense who supports capital punishment. I swear I heard something just like that today. Look how long Hershey ran Selective Service. Blacks embrace capitalism, the most unnatural and

235

outstanding example of man against himself that history can offer. After the Civil War, the form of slavery changed from chattel to economic slavery, and we were thrown onto the labor market to compete at a disadvantage with poor whites. Ever since that time, our principal enemy must be isolated and identified as capitalism. The slaver was and is the factory owner, the businessman of capitalist Amerika, the man responsible for employment, wages, prices, control of the nation's institutions and culture. It was the capitalist infrastructure of Europe and the U.S. which was responsible for the rape of Africa and Asia. Capitalism murdered those 30 million in the Congo. Believe me, the European and Anglo-Amerikan capitalist would never have wasted the ball and powder were it not for the profit principle. The men, all the men who went into Africa and Asia, the fleas who climbed on that elephant's back with rape on their minds, richly deserve all that they are called. Every one of them deserved to die for their crimes. So do the ones who are still in Vietnam, Angola, Union of South Africa (U.S.A.!!). But we must not allow the emotional aspects of these issues, the scum at the surface, to obstruct our view of the big picture, the whole rotten hunk. It was capitalism that armed the ships, free enterprise that launched them, private ownership of property that fed the troops. Imperialism took up where the slave trade left off. It wasn't until after the slave trade ended that Amerika, England, France, and the Netherlands invaded and settled in on Afro-Asian soil in earnest. As the European industrial revolution took hold, new economic attractions replaced the older ones; chattel slavery was replaced by neoslavery. Capitalism, "free" enterprise, private ownership of public property armed and launched the ships and fed the troops; it should be clear that it was the profit motive that kept them there.

It was the profit motive that built the tenement house and the city project. Profit and loss prevents repairs and maintainance. Free enterprise brought the monopolistic chain store into the neighborhood. The concept of private ownership of facilities that the people need to exist brought the legions of hip-shooting, brainless pigs down upon our heads, our homes, our streets. They're there to protect the entrepreneur!! His chain store, and his property that you are renting, his bank.

If the entrepreneur decides that he no longer wants to sell you food, let's say, because the Yankee dollar that we value so dearly has suddenly lost its last thirty cents of purchasing power, private ownership means that the only way many of the people will eat is to break the law. Fat Rat Daley has ordered all looters shot.

Black capitalism, black against itself. The silliest contradiction in a long train of spineless, mindless contradictions. Another painless, ultimate remedy: be a better fascist than the fascist. Bill Cosby, acting out the establishment agent—what message was this soul brother conveying to our children? *I Spy* was certainly programmed to a child's mentality. This running dog in the company of a fascist with a cause, a flunky's flunky, was transmitting the credo of the slave to our youth, the mod version of the old house nigger. We can never learn to trust as long as we have them. They are as much a part of the repression, more even than the real live, rat-informer-pig. Aren't they telling our kids that it is romantic to be a running dog? The kids are so hungry to see the black male do some shooting and throw some hands that they can't help themselves from identifying with the quislings. So first they turn us against ourselves, precluding all possibility of trust, then fascism takes any latent divisible forces and develops them into divisions in fact: racism, nationalism, religions.

You have Spic, Dago, Jew, Jap, Chink, Gook, Pineapple, and the omnibus nigger to represent the nations of Africa. The point being that it is easier to persuade that little man who joined the army to see the world and who has never murdered before to murder a Gook. Well, it's not quite like murdering a man. Polack, Frog, Kraut, etc.

The wheels just fell off altogether in the thirties. People in certain circles like to forget it, and any reference to the period

237

draws from these circles such defensive epithets as "old-fashioned," "simple old-style socialism," and "out of date." But fashion doesn't concern me, I'm after the facts. The facts are that no one, absolutely no one in the Western world, and very few anywhere else (this includes even those who may have been born yesterday), is unaffected by those years when capitalism's roulette wheel locked in depression. It affected every nation-state on earth. Of course Russia had no stock market and consequently no business cycle, but it was affected by the war that grew out of the efforts to restart the machines and by the effect it had on other nations with which Russia has had to deal. Relativism enters. Since international capitalism was at the time in its outward peak of expansion, there were no African, Asian, or Latin lands organized along nation-state lines that were not adversely affected. Every society in the world that lived by a money economy was part of the depression. Although Russia had abandoned the forms and vacillations of capitalism, it too was damaged due to the principles of relativism.

If there is any question whether those years have any effect on, or relevance to now, just consider the effect on today's mentality. Had the world's people been struck with hereditary cretinism all at once, instead of Adam Smith's "invisible hand," the analogy couldn't be more perfect. I mean cretinism in its literal, medical sense: a congenital deficiency in the secretions of the thyroid gland resulting in deformity and idiocy. Causation links that depression with World War II. The rise to power of Europe's Nazis can be attributed to the depression. The WASP fascists of Amerika secretly desired a war with Japan to stimulate demand and control unemployment. The syllogism is perfect.

So question and analyze the state of being of Europe's Jews who survive. Do the same with the people of Hiroshima and Nagasaki. But we don't have to isolate groups. Causation and relativism link everyone inescapably with the past. None of the righteous people would even be alive had their parents died of

238

the underconsumption of that period or the desperate fascist chicanery aimed at diverting the lower classes from the economic reality of class struggle. The Nazis actually succeeded in foisting upon the lower-class Germans and some of the other European national groups the notion that their economic plight was due not to bad economic principles but caused by the existence of Jews within the system and the shortage of markets (colonies). The obvious intent being to put lower-class, depressed German against lower-class Jew, instead of exploited lower-class German against privileged upper-class German.

The Amerikan fascist used a thousand similar devises, delaying maneuvers, to prevent the people from questioning the validity of the principles upon which capitalism is founded, to turn the people against themselves, people against people, people against other groups of people. Always they will promote competition (while they cooperate), division, mistrust, a sense of isolation. The antipodes of love. The M.O. of the fascist arrangement is always to protect the capitalist class by destroying the consciousness, the trust, the unity of the lower classes. My father is in his forties today; thirty-five years ago he was living through his most formative years. He was a child of the Great Depression. I want you to notice for later reference that I emphasize and differentiate *Great* Depression. There were many more international, national, and regional depressions during the period in history relevant to this comment.

There are millions of blacks of my father's generation now living. They are all products of a totally depressed environment. All of the males have lived all of their lives in a terrible quandary; none were able to grasp that a morbid economic deprivation, an outrageous and enormous abrasion, formed the basis of their character.

My father developed his character, convention, convictions, his traits, his life style, out of a situation that began with his mother running out. She left him and his oldest brother on the

239

corner of one of the canyons in East St. Louis. They raised themselves, in the streets, then on a farm somewhere in Louisiana, then in CCC camps. This brother, my father, had no formal education at all. He taught himself the essentials later on. Alone, in the most hostile jungle on earth, ruled over by the king of beasts in the first throes of a bloody and protracted death. Alone, in the most savage moment of history, without arms, and burdened by a black face that he's been hiding ever since.

I love this brother, my father, and when I use the word "love" I am not making an attempt at rhetoric. I am attempting to express a refulgent, unrestrained emanation from the deepest, most durable region of my soul, an unshakable thing that I have never questioned. But no one can come through his ordeal without suffering the penalty of psychosis. It was the price of survival. I would venture that there are no healthy brothers of his generation, *none at all.*

The brother has reached the prime of his life without ever showing in my presence or anywhere, to my knowledge, an overt manifestation of *real* sensitivity, affection, or sentiment. He has lived his entire life in a state of shock. Nothing can touch him now, his calm is complete, his immunity to pain is total. When I can fix his eyes, which is not often since when they aren't closed they are shaded, I see staring back at me the expressionless mask of the zombie.

But he must have loved us, of this I am certain. Part of the credo of the neoslave, the latter-day slave, who is free to move from place to place if he can come by the means, is to shuffle away from any situation that becomes too difficult. He stayed with us, worked sixteen hours a day, after which he would eat, bathe and sleep—period. He never owned more than two pairs of shoes in his life and in the time I was living with him never more than one suit, never took a drink, never went to a nightclub, expressed no feelings about such things, and never once reminded any one of us, or so it seemed, never expected any notice of the fact that he was giving to us all of the life

240

force and activity that the monster-machine had left to him. The part that the machine seized, that death of the spirit visited upon him by a world that he never influenced, was mourned by us, and most certainly by me, but no one ever made a real effort to give him solace. How do you console a man who is unapproachable?

He came to visit me when I was in San Quentin. He was in his forties then too, an age in men when they have grown full. I had decided to reach for my father, to force him with my revolutionary dialectic to question some of the mental barricades he'd thrown up to protect his body from what to him was an undefinable and omnipresent enemy. An enemy that would starve his body, expose it to the elements, chain his body, jail it, club it, rip it, hang it, electrify it, and poison-gas it. I would have him understand that although he had saved his body he had done so at a terrible cost to his mind. I felt that if I could superimpose the explosive doctrine of self-determination through people's government and revolutionary culture upon what remained of his mind, draw him out into the real world, isolate and identify his real enemies, if I could hurl him through Fanon's revolutionary catharsis, I would be serving him, the people, the historical obligation.

San Quentin was in the riot season. It was early January 1967. The pigs had for the last three months been on a search-and-destroy foray into our cells. All times of the day or night our cells were being invaded by the goon squad: you wake up, take your licks, get skin-searched, and wait on the tier naked while they mangled your few personal effects. This treatment, fear therapy, was not accorded to all however. Some Chicanos behind dope, some whites behind extortionate activities were exempted. Mostly, it came down on us. Rehabilitational terror. Each new pig must go through a period of in-service training where he learns the Gestapo arts, the full range of anti-body tactics that he will be expected to use on the job. Part of this in-service training is a crash course in close-order combat where the pigs are taught how to use club

241

and sap, and how to form and use the simpler karate hands, where to hit a man with these hands for the best (or worst) effect.

The new pigs usually have to serve a period on the goon squad before they fall into their regular role on the animal farm. They are always anxious to try their new skills—"to see if it really works"—we were always forced to do something to slow them down, to demonstrate that violence was a two-edged sword. This must be done at least once every year, or we would all be as punchy and fractured as a Thai Boxer before our time was up. The brothers wanted to protest. The usual protest was a strike, a work stoppage, closing the sweatshops where industrial products are worked up for two cents an hour. (Some people get four cents after they've been on the job for six months.) The outside interests who made the profits didn't dig strikes. That meant the captain didn't like them either since it meant pressure on him from these free-enterprising political connections.

January in San Quentin is the worst way to be. It's cold when you don't have proper clothing, it's wet, dreary. The drab green, barred, buttressed walls that close in the upper yard are sixty to seventy feet high. They make you feel that your condition may be permanent.

On the occasion I wish to relate, my father had driven all night from Los Angeles alone; he had not slept more than a couple of hours in the last forty-eight.

We shook hands and the dialectic began. He listened while I scorned the diabolical dog—capitalism. Didn't it raise pigs and murder Vietnamese? Didn't it glut some and starve most of us? Didn't it build housing projects that resemble prisons and luxury hotels and apartments that resemble the Hanging Gardens on the same street? Didn't it build a hospital and then a bomb? Didn't it erect a school and then open a whorehouse? Build an airplane to sell a tranquilizer tablet? For every church didn't it construct a prison? For each new medical discovery didn't it produce as a by-product ten new biological warfare

242

agents? Didn't it aggrandize men like Hunt and Hughes and dwarf him?

He said, "Yes, but what can we do? There's too many of the bastards." His eyes shaded over and his mind went into a total regression, a relapse back through time, space, pain, neglect, a thousand dreams deferred, broken promises, forgotten ambitions, back through the hundreds of renewed hopes shattered to a time when he was young, roaming the Louisiana countryside for something to eat. He talked for ten minutes of things that were not in the present, people that I didn't know. "We'll have to take something back to Aunt Bell." He talked of places that we had never seen together. He called me by his brother's name twice. I was so shocked I could only sit and blink. This was the guy who took nothing seriously, the level-headed, practical Negro, the work-a-day, never-complain, cool, smooth colored gentlman. They have driven him to the abyss of madness; just behind the white veneer waits the awesome, vindictive black madness. There are a lot of blacks living in his generation, the one of the Great Depression, when it was no longer possible to maintain the black self by serving. Even that had dried up. Blacks were beaten and killed for jobs like porter, bellboy, stoker, pearl diver, and bootblack. My clenched fist goes up for them; I forgive them, I understand, and if they will stop their collaboration with the fascist enemy, stop it now, and support our revolution with just a nod, we'll forget and forgive them for casting us naked into a grim and deleterious world.

The black colonies of Amerika have been locked in depression since the close of the Civil War. We have lived under regional depression since the end of chattel slavery. The beginning of the new slavery was marked by massive unemployment and underemployment. That remains with us still. The Civil War destroyed the *landed* aristocracy. The dictatorship of the agrarian class was displaced by the dictatorship of the manufacturing-capitalist class. The neoslaver destroyed the uneconomic plantation, and built upon its ruins a factory and

243

a thousand subsidiaries to serve the factory setup. Since we had no skills, outside of the farming techniques that had proved uneconomic, the subsidiary service trades and menial occupations fell to us. It is still so today. We are a subsidiary subculture, a depressed area within the parent monstrosity. The other four stages of the capitalist business cycle are: recovery, expansion, inflation, and recession. Have we ever gone through a recovery or expansion stage? We are affected adversely by inflationary trends within the larger economy. Who suffers most when the prices of basic, necessary commodities go up? When the parent economy dips into inflation and recession we dip into subdepression. When it goes into depression, we go into total desperation. The difference between what my father's generation went through during the *Great* Depression and what we are going through now is simply a matter of degree. We can sometimes find a service to perform across the tracks. They couldn't. We can go home to Mama for a meal when things get really tight. They couldn't. There's welfare and housework for Mama now. Then there was no such thing as welfare.

Depression is an economic condition. It is a part of the capitalist business cycle, a necessary concomitant of capitalism. Its colonies—secondary markets—will always be depressed areas, because the steadily decreasing labor force, decreasing and growing more skilled under the advances of automation, casts the unskilled colonial subject into economic roles that preclude economic mobility. Learning the new skills even if we were allowed wouldn't help. It wouldn't help the masses even if they learned them. It wouldn't help because there is a fixed ceiling on the labor force. This ceiling gets lower with every advance in the arts of production. Learning the newer skills would merely put us into a competition with established labor that we could not win. One that we don't want. There are absolutely no vacuums for us to fill in the business world. We don't want to capitalize on people anyway. Capitalism is the enemy. It must be destroyed. There is no other recourse.

244

The System is not workable in view of the modern industrial city-based society. Men are born disenfranchised. The contract between ruler and ruled perpetuates this disenfranchisement.

Men in positions of trust owe an equitable distribution of wealth and privilege to the men who have trusted them. Each individual born in these Amerikan cities should be born with those things that are necessary to survival. Meaningful social roles, education, medical care, food, shelter, and understanding should be guaranteed at birth. They have been part of all civilized human societies—until this one. Why else do men allow other men to govern? To what purpose is a Department of Health, Education, and Welfare, or of Housing and Urban Development, etc? Why do we give these men power over us. Why do we give them taxes? For nothing? So they can say that the world owes our children nothing? This world owes each of us a living the very day we are born. If not we can make no claims to civilization and we can stop recognizing the power of any administrator. Evolution of the huge modern city-based society has made our dependence upon government complete. Individually, we cannot feed ourselves and our children. We cannot, by ourselves, train and educate them at home. We cannot organize our own work inside the city structure by ourselves. Consequently, we must allow men to specialize in coordinating these activities. We pay them, honor them, and surrender control of certain aspects of our lives to them so that they will in return take each new, helpless entry into the social group and work on him until he is no longer helpless, until he can start to support himself and make his contribution to the continuity of the society.

If a man is born into Amerikan society with nothing coming, if the capitalist creed that runs "The world doesn't owe you a living" is true, then the thing that my father's mother did is not outrageous at all. If it is true that government shouldn't organize then the fact that my father had no place to seek help until he could help himself has little consequence. But it would also mean that we are all in the grip

245

of some monstrous contradiction. And that we have no more claim to civilization than a pack of baboons.

What is it then that *really* destroyed my father's comfort, that doomed his entire generation to a life without content? What is it that has been working against my generation from the day we were born through every day to this one?

Capitalism and capitalist man, wrecker of worlds, scourge of the people. It cannot address itself to our needs, it cannot and will not change itself to adapt to natural changes within the social structure.

To the black male the losses were most tragic of all. It will do us no good to linger over the fatalities, they're numberless and beyond our reach. But we who have survived must eventually look at ourselves and wonder why. The competition at the bottom of the social spectrum is for symbols, honors, and objects; black against itself, black against lower-class whites and browns, virulent, cutthroat, back-stabbing competition, the Amerikan way of life. But the fascists cooperate. The four estates of power form a morbid lone quadrangle. This competition has destroyed trust. Among the black males a premium has been placed on distrust. Every other black male is viewed as the competition; the wise and practical black is the one who cares nothing for any living ass, the cynic who has gotten over any principles he may have picked up by mistake. We can't express love on the supposition that the recipient will automatically use it against us as a weapon. We're going to have to start all over again. This next time around we'll let it all hang out, we'll stop betraying ourselves, and we'll add some trust and love.

I do not include those who support capitalism in any appreciable degree or who feel they have something to lose with its destruction. They are our irreconcilable enemy. We can never again trust people like Cosby, Gloves Davis,* or the

---

*The black Chicago policeman who was reported to have shot Fred Hampton.

old Negro bus driver who testified in the Huey Newton trial. Any man who stands up to speak in defense of capitalism must be slapped down.

Right now our disease must be identified as capitalist man and his monstrous machine, a machine with the senseless and calloused ability to inflict these wounds programmed into its every cycle.

I was born with terminal cancer, a suppurating, malignant sore that attacked me in the region just behind the eyes and moves outward to destroy my peace.

It has robbed me of these twenty-eight years. It has robbed us all for nearly half a millennium. The greatest bandit of all time, we'll stop him now.

Recall the stories you've read about the other herd animals, the great Amerikan bison, the caribou or Amerikan reindeer.

The great Ameikan bison or buffalo—he's a herd animal, or social animal if you prefer, just like us in that. We're social animals, we need others of our general kind about us to feel secure. Few men would enjoy total isolation. To be alone constantly is torture to normal men. The buffalo, cattle, caribou, and some others are like folks in that they need company most of the time. They need to butt shoulders and butt butts. They like to rub noses. We shake hands, slap backs, and rub lips. Of all the world's people we blacks love the company of others most, we are the most socialistic. Social animals eat, sleep, and travel in company, they need this company to feel secure. This fact means that socialistic animals also need leaders. It follows logically that if the buffalo is going to eat, sleep, and travel in groups some coordinating factor is needed or some will be sleeping when others are traveling. Without the leader-follower complex, in a crisis the company would roar off in a hundred different directions. But the buffalo did evolve the leader-follower complex as did the other social animals; if the leader of a herd of caribou loses his footing and slips to his death from some high place, it is very likely that the whole herd will die behind.

247

The leader-follower complex. The hunter understood this. Predatory man learned of the natural occurrence of leadership in all of the social animals; that each group will by nature produce a leader, and to these natural leaders fall the responsibility for coordination of the group's activity, organizing them for survival. The buffalo hunter knew that if he could isolate and identify the leader of the herd and kill him first, the rest of the herd would be helpless, at his mercy, to be killed off as he saw fit.

We blacks have the same problem the buffalo had; we have the same weakness also, and predatory man understands this weakness well.

Huey Newton, Ahmed Evans, Bobby Seale, and the hundreds of others will be murdered according to the fascist scheme.

A sort of schematic natural selection in reverse: Medgar Evers, Malcolm X, Bobby Hutton, Brother Booker, W. L. Noland, M. L. King, Featherstone, Mark Clark, and Fred Hampton—just a few who have already gone the way of the buffalo.

The effect these moves from the right have had on us is a classic textbook exercise in fascist political economy. At the instant a black head rises out of our crisis existence, it's lopped off and hung from the highest courthouse or newspaper firm. Our predetermined response is a schizophrenic indifference, withdrawal, and an appreciation of things that do not exist. "Oh happy days. Oh happy days. Oh happy days." Self-hypnotically induced hallucinations.

The potential black leadership looks at the pitiable condition of the black herd: the corruption, the preoccupation with irrelevance, the apparent ineptitude concerning matters of survival. He knows that were he to give the average brother an M-16, this brother wouldn't have anything but a club for a week. He weighs this thing that he sees in the herd against the possible risks he'll be taking at the hands of the fascist monster and he naturally decides to go for himself, feeling that he can't help us because we are beyond help, that he may as well get something out of existence. These are the "successful Negroes," the opposite of the "failures." You find them on the ball courts and fields, the stage, pretending and playing children's games. And looking for all the world just as pitiable as the so-called failures.

We were colonized by the white predatory fascist economy. It was from them that we evolved our freak subculture, and the attitudes that perpetuate our conditions. These attitudes cause us to give each other up to the Klan pigs. We even on occasion work gun in hand right with them. A black killed Fred Hampton; blacks working with the CIA killed Malcolm X; blacks are plentiful on the payroll of the many police forces that fascism must employ to protect itself from the people. These fascist subcultural attitudes have sent us to Europe, Asia (one-fourth of the fatalities in Vietnam are black fatalities), and even Africa (the Congo during the Simba attempt to establish people's government) to die for nothing. In the recent cases of Africa and Asia we have allowed the neoslaver to use us to help enslave people we love. We are so confused, so foolishly simple that we not only fail to distinguish what is generally right and what is wrong, but we also fail to appreciate what is good and not good for us in very personal matters concerning the black colony and its liberation. The ominous government economic agency whose only clear motive is to further enslave, number, and spy on us, the black agency subsidized by the government to infiltrate us and retard liberation, is accepted, and by some, even invited and welcomed, while the Black Panther is avoided and hard-pressed to find protection among the people. The Black Panther is our brother and son, the one who wasn't afraid. He wasn't so lazy as the rest, or so narrow and restricted in his vision. If we allow the fascist machine to destroy these brothers, our dream of eventual self-determination and control over the factors surrounding our survival is going to die with them, and the generations to come will curse and condemn us for irresponsi-

249

ble cowardice. I have a young couragous brother whom I love more than I love myself, but I have given him up to the revolution. I accept the possibility of his eventual death as I accept the possibility of my own. Some moment of weakness, a slip, a mistake, since we are the men who can make none, will bring the blow that kills. I accept this as a necessary part of our life. I don't want to raise any more black slaves. We have a determined enemy who will accept us only on a master-slave basis. When I revolt, slavery dies with me. I refuse to pass it down again. The terms of my existence are founded on that.

Black Mama, you're going to have to stop making cowards: "Be a good *boy*"; "You're going to worry me to death, *boy*"; "Don't trust those niggers"; "Stop letting those bad niggers lead you around, *boy*"; "Make you a dollar, *boy*." Black Mama, your overriding concern with the survival of our sons is mistaken if it is survival at the cost of their manhood.

The young Panther party member, our vanguard, must be embraced, protected, allowed to develop. We must learn from him and teach him; he'll be full grown soon, a son and brother of whom we can be proud. If he sags we'll brace him up, when he takes a step we'll step with him, our dialectic, our communion in perfect harmony, and there'll never, never be another Fred Hampton affair.

Power to the people.

George

APRIL, 1970
17

Dear Fay,

Slavery is an economic condition. Today's neo-slavery must be defined in terms of economics. The chattel is a property, one man exercising the property rights of his established economic order, the other man as that property. The owner can move that property or hold it in one square yard of the earth's surface; he can *let* it breed other slaves, or *make* it breed other slaves; he can sell it, beat it, work it, maim it, fuck it, kill it. But if he wants to keep it and enjoy all of the benefits that property of this kind can render, he must feed it sometimes, he must clothe it against the elements, he must provide a modicum of shelter. Chattel slavery is an economic condition which manifests itself in the total loss or absence of self-determination.

The new slavery, the modern variety of chattel slavery updated to disguise itself, places the victim in a factory or in the case of most blacks in support roles inside and around the factory system (service trades), working for a wage. However, if work cannot be found in or around the factory complex, today's neoslavery does not allow even for a modicum of food and shelter. You are free—to starve. The sense and meaning of slavery comes through as a result of our ties to the wage. You must have it, without it you would starve or expose yourself to the elements. One's entire day centers around the acquisi-

251

tion of the wage. The control of your eight or ten hours on the job is determined by others. You are left with fourteen to sixteen hours. But since you don't live at the factory you have to subtract at least another hour for transportation. Then you are left with thirteen to fifteen hours to yourself. If you can afford three meals you are left with ten to twelve hours. Rest is also a factor in efficiency so we have to take eight hours away for sleeping, leaving two to four hours. But—one must bathe, comb, clean teeth, shave, dress—there is no point in protracting this. I think it should be generally accepted that if a man (or woman) works for a wage at a job that he doesn't enjoy, and I am convinced that no one could enjoy any type of assembly-line work, or plumbing or hod carrying, or any job in the service trades, then he qualifies for this definition of neoslave. The man who owns the factory or shop or business runs your life; you are dependent on this owner. He organizes your work, the work upon which your whole life source and style depends. He indirectly determines your whole day, in organizing you for work. If you don't make any more in wages than you need to live, you are a neoslave. You qualify if you cannot afford to leave California for New York. If you cannot visit Zanzibar, Havana, Peking, or even Paris when you get the urge, you are a slave. If you're held in one spot on this earth because of your economic status, it is just the same as being held in one spot because you are the owner's property. Here in the black colony the pigs still beat and maim us. They murder us and call it justifiable homicide. A brother who had a smoking pipe in his belt was shot in the back of the head. Neoslavery is an economic condition, a small knot of men exercising the property rights of their established economic order, organizing and controlling the life style of the slave as if he were in fact property. Succinctly: an economic condition which manifests itself in the total loss or absence of *self*-determination. Only after this is understood and accepted can we go on to the dialectic that will help us in a remedy.

A diagnosis of our discomfort is necessary before the surgery; it's always necessary to justify the letting of blood.

And we don't want the knife to damage any related parts that could be spared for later use.

The pig is an instrument of neoslavery, to be hated and avoided; he is pushed to the front by the men who exercise the unnatural right over property. You've heard the patronizing shit about the thin blue line that protects property and the owners of property. The pigs are not protecting you, your home, and its contents. Recall they never found the TV set you lost in that burglary. They're protecting the unnatural right of a few men to own the means of all of our subsistence. The pig is protecting the right of a few private individuals to own public property!! The pig is merely the gun, the tool, a mentally inanimate utensil. It is necessary to destroy the gun, but destroying the gun and sparing the hand that holds it will forever relegate us to a defensive action, hold our revolution in the doldrums, ultimately defeat us. The animal that holds the gun, that has loosed the pig of war on us, is a bitter-ender, an intractable, gluttonous vulture who must eat at our hearts to live. Midas-motivated, never satisfied, everything he touches will turn into shit! Slaying the shitty pig will have absolutely no healing effect at all, if we leave this vulture to touch someone else. Spare the hand that holds the gun and it will simply fashion another. The Viet soldier has attacked and destroyed the pigs and their guns, but this alone has not solved his problems. If the Cong could get to the factories and the people who own and organize them, the war would end in a few months. All wars would end. The pigs who have descended upon the Vietnamese colony are the same who have come down on us. They come in all colors, though they are mainly white. Culturally (or anticulturally), they have the same background and the same mentality. They have the same intent: to preserve the economically depressed areas of the world as secondary markets and sources of cheap raw materials for the Amerikan fascist. The black colonies inside the Amerikan fascist state are secondary markets and sources of cheap raw materials. In our case this cheap raw material is our bodies, giving all of the benefits that property of this kind can render. How much more in wages would they have to pay a white, unionized garbage collector? And black mama tricks for ten-and-two?

Right behind the expeditionary forces (the pigs) come the missionaries, and the colonial effect is complete. The missionaries, with the benefits of christendom, school us on the value of symbolism, dead presidents, and the rediscount rate. The black colony lost its conscience to these missionaries. Their schools, their churches, their newspapers and other periodicals destroyed the black conscience and made it almost impossible for us to determine our own best interest.

The cultural links to the established capitalist society have been a lot closer than we like to admit. In the area of culture (I am using this word in the narrow sense out of necessity), we are bonded to the fascist society by chains that have strangled our intellect, scrambled our wits, and sent us stumbling backward in a wild, disorganized retreat from reality. We don't want their culture. We *don't* want a piece of that pie. It's rotten, putrid, repulsive to all the senses. Why are we rushing to board a sinking ship? When we join hands with the established fascist scum in any way, it gives the people of the world, the righteous people of the Congo, Tanzania, Sudan, of Cuba, China, Vietnam, etc., the legitimate right to hate us too.

The Swedish people and their government hate the Amerikan fascist (as almost every civilized state must). They show their loathing every chance they get. The Amerikan government dresses some black clown in a stovepipe hat and sends him over as an ambassador. This black cat isn't representing the black colony. He's representing the pigs. The Swedes throw bricks at him and call for the "nigger" to go home.

Chances are that the old slave they sent to Sweden never spent a night in the ghetto but still he represents the black oppressed. So when the slave turns up in his tails and stovepipe lid, a distorted imitation of the genuine fool (tomfool?), the hatred felt so deeply for the Amerikan fascist state by the Swedes is transferred onto us!

The government buys and trains these running dogs very

254

carefully, and sends them scrambling, tails and all, outward to represent the establishment. Whole kennels are sent to the African nations on the ambassadorial level (and lower, of course) on the supposition that the people of these nations will be able to relate better to a black face. The leaders of these nations, if they can be counted among the righteous, are never impressed, but this sort of thing affects the African masses deeply. Several years ago, in one of the central African states, a gathering of the people marched against the local representatives of the Amerikan government, the USIA, over an issue that won't come to mind now (there have been so many)—but they were resentful enough to carry their protest demonstration to violent extremes. They threw bricks and fire and called for the slavers' blood. They tore down the Yankee rag and danced on it, spit on it, and were about to burn it. They would have burned it and gone on to sack and burn the fascist propaganda center, but the running dog, the tomfool, stopped them, harangued them in the voice of the ventriloquist, and ran Old Glory back to its familiar station—obstructing the sun. They should have hung that nigger from the flagpole by the fat part of his neck, for that black ventriloquist threw up one more barrier to the communion that we must establish with the other oppressed peoples of the world.

They send us to school to learn how to be so disgusting. We send our children to places of learning operated by men who hate us and hate the truth. It is clear that *no school* would be better. Burn it; all the fascist literature, burn that too. Then equip yourself with the Little Red Book. There is no other way to regain our senses. We must destroy Johnson Publications and the little black tabloids that mimic the fascist press even to their denunciations of black extremists. Burn them or take them over as people's collectives, and give the colonies a dynamite case of self-determination, anticolonialism, and Mao think!!!!!

I attended my last year of high school at Bayview High - that's in San Quentin where I did seven years of the last ten that I have spent in jail. The schools in the joint are no different

255

than those out there in the colony at large, with the exception that they are not coeducational. We use the same fascist textbooks that contain the same undercurrent of racism and overtones of nationalism. The missionaries themselves are the same.

At the time, my eventual release on parole was conditional to my finishing high school, and of course being a good boy, never showing any anger, or displeasure, or individuality. I was trying to fake it. I would never have been in the mission school otherwise. I was working in the daytime and attended school evenings.

The biology wasn't too bad. The instructor seldom ventured an opinion outside the subjects related to science, but he was exceptional. I attribute this to the fact that he was somewhat younger than the other pundits. Each of them had a fixed opinion on every material and metaphysical feature of the universe. Colonel Davis in history was outstanding for two very typical characteristics of his profession, temperament and foolishness. True to his persuasion, this jackass was so patriotic and Republican that he actually proposed we begin and end each class with a pledge of allegiance to the flag from a kneeling position. He was tall and square and gray-blond, a veteran of several declared and undeclared Yankee wars. If you passed the flag without a genuflection you had this fool to fight. I sat through his shit for a month; Amerika the beautiful, the righteous, the only nation on earth where everyone can afford a flush toilet and a traffic ticket. All Russians were fat Tartars, the Japanese were copyists, Arabs couldn't fight and neither could the French. All Africans were primitives who didn't know when they were well off. Vietnamese were just niggers with slant eyes (there were four blacks in the class). The Chinese were so stupid that they couldn't feed themselves. Inevitably they would have to return to the good old days and ways of the rickshaw, pigtail, the coolie, opium dens, and cathouses. I took this shit with a stony calm for one month. I tried to get out of the class five or

256

six times, but you have to have a clear life-and-death situation to get out of anything once you get in. This is in keeping with the overall prison conspiracy, i.e., you have no will, you have no choice or control, so be wise—surrender. There's this sign hanging everywhere your eyes may happen to rest, begging: "O lord, help me to accept those things I cannot change." A life-death situation is necessary to get out; that's just what I had but I couldn't admit to it—looks bad on the parole board report. I tried to keep a head between myself and this representative of the great silent majority, failing this I would fix my eyes on one of the six flags in the room (one in each corner, two on the desk) and try to endure. Me and this cat fell all the way out in the end. I never planned it that way, in fact my plan was to hide my "face" and hang on. The session we had was completely spontaneous, it started in the opening minutes of our two-hour class. This silent majority had just completed a hymn to the great Amerikan corporate monster with the line "Now haven't we all the right to be proud?" I said, "No." The guy glanced at me, blinked, looked away, and kept right on with his eulogy. My answer didn't register with him; he heard me but he was positive that he heard me wrong. In the cloister of this man's mind, my displeasure, my dissatisfaction was just too impossible to be true. The good colonel had been explaining that corporate capitalism, the end result of a long evolutionary chain of other economic arrangements, was as perfect and flawless a system as man can ever hope to achieve. It was the only economic order that allowed for man's natural inclinations. The barbarous nations of Asia and Africa who had abandoned it for planned economics would ultimately fail since the incentive motive inherent within the capitalist ideal was missing. Without the profit-and-loss incentive, production will remain low and eventually fail. I stood up, sat on the back of my desk, put one foot on the seat, and told this cat that he had just told "another" lie. I don't know why I was doing this. I even felt a thrill of sympathy for the fool at first. His mouth dropped

257

open like a shark's, his ears and forehead and nose showed that he was as red-blooded an Amerikan as anyone could ever become. In an unconscious impulse his hands locked themselves around the base of the two flagpoles on his desk, as if to protect the little pieces of colored rag from the impudent and unpatriotic nigger who did-just-blaspheme!

"What'd you say, boy?" I said, "You've been lying for a month now about 'work ethics' and 'voting processes' and 'economic incentives,' you've been lying all your life really, and now I want to question some of this stuff. Can you stand it?"

I didn't wait for an answer, but continued, "I've worked in factories here in this country, on assembly lines, doing production work. I've made some study of mass production procedures in heavy and light industry, and I've looked into political economy in general, and I'm certain that in everything you've said in here for the last month there was a conscious intent to misrepresent the truth, to present only those parts of the truth that supported your contentions or to omit it altogether. This thing about incentive, if it's a factor in production, in order for it to influence the volume of production, or the quality, it's pretty clear that this incentive must find some way of communicating itself down to the worker. I can understand an owner or executive having the desire to make money—profit—but since ambition is a very personal thing, how does it affect the attitude and productivity of the worker? His wage will be the same if he works hard, not so hard, or not hard at all, and it is ultimately on how hard the worker works that volume and quality depends."

He leaned back in his chair, ran his hands through his hair, palpitated about the nose and upper lip, looked at his flag, and then at me, and answered, "Yes, well, in our factory setups we have quotas to meet and foremen and efficiency experts to see that they are met."

"You did say quotas? That sounds like something from one of Fidel's public addresses—you know, sugar quotas—the

258

difference of course being that Fidel is depending on a cooperation that springs from a sense of participation, and perhaps the knowledge that the volume and quality of production determines their general well-being, rather than the personal fortunes of an owner or small group of owners. In the factories that I worked in and have observed the principal interest of most of the workers was coffee and lunch breaks or quitting time; we watched the clock, watched out for the foreman and other spies, and made as many trips to the toilet as we could possibly expect to get away with. Although the profit motive may excite owner and supervisor to invest and organize for production, the index of productivity is determined by the attitudes of the worker in a plant that is not totally automated and even then it would depend on the workers in the machine, tool, and maintenance sectors to a great extent. This being the case, it is the diametrical opposite of your contention that is true. There is *less* real incentive. Based on the impulse to gain benefits, inherent within the modern form of capitalism, it's clear to me that the worker who felt that the machine, the factory, all factories were in part his own would be very much concerned about productivity and quality of product, much more concerned than one who has no more at stake than an inadequate wage."

"But you missed the meaning of my statement." This is him talking now. "The spur of profit and the fear of loss are the motivations that have made the capitalist system of production efficient. It automatically checks the marginal facilities and factors of production. It is responsive to demand and supply, i.e., the demands of the *consumers* and the availability of materials, and this responsiveness is automatic, built in, an inherent part of the system."

I replied that "the same can be said for any system of political economy. With planned, people's economics, however, the automatic feature is dropped and demand is not stimulated artifically in the Madison Avenue sense. It's fatuous and misleading to claim profit-and-loss motivation a feature of

259

capitalism only. It is a feature of all economies in all time past and present. The only difference is that with capitalism the spur is driven into the flanks of the people by a relatively few individuals who by chance or bent of ferocity have been able to make fraudulent claims on the rights to profit, the rights to benefit from wealth created by *labor* first, applied to materials from *man's* (plural possessive) source of life support—nature. In the People's Republics of Africa, Asia, and Eastern Europe this right to profit—to benefit from their labor and their land—is being returned to the people. The *people* are spurred by the profit motive collectively; a situation far more conducive to productivity since ultimately productivity depends on the attitude of the individual worker. Proportionally China has achieved more economically in twenty years than the U.S. has in two hundred. They had the advantage of being able to avoid the terrible mistakes made by the U.S. and Western Europe in those two hundred years, but a comparison between today's China and let's say today's India and Indonesia, where they have developed nothing economically, will point up clearly which system is best oriented to meet the needs of the people. The leadership in India stayed with capitalism (private enterprise) when China turned to revolutionary people's socialism with communism projected for the future. I am certain that everyone in this room has the intelligence to understand that India's rice riots and street sleepers are not indications that *China* has taken the wrong road."

"But they're starving in China," he said with great vehemence, on his feet with his hair streaming over his forehead, fists balled, chest out, shoulders thrown back.

"No one starves in China, that's your ignorance speaking now. You were probably just lying before, but it is possible that you are ignorant enough to think that people starve in China still, because they were starving in such great numbers when you were there in the forties serving the fascist military-industrial establishment. You people's ignorance on

260

these matters has prompted the Chinese and other third world nations to the observation that you all live behind a veritable curtain of ignorance. There are more people starving in the U.S., in the Black Belt of southeastern U.S. in all the large cities, in the Appalachian Mountains and grape fields of California than in any other country on earth with the possible exception of India. China sends grain to other countries on a long-term, interest-free-loan basis. Vietnam, Egypt, Pakistan, and some others are eating Chinese surplus food supplies right now."

"Nigger they just bought a hundred thousand tons of wheat from Canada last month."

"You did say they 'bought' it, it means that they must be doing pretty well; the principle of economic advantage means that the people in their respective areas, nations if you prefer, with their respective differences in climate and topography should produce that thing which is easy and natural for them to produce. With proper organization they will be able to produce a surplus of this thing that they produce well. It is this surplus that the well-ordered society (of today at least) uses to exchange for the things that they cannot produce economically. China bought that wheat from Canada with other food products and raw materials that Canada needed. That deal last month was simply good economics on China's part. Canada buys beef from Argentina. Does that mean that Canada is about to collapse economically? Nothing stays the same, not even for an instant. If a thing isn't growing, it's decaying. People's government has been on the march since the close of World War II everywhere, building, developing, challenging, and defeating the capitalist-based systems that function on servitude of the people. The inevitable failure will be with capitalism, the guns of Vietnam will sound the death knell of capitalism. We know how to fight you now; capitalism is dying right here tonight, look at yourself, you're defeated." He was advancing on me in his Marquis of Queensberry boxing stance. I got out of the class *that night*, I haven't been able to

261

get out of the joint, however.

We don't want people like Davis teaching the children, he has himself been educated into inanity. His favorite platitude was that Amerikans "enjoy hard work, desire gainful employment, and have the natural inclination to be thrifty and save." This is a shot against the automated welfare state. He believes that Amerikans would rather work with their hands than use a machine that could do the same work better and faster. Sounds pretty silly to me. I certainly don't *like to work*. No one could honestly enjoy the monotony of an assembly line. And the garbage collecting, the street sweeping, the window washing. I'm all for the machines taking over in every sector of the economy where they can be applied. I wouldn't have the least difficulty in finding something to do with my time. As long as my check comes by mail, as long as I didn't have to stand in some line somewhere to pick it up, I would never have a complaint. To eat bread "in the sweat of thy face" was intended as a curse. The conservatives (of their privilege) would have us now believe that work is great fun. The capitalist Eden fits my description of hell.

To destroy it will require cooperation and communion between our related parts; communion between colony and colony, nation and nation. The common bond will be the desire to humble the oppressor, the need to destroy capitalist man and his terrible, ugly machine. If there were any differences or grievances between us in the black colonies and the peoples of other colonies across the country, around the world, we should be willing to forget them in the desperate need for coordination against Amerikan fascism.

International coordination is the key to defeating this thing that must expand to live. Our inability to work with other peoples, other slaves who have the same master, is a consequence of the inferiority complex we have been conditioned into. We're afraid that in the process the Chinese will *trick us*, or the white folks who support socialism and liberation of all the Amerikan colonies really just want to use

262

us, *trick us.* "We can't trust them, they'll *trick us.*" Well, if we're tricks we can expect to get tricked and we should rightly be afraid. This paranoia is a carry-over from the days when a white face in a black crowd meant that the white brain was controlling things. It is a carry-over from the days when some of us felt that nothing could function properly without the presence of a white brain, when we were sufficiently convinced of our own inferiority to allow them to take us over. Now as things stand in the new light of different days, with our revolution in the doldrums, our struggles counterpoised by vicious political kills and avalanches of propaganda, terror, and tokenism, we must overcome the paranoia. It is based on lack of confidence in our ability to control situations. Yet no one can take us over or betray our interests if we are vigilant and aggressively intelligent. We must accept the spirit of the true internationalism called for by Comrade Che Guevara. It is not a matter of trusting anyone, though I personally find that I can still trust certain general types of people since I am of that people. I am also assured of my ability to detect in advance any atavistic changes that portend betrayal. It isn't just a matter of trusting the goodwill of other slaves and other colonies and other peoples, it is simply a matter of *common need.* We need allies, we have a powerful enemy who cannot be defeated without an allied effort! The enemy at present is the capitalist system and its supporters. Our prime interest is to destroy them. *Anyone* else with this same interest must be embraced, we must work with, beside, through, over, under anyone, regardless of their external physical features, whose aim is the same as ours in this. Capitalism must be destroyed, and after it is destroyed, if we find that we still have problems, we'll work them out. That, the nature of life, struggle, permanent revolution; that is the situation we were born into. There are other peoples on this earth. In denying their existence and turning inward in our misery and accepting any form of racism we are taking on the characteristic of our enemy. We are resigning ourselves to defeat. For in forming a conspiracy aimed at the destruction of the system that holds us all in the throes of a desperate insecurity we must have coordinating elements connecting us and our moves to the moves of the other colonies, the African colonies, those in Asia and Latin Amerika, in Appalachia and the southwestern bean fields. If it is more expediant for a white revolutionary to neutralize a certain area, should I deny him the opportunity to contribute by withholding the protective influence of my cooperation?! If I did it would make me a fool and a myopic coward—a trick.

The revolutionary of Vietnam, this brother is so tried, so tested, so clearly antifascist, anti-Amerikan, that I must be suspicious of the sincerity of any black who claims anti-Amerikanism and antifascism but who cannot embrace the Cong. The Chinese have aided every anticolonial movement that has occurred since they were successful in their own, particularly the ones in Africa. They have offered us in the Amerikan colonies any and all support that we require, from hand grenades to H-bombs. Some of us would deny these wonderful and righteous people. I accept their assistance in my struggle with our mutual enemy. I accept and appreciate any love that we can build out of our relation in crisis. I'll never, never allow my enemy to turn my mind or hand against them. The Yankee dog that proposes to me that I should join him in containing the freedom of a Vietnamese or a Chinese brother of the revolution is going to get spat on. I don't care how much he has to offer in the way of short-term material benefits.

We must establish a true internationalism with other anticolonial peoples. Then we will be on the road of the true revolutionary. Only then can we expect to be able to seize the power that is rightfully ours, the power to control the circumstances of our day-to-day lives.

The fascist must expand to live. Consequently he has pushed his frontiers to the farthest lands and peoples. This is an aspect of his being, an ungovernable compulsion. This perverted mechanical monster suffers from a disease that

264

forces him to build ugly things and destroy beauty wherever he finds it. I just read in a legal newspaper that 50 percent of all the people ever executed in this country by the state were black and 100 percent were lower-class poor. I'm going to bust my heart trying to stop these smug, detenerate, primitive, omnivorous, uncivil... and anyone who would aid me, I embrace you. We of the black Amerikan colony must finally take courage, control our fear, and adopt a realistic picture of this world and our place within it. We are not fascist, or Amerikans. We are an oppressed, economically depressed colonial people. We were brought here, from Africa and other parts of the world of palm and sun, under duress, and have passed all our days here under duress. The people who run this country will never *let* us succeed to power. Everything in history that was of any value was taken by force. We must organize our thoughts, get behind the revolutionary vanguard, make the *correct* alliances this time. We must fall on our enemies, the enemies of all righteousness, with a ruthless relentless will to win! History sweeps on, we must not let it escape our influence *this time*!!!!

I am an extremist. I call for extreme measures to solve extreme problems. Where face and freedom are concerned I do not use or prescribe half measures. To me life without control over the determining factors is not worth the effort of drawing breath. Without self-determination I am *extremely* displeased.

International capitalism cannot be destroyed without the extremes of struggle. The entire colonial world is watching the blacks inside the U.S., wondering and waiting for us to come to our senses. Their problems and struggles with the Amerikan monster are much more difficult than they would be if we actively aided them. We are on the inside. We are the only ones (besides the very small white minority left) who can get at the monster's heart without subjecting the world to nuclear fire. We have a momentous histroical role to act out if we will. The whole world for all time in the future will love us and remember us as the righteous people who made it possible for the world to live on. If we fail through fear and lack of aggressive imagination, then the slaves of the future will curse us, as we sometimes curse those of yesterday. I don't want to die and leave a few sad songs and a hump in the ground as my only momument. I want to leave a world that is liberated from trash, pollution, racism, poverty nation-states, nation-state wars and armies, from pomp, bigotry, parochialism, a thousand different brands of untruth, and licentious usurious economics.

We must build the true internationalism now. Getting to know people under crisis is the best way to learn them. Crisis situations show up their weakness and strength. They outline our humanity in vivid detail. If there is any basis for a belief in the universality of man then we will find it in this struggle against the enemy of all mankind.

George

MARCH, 1970
17

Dear Z.,

Very pleasant surprise for me seeing you again. Old friends are rare. Thank you for your concern and convey my further thanks to your mother. I know you both surrendered your holiday time to be present. The people are becoming very responsive, encouraging to say the least; we love you all.

You have certainly matured into a fine-looking young woman. I knew you would, you were a beautiful baby. Return this form and write me a letter (at the same time) and run it all down: school, politics, futurities. I want to know it all, all that you don't mind the officials knowing also, that is.

You may also have a half hour with me here, when you can get one. But that is all, and that only if you don't mind the civil service sitting in.

This is my tenth year of this, actually my twenty-eighth, but I was too numb to feel the first eighteen. All for the events of one riotous day, fifteen minutes to be exact. And now they would take all of the rest; you are aware that 4500* means automatic death penalty. One intimation of displeasure and the anti-bodies rush to destroy you. Well I am posiuvely

*The number of the California statute which makes the death penalty mandatory for any inmate serving a life sentence who is convicted of assault on a noninmate.

displeased and since I am positively destined to remain so. Return this form with all dispatch, I would like very much to relate and exchange.

Someone may have to get hurt but Power to the People.

George

MARCH, 1970
27

Dear Z.,

I've been attempting to establish correspondence with you for several years now. However, being locked up in close confinement has kept me in a position in which I've not been able to ascertain your full address (I still don't have the Zip Code). Now I have been able to learn which one of your parents' names you use officially. The chaplain here was kind enough to help me. Did he talk to you yet? When he does, thank him, for he went to some lengths to help us.

I was very pleasantly surprised to hear from the chaplain that you live so close to the prison. The only exchange I've had with intelligent females or any female outside my family in all these years is limited to the brief self-conscious glances of the visiting room. My lawyer is the first woman I've talked to since my arrest!! That must be the record.

Distressing is only a mild way of putting the events of these last 106 (106 years). I haven't been able to adjust. They adjust, they keep telling me. I keep trying to tell them this just isn't the kind of thing I favor. I've been picked up and swept along by events long gone out of control. Perhaps in the next 106 I'll be able, with an assist from wonderful people like your mother and you, to win enough of the control factor to get out and make the existence of places like this unnecessary.

I do have plenty of time. I'm in my cell 23½ hours a day. I try to employ all of it (except the three in which I sleep) in something related to antithesis, but there remain long periods of wasted time in this twenty-three-hour day, back to bed, one foot stacked lengthwise atop the other, gazing into the light. It would save my eyes and ease my mind a great deal to have long, informal, newsy, and perhaps endearing messages reaching me here, from time to time, from San Jose. If we can reach each other through all of this, fences, fear, concrete, steel, barbed wire, guns, then history will commend us for a great victory won. If so—it will be your generosity and my good fortune.

George

APRIL, 1970
3

Dear Z.,

I have your message here beside me now, it was delivered ten minutes ago. I do not think Nkrumah has failed either. As for me, I plan to save all of your correspondence so that when we are old people, and our enemies are no more, we can steep ourselves in it again, in an atmosphere where all the related parts are in harmony, and we can recall the fearful, traumatic, and desperate days at the barricade without rancor.

Did you receive the message I sent you last Thursday? Let me know; we'll be forced to confirm each of our letters, you know. Did you mail this one that I have now Thursday April 2 or March 27? If the former, it took only one day to reach me. I cannot read the postmark. It's too faint.

I dug the poem. I suspect that we are of kindred spirits, soldier; my mother and sisters say so, though they never really understood me. But I will forgive them, they will learn better.

We will have much to discuss in the days ahead, if what I suspect is true; history sweeps on apace and we mustn't let it escape our influence this time. I have messages from Narodnik and Nihilist, they are man and woman, coefficients in the production of . . . one cannot exist without the other. Narodnik excites a defense reflex within the beast; the beast encircles, infiltrates, and will destroy Narodnik. Without

Nihilist to enforce and protect, pure nonviolence is a false ideal, a contradiction.

Send me some photographs of you and your family. I liked the card. That is the sort of thing I need to take me out of this cell on occasion and remind me that the world could be beautiful.

You take care of yourself, I need you; you have my sincere regard, soldier.

George

APRIL, 1970
11

Dear Z.,

I received your letter late this afternoon. I've picked it up twenty-five times since then, reading things into it, holding it to my nose, fixing myself on the picture I have of you in my mind.

I am very pleased to have someone so warm, and so soft, and so lovely come into my miserable life; I haven't met *any* selfless, intelligent (mentally liberated), and aggressive women before now, before you. I knew that you existed but I had never had the pleasure. I am uneasy thinking that you may be attracted to the tragedy of me. I hope not, because my response to you is perfectly personal, your eyes, your voice, your walk, hands, mouth. It just occurred to me that I've never noticed any of these things in Frances or Penny or Delora. I like you a lot.

But I am in such a hurry!

My life is so disrupted, so precarious, my inclinations so oriented to struggle that anyone who would love me would have to be bold indeed—or out of their head. But if you're saying what I think you are saying, I like it. (If I have flattered myself please try to understand.) I like the way you say it also; over the next few months we'll discuss the related problems. By the time I've solved these minor ones that temporarily limit my movements, we'll have also settled whether or not it is selfish for us to seek gratification by reaching and touching and holding; does the building of a bed precede the love act itself? Or can we "do it in the road" until the people's army has satisfied our territory problem? That is important to me, whether or not you are willing to "do it in the road." You dig, I'm more identifiable with Ernesto than with Fidel. When this is over I immediately go under.

I want to see you! I understand the problems involved, money and transportation, but use your imagination, soldier. Are you getting your social security; That should hold you until you find work. I hate to appear selfish, but you have destroyed my peace here. I have a lot to tell you and some questions.

I'll love you till the wings fly off at least, perhaps beyond. My love could burn you, however, it runs hot and I have nearly half a millennium stored up. Mine is a perfect love, soft to the touch but so hot, hard, and dense at its center that its weight will soon offset this planet.

George

16

Dear Z.,

Did you receive my love letter? I wrote it on the eleventh or twelfth.

Jon likes you and your mother, but he does indeed like you. I wish very much that I could have been around him when he was growing up. He had a hard time identifying himself. He was forced to beat on some of the blacks because of the big green eyes (used to be blue!) and gold hair. He had to beat on the whites because he was a nigger. They used to write me about it, the others, but everyone in that house in Pasadena is so hare-brained. Well, he had to work out his problems on his own. That he turned out to be a beautiful black man-child is testimony of his own dogged strength. I love him more dearly than I love myself.

I've been thinking of you. Write me; I know how hard you are working and understand the limitations regarding time, but when you get a moment, between rounds, remember that I want to hear from you. Send the photographs I asked for too.

Power to the People. Love—

George

18

Dear Z.,

    I have your message of April 16 in here with me now.

Arms, holds, and understanding—me and you.

Your mother must be a wonderful person, or perhaps it was the revolution, or maybe some guy, whatever. This guy thanks the forces that be for forming you so that you favor me.

Communion can never be selfish. they are opposing terms, diametrical opposites, one the antithesis of the other, communion across the cultures, the nations, the planets, the universe—that's the name of our thing.

The question that I posed, as I think about it, was a ghost from the really dark days, when all of my smiles were merely gestures to put people at their ease. I was motivated then by disgust alone and *anything* that distracted me from a work-filled twenty-one-hour day was considered a hindrance, an obstacle, or an object of self-interest. I thought of individual relationship as a flight from the existential reality of individual responsibility to the whole, to the people. I considered it selfish to look for some individual to touch and hold and understand, because *all* of my time belonged to *all* of the people. That the deep, burning incessant thing centered in my guts was hatred alone, that people who (especially in the joint) looked for another individual to relate to, instead of the

274

people's struggle—ful! time, was lonely, was weak.

But I've gone through some changes since then, I saw and read about Angie Davis and some other females of our kind, and I realized that perhaps it was possible that this country has produced some females like those of Cuba or Vietnam.

When you reentered my little cloister last year I was more than ready for such an encounter. The look of love from a rebel breed—I like it. I'm weak.

George

APRIL, 1970
27

Dear Z.,

This is just a "thinking of you" note, because I was thinking of you.

It occurred to me how keen you were ten years ago when I was out, and we were both eighteen. I've envied you that intelligence over these years. Had I been fortunate enought to have had someone to relate to my need in that area, perhaps things would have been different. But far from me to complain. I probably wouldn't have listened anyway.

Don't compare yourself to me in such things as sleep and endurance. I don't sleep any more than I do because I can't really. I just don't like the idea of lying around unconscious for hours and then too my metabolism is pitched so high that I actually need activity to feel well.

I do know what you meant about beauty, the pleasant

features that remain to us in this life; I haven't seen many personally, but I know they exist, otherwise you wouldn't exist, F., your mother and the will to resist and win couldn't exist—evil can never take full control. But for me you are my first beautiful, really beautiful experience, honestly you are.

And you'll just have to relent—on the issue of photographs. Give F. some of the family, kids and all. I know where you're at, and I dig it, but consider where I'm at.

I love that guy T. Are there many like him and M. You know about M. Well, he was one out of a thousand (it took great courage). Are the ratios that bad everywhere? I'm sure you know what I want here. With people like these around, my job won't be half as hard as I've always anticipated.

I must be about my work, comrade, and no more reference to my ability to accept love. Perhaps my sensibilities are somewhat dulled but not like that. I'll never fail you—it just won't happen.

Sincerely in Love and Revolution,

George

2

Dear Z,

Time seems to be passing much faster these last few months. Wonder where it's running to, what's building? Will I be able to control the outcome of whatever . . .

This is for certain, it's going to get worse. Things will become much more difficult before anything good can come of this. People like Nixon and the ventriloquists that make him speak hold forth by default. The good element has not contested them vigorously; for the very same natural reason that allows flotsam to rise to the surface these people have come by the means and power to cause great discord and suffering. "They met little resistance on their way up." "Good people don't like to cut throats." This unnatural arrangement that allows the sediment to remain on the top while the cream rests on the bottom can be righted in one way only. The VC have the idea. They understand a trial of combat, an ordeal by fire. You simply can't reason with people like them, they have too much to lose by being reasonable.

They make my head ache; I must get off the subject.

Your "Little Soulful Tune" did make me smile. I must confess that you have startled me on occasion, the kinship, your sensitivity, almost like we've lived all of it before. You know me too well. I suspect you've been peeping with those big delightfully sad eyes into my sad soul. Beautiful sister, desirable woman, quintessence of revolutionary woman, ne plus ultra of the new rebel breed, if I didn't take you into my heart, and if I didn't find myself loving you, and if this love wasn't as easy and natural as breathing, there would be something very wrong with me.

Things have fallen apart, haven't they; that realization must come to all of us, it is a prerequisite to remedy. Send it to me a piece at a time in your letters, it's best that way.

Take care of yourself, this cat needs you.

Love,

George

MAY, 1970
8

Dear Joan, *

You may never read this letter—my correspondence is being limited at present to those approved prior to my most recent troubles. However, this limiting policy is not legal, nor has it been clearly stated. So if this message reaches you, be informed that I have also sent with it a request to have you placed permanently on my visiting and mailing list. It is a formality that the state requires we go through in order to further assure its complete control over our lives here. But I don't mind. Ever since the earliest days of my youth, you should recall, my foremost wish was to have a big brother.

*A member of the Soledad Defense Committee.

These people are on my trail this time. Mama probably discussed with you the other incidents that occurred while I was in San Quentin. What do you think? I try to be a good boy and help other boys to be good, and this sort of thing is my reward. I get accused of everything that cannot be positively established elsewhere, but I mustn't complain too much, it isn't allowed.

I know you have to work pretty hard and consequently haven't much time to yourself, but if you have any at all I could use it. You did such a wonderful job with your own children, I'm thinking that you could probably help my mama's children. Me in particular.

But more seriously, old friend, Mama told me of your concern, thanks. We have plenty of support in this, your youngest daughter as you probably know came to a couple of the appearances. I tried to contact her or establish her as a regular correspondent but we got lost in a confusion of red tape. She is a lovely young woman. Give my regards.

When were you last in Chicago? I have heard that the place we stayed in and all the surrounding neighborhood has been completely rebuilt, city-owned projects. They should have done that fifty years ago. I still dream about that place sometimes. Big Brother chasing me in slow motion down alleys, over the roofs, busting their windows with my slingshot.

Send me lots of brightly colored postcards and some pictures of the family. And if you get a few minutes you can tell me of your impressions of this fierce world. Oh, if that girl is still at home, I want you to try and fatten her up—just a little.

George

1970

Angela, *

  I am certain that they plan to hold me incommunicado. All of my letters except for a few to my immediate family have come back to me with silly comments on my choice of terms. The incoming mail is also sent back to the outside sender. The mail which I do receive is sometimes one or two weeks old. So, my sweet sister, when I reach you, it will be in this manner.

  ... I'm going to write on both sides of this paper, and when I make a mistake I'll just scratch over it and continue on. That is my style, completely informal.

  Was that your sister with you in court? If so, she favored you. Both very beautiful people. You should have introduced me.

  They are going to take your job, I know they are—anything else would be expecting too much. They can't, however, stop you from teaching in public institutions, can they?

  They hate us, don't they? I like it that way, that is the way it's supposed to be. If they didn't hate me I would be doing something very wrong, and then I would have to hate myself. I prefer it this way. I get little hate notes in the folds of my newspaper almost every day now. You know, the racist stuff, the traditional "Dear nigger" stuff, and how dead I am going to be one day. They think they're mad at me now, but it's nothing compared to how it will be when I really get mad

*Angela Y. Davis

280

myself. . . .

Pigs are punks, Angela. We've made a terrible mistake in overestimating these people. It reflects on us badly that we have allowed them to do the things they have done to us. Since they are idiots, what does that make us. I just read Bobby Seale's account of that scene in Chicago (Ramparts, June '70). It started in San Francisco with that "flight to evade charge. One of the pigs commented that "this was so easy." But it shouldn't have been. Brothers like that are the best of us. It shouldn't have gone down like that. We should never make it easy for them—by relaxing—at this stage of the educational process. Examples are crucially important. Well that's the name of the game right now.

I have ideas, ten years' worth of them, I'd like all those brothers on Fiftieth Street to be aware of them. Tell Fay Stender to give you a copy of my thoughts on Huey Newton and politics. . . . At the end of these writings, titled "Letter to Huey Newton," there should be a note on revolutionary culture and the form it should take in the black Amerikan colonies. That was the best section. Without that section the power would be lost. Fay and I don't agree altogether on political methods. But that is only because we are viewing things from very different levels of slavery. Mine is an abject slavery.

I think of you all the time. I've been thinking about women a lot lately. Is there anything sentimental or otherwise wrong with that? There couldn't be. It's never bothered me too much before, the sex thing. I would do my exercises and the hundreds of katas, stay busy with something . . . this ten years really has gone pretty quickly. It has destroyed me as a person, a human being that is, but it was sudden, it was a sudden death, it seems like ten days rather than ten years.

Would you like to know a subhuman. I certainly hope you have time. I'm not a very nice person. I'll confess out front, I've been forced to adopt a set of responses, reflexes, attitudes that have made me more kin to the cat than anything else, the

281

big black one. For all of that I am not a selfish person. I don't think so anyway, but I do have myself in mind when I talk about us relating. You would be the generous one, I the recipient of that generosity.

They're killing niggers again down the tier, all day, every day. They are killing niggers and "them protesters" with small workings of mouth. One of them told a pig today that he was going to be awful disappointed with the pig if the pig didn't shoot some niggers or protesters this evening when he got off work. The pig found it very amusing. They went off on a twenty minute political discussion, pig and his convict supporter. There is something very primitive about these people. Something very fearful. In all the time I've been down here on Maximum Row, no brother has ever spoken to one of these people. We never speak about them, you know, across the cells. Every brother down here is under the influence of the party line, and racist terms like "monky" have never been uttered. All of these are beautiful brothers, ones who have stepped across the line into the position from which there can be no retreat. All are fully committed. They are the most desperate and dauntless of our kind. I love them. They are men and they do not fight with their mouths. They've brought them here from prisons all over the state to be warehoused or murdered. Whichever is more expedient. That Brother Edwards who was murdered in that week in January told his lawyer that he would never get out of prison alive. He was at the time of that statement on Maximum Row, Death Row, Soledad, California. He was twenty-one years old. We have made it a point to never exchange words with these people. But they never relent. Angela, there are some people who will never learn new response. They will carry what they incorporated into their characters at early youth to the grave. Some can never be educated. As an historian you know how long and how fervently we've appealed to these people to take some of the murder out of their system, their economics, their propaganda. And as an intelligent observer you must see how our appeals were received. We've wasted many generations and oceans of blood trying to civilize these elements over here. It cannot be done in the manner we have attempted it in the past. Dialectics, understanding, love, passive resistance, they won't work on an activistic, maniacal, gory pig. It's going to grow much worse for the black male than it already is, much, much worse. We are going to have to be the vanguard, the catalyst, in any meaningful change.

When generalizing about black women I could never include *you* in any of it that is not complimentary. But my mother at one time tried to make a coward of me, she did the same with Jon. She is changing fast under crisis situation and apocalyptic circumstance. John and Fleeta's mothers did the same to them, or I should say tried. And so did every brother's mother I've ever drawn out. I am reasonably certain that I can draw from every black male in this country some comments to substantiate that his mother, the black female, attempted to aid his survival by discouraging his violence or by turning it inward. The blacks of slave society, U.S.A., have always been a matriarchal subsociety. The implication is clear, black mama is going to have to put a sword in that brother's hand and stop that "be a good boy" shit. Channel his spirit instead of break it, or to break it I should say. Do you understand? *All* of the sisters I've ever known personally and through other brothers' accounts begged and bullied us to look for *jobs* instead of being satisfied with the candy-stick take. The strongest impetus a man will ever have, in an individual sense, will come from a woman he admires.

When "Soul" did that feature on you, I discussed you with some the comrades. One of them asked me what my response would be if it were my job to guard your body (for the party) from the attack of ten armed pigs. I told them my response would be to charge. There would be eleven people hurting but you wouldn't be one of them. Everyone agreed it was the correct response.

As an individual, I am grateful for you. As the black male, I hope that since your inclination is to teach you will give serious consideration to redeeming this very next generation of black males, by reaching for today's black female. I am not too certain about my generation. There are a few, and with these few we will keep something. But we have altogether too many pimps and punks, and black capitalists (who want a piece of the putrescent pie). There's no way to predict. Sometimes people change fast. I've seen it happen to brothers overnight. But then they have to learn a whole new set of responses and attack reflexes which can't be learned overnight. So cats like me who have no tomorrows have to provide examples. I have an ideal regarding tomorrow, but I live an hour at a time, right in the present, looking right over my nose for the trouble I know is coming.

There is so much that could be done, right now. . . . But I won't talk about those things right here. I will say that it should never be easy for them to destroy us. If you start with Malcolm X and count *all* of the brothers who have died or been captured since, you will find that not even one of them was really *prepared* for a fight. No imagination or fighting style was evident in any one of the incidents. But each one that died professed to know the nature of our enemies. It should never be so easy for them. Do you understand what I'm saying? Edward V. Hanrahan, Illinois State Attorney General, sent fifteen pigs to raid the Panther headquarters and murder Hampton and Clark. Do you have any idea what would have happened to those fifteen pigs if they had run into as many Viet Cong as there were Panthers in that building. The VC are all little people with less general education than we have. The argument that they have been doing it longer has no validity at all, because they were doing it just as well when they started as they are now. It's very contradictory for a man to teach about the murder in corporate capitalism, to isolate and expose the murderers behind it, to instruct that these madmen are completely without stops, are licentious, totally depraved—and then not make adquate preparations to defend himself from

284

the madman's attack. Either they don't really believe their own spiel or they harbor some sort of subconscious death wish.

None of this should have happened as it did. I don't know if we'll learn in time or not. I am not well here. I pretend that all is well for the benefit of my family's peace of mind. But I'm going to cry to you, so you can let the people on Fiftieth Street know not to let this happen to them, and that they must resist that cat with *all* of their strength when he starts that jail talk.

When the menu reads steak we get a piece of rotten steer (I hope) the size of a quarter. When it reads cake we get something like cornbread. Those are the best things served. When two guys fight, the darker guy will get shot. To supplement their incomes the pigs will bring anything into the prison and sell it to the convict who smuggles money in from his visits. Now black people don't visit their kin in the joint much and those that do can't afford to give up any money. So we have less of everything that could make life more comfortable —and safe (weapons are brought in too). Pigs are fascist right out front, the white prisoner who is con-wise joins the Hitler party right here in the joint. He doesn't have to worry about the rules, he stays high. When he decides to attack us, he has the best of weapons (seldom will a pig give a con a gun, though. It has happened, however, in San Quentin three times to my knowledge. But they will provide cutlery and zip guns). The old convict code died years ago. These cons work right with the police against us. The only reason that I am still alive is because I take everything to the extreme, and they know it. I never let any of them get within arm's reach, and their hands must be in full view. When on the yard I would stay close to something to get under. Nothing, absolutely nothing comes as a surprise to me. There is much to be said about these places but I must let this go right now or I won't be able to post it until tomorrow. In the event that you missed it, (my writing is terrible, I know), I think a great deal of you. This is one slave

285

that knows how to love. It comes natural and runs deep. Accepting it will never hurt you. Free, open, honest love, that's me.

Should you run into Yvonne* tell her that I love her also and equally. Tell her that I want to see her, up close. Tell her I'm not a possessive cat, never demanding, always cool, never get upset until my (our) face and freedom get involved. But make her understand that I want to hold her (chains and all) and run my tongue in that little gap between her two front teeth. (That should make her smile.)

Power to the People!

George

*Yvonne is Angela Davis's middle name.

MAY, 1970
21

Dear Angela,

I think about *you all of the time.* I like thinking about you, it gives me occasion for some of the first few really deeply felt ear-to-ear grins. And I've had to increase the number of my daily push-ups by half. That will make me stronger. The contact has been good for me in a hundred ways.

But then my thoughts return to your enemies. They are

286

mine too, of course, but thinking of them as your enemies calls up the monster in me, the dark, terrible things that I keep hidden in the pit, fanged, clawed, armored—they are more awful by far when you become involved. I've been finding and developing these things for many years now. As soon as you isolate, identify, and number your enemies I'll set these things loose on them. And you won't be disappointed this time, I promise, sweet sister. This time nothing will be held back .... Your enemies will be made humbler and wiser men.

Jon is a young brother and he is just a little withdrawn, but he is intelligent and loyal. ... He is at that dangerous age where confusion sets in and sends brothers either to the undertaker or to prison. He is a little better off than I was and than most brothers his age. He learns fast and can distinguish the real from the apparent, provided someone takes the time to present it. Tell the brothers never to mention his green eyes and skin tone. He is very sensitive about it and he will either fight or withdraw. Do you understand? You know that some of us don't bother to be righteous with each other. He has had a great deal of trouble these last few years behind that issue. It isn't right. He is a loyal and beautiful black man-child. I love him.

This shit is starting to thicken. Six in Georgia, two in Jackson, hard hats, counterdemonstrations, much like Germany in the thirties. That thing in Georgia and the one in Jackson were like turkey shoots. We die altogether too easy. Each one of those brothers has fathers, blood brothers, sisters, and mamas. But it's safe to assume that no positive response will be made, no eye-for-eye reprisal. Something very wrong has swept over us. We've grown so accustomed to seeing murder done to us that no one takes it seriously anymore. We've grown numb, immune to the pain. Charles Evers and the entire world knows who killed Medgar Evers, the murderer is still walking the streets. . . .

Perhaps I shouldn't even recognize people like Whitney Young except as enemies, but the shit that they sling around

287

does fall on some of us and consequently must be counter-poised. He has now gone on record as thinking that we "should arm ourselves, but strictly for defense only." But then he goes on to contradict himself by commenting that if we used arms it would be like suicide. His words: "a beer can against a tank." Well, how does one defend himself from an attacker without at some point launching a counterattack—especially when guns are the choice of weapons! . . .

There is an element of cowardice, great ignorance, and perhaps even treachery in blacks of his general type. And I agree with Eldridge and Malcolm, we *are not* protecting unity when we refrain from attacking them. Actually it's the reverse that's true. We can never have unity as long as we have these idiots among us to confuse and frighten the people. It's not possible for anyone to still think that Western mechanized warfare is absolute, not after the experiences of the third world since World War II. The French had tanks in Algeria, the U. S. had them in Cuba. Everything, I mean every trick and gadget in the manual of Western arms, has been thrown at the VC and they have thrown them back, twisted and ruined; and they have written books and pamphlets telling us how we could do the same. It's obvious that fighting ultimately depends upon men, not gadgets. So I must conclude that those who stand between us and the pigs, who protect the marketplace, are either cowards or traitors. Probably both. . . .

One way of indirectly detecting the traitor is to draw him out regarding our enemies' *enemies.* Young and all the other of those running dogs attack the white left. Young attacked the Chicago Seven and the other whites of the left who want to help us destroy fascism. So did LeRoi Jones on national TV in the company of Anthony Imperiale, a white racist KKKer, and a lot of high police officials. So what's happening with a guy who says he is for us but not against the government? Or one who says he's for us and against *all* whites—except the ones who may kick his ass? There is a great deal of cowardice and treachery and confusion here. The black bourgeoisie (pseudo-

288

bourgeoisie), the right reverends, the militant opportunists, have left us in a quandary, rendered us impotent. How ridiculous we must sem to the rest of the black world when we beg the government to investigate their own protective agencies. Aren't the wild hip-shooting pigs loose among us to protect the property rights of the people who formed the government? I've been sitting in here ten years watching that kind of shit go down. It's always the same blacks. I am sure that it's intentional. They're not with us, you understand. Experience, trial and error, would have changed them if they were. Who is the black working for, who does he love when he screams "Honky"? He would throw us into a fight where we would be outnumbered 1 to 14 (counting the blacks who would fight with/for the other side in a race war. War on the honky, it's just another mystification, if not an *outright* move by the fascist. I *don't know,* I don't pretend to clairvoyance, I can't read *all* thoughts, and I do know some whites that I wouldn't count as enemies, but if *all* whites were my enemies would it make sense for me to fight them all at the same time? The blanket indictment of the white race has done nothing but perplex us, inhibit us. The theory that all whites are the immediate enemy and all blacks our brothers (making them loyal) is silly and indicative of a lazy mind (to be generous, since it could be a fascist plot). It doesn't explain the black pig; there were six on the Hampton-Clark kill. It doesn't explain the black paratroopers (just more pigs) who put down the great Detroit riot, and it doesn't explain the pseudo-bourgeois who can be found almost everywhere in the halls of government working for white supremacy, fascism, and capitalism. It leaves the average brother confused. In Detroit they just didn't know what to do when they encountered the black paratroopers. They were so stunned when they saw those black fools shooting at them that they probably never will listen to another black voice regardless of what it's saying.

If I were at large and wanted to help revolutionize the black community so that in as short a time as possible it would be made ready to take up the vanguard in an *antiestablishment* war, I would start like this: 1. Lay my hands on some money any way I could. 2. Quietly, without even a hint of political flavoring, I would have my fronts open as many skeet, trap, rifle, and pistol ranges as I could rent space for in and around the black community. I would operate these places at cost and advertise. 3. Next door to these places (figurative) I would quietly, without political flavoring, open schools that deal with the close-order combat arts, ostensibly as a community project to keep the children off the streets. The real intent, of course, is to instill the "attack as defense" idea that we lost somewhere along the line. 4. Apart from the two business ventures just mentioned, I would provide myself with printing or copying machines, and make the salient points of urban guerilla warfare, antitank warfare, and revolutionary culture as easy to get, as close to hand, as a glass of water.

Now that just-mentioned activity would be aside from the hard and seriously needed revolutionary work discussed early this morning, and the stuff you will find in the writings I mentioned in my last letter.

"One doesn't wait for all conditions to be right to start the revolution, the forces of the revolution itself will make the conditions right." Che said something like this. Write me and let me have it straight.

Power to the People.

I love you, little sister.

George

290

22

Dear Joan,

They approved us for both correspondence and visits. Something really bad must be about to come down on me. This is the first time in a long train of efforts that I actually received my issue.

It's good, and I want to hear from you whenever you get time. Did you get that thing from John Thorne?

When I'm not working on my defense I like to be doing something like this. Ideals and ideas grow and become more definite when one attempts to explain them to others who will try to understand.

You know that my family has never understood me very well before, they are trying to now, but for years I had no line at all, to the outside prison. It was almost like being held incommunicado. Incommunicado, it's almost destroyed me.

So I thank you, madam. None of us could have made it this far without folks like yourself. We would be hunting each other over the ruins.

Will you tell me all that you have experienced in these years of our separation? It will help me to answer some of the questions my mind has posed to itself recently. Everything, events and how they impressed you. We don't have to worry about the censor and my record, they already are informed that I am a dirty, real dirty red, and they have already made their plans to stone me. I will stop them of course, but at this level of the fight there is almost nothing for you to say that would compromise me any more than I already am.

Then, too, they can kill me once more only (we cats live nine times, I've started on my ninth). And since they seem determined to take this last little bit from me I have nothing to lose. So we can bring it right down front. I will anyway.

Dialectical materialism is my bag. I identify with anyone who hates just one fascist. I don't want a piece of the pie, I don't want all of it even. I think it's rotten, should be discarded, we should start all over again. This new start should be made without individualism (read isolation), mysticism (read religion), with a modification of the language for the purpose of removing the concept of possession (read capitalism), without the hard-hat mentality (read William F. Buckley, *Playboy*, *C*entral *I*ntelligence *A*gency).

The Buckleys, Babbitts, the snobs who are thoroughly convinced of their ability to bluff it through, I'll have to pull their arms off; and hope that without their negative influence you will be able to educate the rest (note that I didn't say reeducate). Power to the People. Love from your friend,

George

292

25

Dear Joan,

I have both of your letters right here. I got them about ten minutes ago. One was dated by you May 20, the other May 22.

It is very nice (this is understating it) to see a new hand in here, Joan. Yours is a beautiful hand, and I am gratified (another understatement) that it would bridge the things that separate us and hold me tenderly . . . it's the best proof that I can ever have, all that I need, to assure me that I am still alive and have lived well.

Love's labor—I understand these things, much better than most, always have, but I never could present it in the proper light before. Presentation was the problem. People kept mistaking it for animality, or criminality, and then, less sensibly still, un-Amerikan.

With you, whom I have always thought so much in agreement, I can't fail this time.

There is a great deal to be exchanged between us. There is so much that I really need to know, things that will help me do the theoretical work for a treatise in which I intend to prove that if there is still basis for a belief in the brotherhood of man, it must be discovered in this struggle for control of this country's direction.

Since I've been an adult (mentally), I've never had the opportunity to question a mature, intelligent, and, most important, objective person of your particular distinctness (class, race, sex). When I can do so without compromising either of us I will pose some very sensitive, exploring queries. On these things I will first want the detached, statistical evidence, and then what you feel to be so. If I overload you—well, it's just my style, I encircle and pull. It means simply that I think a great deal of you. And I am in such a hurry.

Give John T. the pocketbook edition of *A Dying Colonialism, The Wretched of the Earth, Black Face White Mask,* Malcolm's *Autobiography* (the other was borrowed) and *Malcolm Speaks.* Also, if they can be found in pocketbook form, African Genesis and *The Territorial Imperative* by Robert Ardrey. Do you know who Leakey is, the anthropologist? I need him and Ruth Benedict too. She wrote among other things *Races.* She was a very wonderful woman, much like yourself in many ways.

You can and must send photographs of the family, yourself, and friends. They took all that I had when they started this stuff in January. All my books, everything. We'll have to test them on the clippings, if not just give them to John T. Then, my friend, anything that you feel that I need to know, send it, say it, by all means. You have in me a receptive, completely liberated mind.

Love and Light.

George

294

MAY, 1970
26

Dear Joan,

I have your message of the twenty-fifth already!
Things have improved in this respect. You are quite an
experience for me also, a very new thing altogether. I would
say fresh—how do you state newness, I can only understate it
again. Pleasure? To express it I'll confess that with these three
messages—delicate intrusions on my sobriety—you have re-
defined all of those care elements. It has been a long time since
I've heard anything whispered, the banshee drowns such things
out—it has started to dim.

You have a very fortunate boss. I'm sure he must
understand how rarely those kind of contacts (too cold—how
about contract or covenant, perhaps bond? yes, a bond), I'm
sure he appreciates how uncommon they are.

I've changed my mind, when I need statistics I'll address
myself to Liz—don't by shy—the years of our separation mean
nothing to me. I remain as I was (arms are somewhat longer),
and we should have a division of labor according to character
and disposition, some passion—certainly in order.

Will you excuse me when these letters appear a little
informal, the scratching in and out? It doesn't mean that I am

295

lazy, it's an effect of my haste. I'm in a great race against time (justifiable homicide). But let's discuss the division of labor. It's essential to competent organisms. We are in step with each other. Hearts and heads, nervous equipment, arms, hands, extensions of the hand (sword and pen), *passion.* I am sure that you know they must all function according to ability in perfect harmony, the organism can't survive in good health and grow without all of its related parts.

There are no principal parts. You conceded that with the "all or none." It means that the small toe is as important to the human organism as the heart. It must be that way: the small toe is essential to balance, and its loss could precede or let's say presage the loss of the foot. Without footing the movements of head and heart become less efficient, the remainder of the organism could survive without the arm but it should never be surrendered without making the strongest possible protest, I won't stand for any loss at all. The instant that my toe is taken, I will lose my head.

We must move along two lines in concert, instruction of the unrighteous and destruction of the unrighteous. Within the structure of these two (and structure is an imperative) components there is a situation for every refinement of character—passion is at the heart of instruction.

I just got a copy of *Malcolm x Speaks* from Fay so you can take that off your list, but send (through John) Malcolm's *Autobiography*. Need it for my legal work.

I haven't changed, I still adore you—

George

28

Dear Angela,

I sincerely hope you understand this situation here with me, the overall thing I mean, you probably do. I don't want to be bash with you, the relative levels of our insecurity are too disparate for me to dwell on feelings, the warm, very personal, elemental thing. I can never express it in this form anyway, but I want you to know, and then we can get on with the work.

I have, like most people, a recurring dream. In this dream there is a great deal of abstract activity. Have you ever seen the pig they have named —— General Something-or-other ——. I don't know why my mind locked on him, but part of this dream is a still shot of my trying to fit a large steel boomerang into his mouth. It switches then to a scene where me and two other brothers T.G. and a brother named H.B., are holding hands to form a large circle, in the ring. Inside the ring formed by the three of us is this guy. He's wearing top hat and tails—stars and stripes—beard and bushy eyebrows. The action part goes like this: Old Sam tries to break out of the circle; we stop him; after about ten tries—we're wearing track shoes—he's ragged as an old mophead. It goes on that way, scenes running

into each other, overlapping, all very pleasing—wish fulfillment?—very gratifying stuff; but the high point, the climax—
well, a tall slim African woman, firelight, and the beautiful
dance of death. This wonderful woman didn't become part of
my dream until last year sometime. I never thought this kind
of environment could produce one like her, but at the same
time I knew that things never could be good with me without
her.

But I promised not to be bash with you. It's crazy, all
women, even the very phenomenal, want at least a promise of
brighter days, bright tomorrows. I have no tomorrows at all.
The worst thing that could have ever happened to the woman
in the dream was letting me touch her. I'll tell you the whole
thing if we can ever find somewhere to relax. . . . Until then I
promise not to bore you. You probably hear these devotions
all day, and with your incentive factors they're probably all
sincere devotions. Let me heap mine on you (with these pitiful
little strokes of the pen) for the last time (unless seized by
ungovernable impulse) with a statement made at the risk of
seeming immodest; but I am modest and I hope that it is
righteous for me to feel that— no one, and much more
meaningful no black, wherever the hurricane has washed up his
broken body, no one at all, can love like I.

In our last communication I made a statement about
women, and their part in revolutionary culture (people's war).
It wasn't a clear statement. I meant to return to it but was
diverted. I understand exactly what the woman's role should
be. The very same as the man's. Intellectually, there is very
little difference between male and female. The differences we
see in bourgeois society are all conditioned and artificial.

I was leading up to the obvious fact that black women in
this country are far more aggressive than black males. But this
is qualified by the fact that their aggression has, until very
recently, been within the system—that "get a diploma boy"
stuff, or "earn you some money." Where it should have been
the gun. Development of the ability for serious fighting and

298

organized violence was surely not encouraged in the black female, but neither was it discouraged, as it was in the case of the black male.

Please don't dismiss this yet. Let me rush to remind you that we have already established that bourgeois society has relegated women in general to a very distinct level of existence, even the slave woman. I'm not about to say they loved you better. Love doesn't even enter this equation, but socially primitive bourgeois thinking and the sex mystique does. First, a woman wasn't considered dangerous. Second, the most important experience in the Amerikan white male's "coming into manhood" was entering the body of the black female. These two circumstances contributed to the longevity and the matriarchal status of black women greatly.

Add to all of this the fact that the black mother wanted to see her son survive in a grim and murderous white male society and the grotesque misshapen pieces come together.

I was saying that if the black mother wants her revenge she will have to stop teaching her sons to fear death. By default she dominates the black subculture, and her son must be the catalyst in any great changes that go down in this country. The head and the fist, no one else has as much to gain.

Power to the People

George

MAY, 1970
29

Dearest Angela,

I'm thinking about you. I've done nothing else all day. This photograph that I have of you is not adequate. Do you recall what Eldridge said regarding pictures for the cell? Give Frances several color enlargements for me. This is the cruelest aspect of the prison experience. You can never understand how much I hate them for this, no one could, I havn't been able to gauge it myself.

Over this ten years I've never left my cell in the morning looking for trouble, never once have I initiated any violence. In each case where it was alleged, it was defense attack response to some aggression, verbal or physical. Perhaps a psychiatrist, a Western psychiatrist that is, could make a case against me for anticipating attacks. But I wasn't born this way. Perhaps this same psychiatrist would diagnose from the overreactions that I am not a very nice person. But again I refer you to the fact that I was born innocent and trusting. The instinct to survive and all that springs from it developed in me, as it is today out of necessity.

I am not a very nice person, I confess. I don't believe in such things as free speech when it's used to rob and defame me.

300

I don't believe in mercy or forgiveness or restraint. I've gone to great lengths to learn every dirty trick devised and have improvised some new ones of my own. I don't play fair, don't fight fair. As I think of this present situation, the things that happen all day, the case they've saddled me with, in retrospection of the aggregate injury—all now drawn against the background of this picture you've given me—no one will profit from this, sister. No one will ever again profit from our pain. This is the last treadmill I'll run. They created this situation. All that flows from it is their responsibility. They've created in me one, irate, resentful nigger—and it's building—to what climax? The nation's undertakers have grown wealthy on black examples, but I want you to believe in me, Angela. I'm going to make a very poor example, no one will profit from my immolation. When that day comes they'll have to bury ten thousand of their own with full military honors. They'll have earned it.

Do you sense how drunk this photograph has made me.

You've got it all, African woman. I'm very pleased, if you don't ask me for my left arm, my right eye, both eyes, I'll be very disappointed. You're the most powerful stimulus I could have.

From now on when you have books for me to read in preparing my motions and jury selection questions, send them through John Thorne, people's lawyer, he is less pressed. And I do want Lenin, Marx, Mao, Che, Giap, Uncle Ho, Nkrumah, and any Black Marxists. Mama has a list. Tell Robert to provide money for them, and always look for the pocket editions, all right? My father—you'll have to try to understand him. He'll be with me in the last days in spite of whatever he says and thinks now. I've told him that I love you, and I told him that if he respects me at all, and wants me to spare his neck at Armageddon, he must be kind to you.

I got a letter from him this evening wherein he called the pigs by their very accurate moniker—pigs—he'll be all right. I see your influence already. But back to the books. With each

301

load of heavy stuff throw in a reference book dealing with pure fact, figures, statistics, graphs for my further education. Also books on the personel and structure of today's political and economic front. I am doing some serious theory work for you concerning the case, dedicated to Huey and Angela. If you understand what I want, let me know. Sister, it's been like being held incommunicado these last ten years. No one understood what I was attempting to do and to say. We belong among the righteous of the world. We are the most powerful. We are in the best position to do the people's work. To win will involve taking a chance, crawling on the belly, naming, numbering, infiltrating, giving up meaningless small comforts, readjusting some values. My life means absolutely nothing without positive control over the factors that determine its quality. If you understand, rush to send all that I've asked for. A load should come in each day. I've read it all, once anyway, but I need it now . . . and time has become very important. I want you to believe in me. I love you like a man, like a brother, and like a father. Every time I've opened my mouth, assumed by battle stance, I was trying in effect to say I love you, African—African woman. My protest has been a small one, something much more effective is hidden in my mind—believe in me Angela. This is one nigger who's got some sense and is not afraid to use it. If my enemies, your enemies, prove stronger, at least I want them to know that they made one righteous African man extremely angry. And that they've strained the patience of a righteous and loving people to the utmost.

I've stopped several times in this writing to exercise, to eat, and it has grown late. I want to get this off tonight. I must know as soon as you get this and the others. Are you sure about your mail? I can imagine that the CIA is reading all your mail before you get it and deciding what you should and shouldn't have. Big Brother. He is rather transparent. I have his number. I know he's a punk, he can't stop me.

302

Should we make a lovers' vow? It's silly, with all my tomorrows accounted for, but you can humor me.

Power to the People!

George

MAY, 1970
30

Dear Joan,

It is early Saturday morning as I write this, I'm using the night-light in front of my cell. This is a rare night, a departure from the ordinary, it's quiet.

It occurs to me that you are probably asleep. But then you may not be, my family was in the area today and I know how disruptive that experience can be.

I just lit my seventy-fifth cigarette of this day. It will be my last—until after breakfast.

I was, before I started this letter, thinking of all the wonderful women in my life, and decided that you should hear from me. I'm doing as I've always done, wish for five, expect three, and get nothing.

I'm a little fat perhaps, but I don't know how I manage that, I eat nothing (for fear of poison). I seldom sleep, and do at least five full hours of martial-type exercises (with plenty of smoke breaks).

At the same time we discover and reach for each other, this opposite factor, within sometimes (just beneath conscious level—let's hope), is working against us. But love is the stronger force—if we just let it hang out unbridled—if it's soft and warm, hug it hard, look for the common features, f—— individualism.

From Dachau with Love,

George

JUNE, 1970
2

Dearest Angela (first among the equals),

This is the fourth attempt to reach you. The others were on paper like this. They all said, "I love you, African Woman," little else. I will continue to try to reach you in this existence that follows. They can't control this.

Once we have some lines established, I'll set down some of my thoughts, but we must hurry. So let me know through someone when I have reached you. The dates will tell you which letters have gotten through or at least they will tell me.

I sent a list of stuff that I needed in that line. If you don't get it, use Georgia's list excepting the Fanon and Ardrey, which I have coming from another quarter. Need reference

304

books too on everything. I've asked my father to provide you with the money for this stuff. He will cooperate with you. But remember we want the pocket editions of everything. These pigs like to steal—if I lose something it's best if it's only something small.

You haven't much time for writing: This is understandable, but always confirm any letters you receive. I worry, and for good reason. There is a great deal of bullshit between us, concrete and steel, fear and barbed wire.

It will not be that way for long. The pig is a dying breed, he is finding it hard to *bluff* people these days. If you *really* need me, I'll rush to your side—right now, through steel, concrete, all that sort of stuff. They are inert, dead, lacking will and intelligence.

Our enemies from the pig right on up to the *Who's Who* level are idiots. Why do we tolerate them? They're not even really bad, because they have the strength which originates in the mind. We've been too merciful, too forgiving, too understanding, but those days are gone forever.

I've heard the term nigger 350 times today. Just a word—but I *don't* understand. All of the cons who use it are little, young, punk types. At least three are outright homosexuals. They're afraid and it's fear that's impelling them. they know that they're so far gone that they have nothing else to lose. They've talked away their lives already.

I guess it's the same way with the pig and the men who make pigs. They know they've gone too far, that forgiveness is impossible. They cannot be reasonable now, because of yesterday's excesses. It's pretty clear, isn't it, what is coming. I accept it, it's beautiful. Tomorrow.

I like the way you do things, I like everything about you.
Love you,

George

305

JUNE, 1970
2

Dear Joan,

I don't know what to say regarding these people. They . . . well I won't say it now. I can't. They would simply return this letter. They sent me a notice saying that you were approved, and how else could you be getting these letters; whoever you talked to on the phone was using an arbitrary, bad-faith, delaying tactic.

I got the book all right, Joan. The long mellow communication with the photos arrived, say, ten minutes ago. Translation unnecessary. Thanks.

I agree with you and Lao-tse (and Mao—who I think acknowledged him somewhere), but I agree with you about feelings and syntax (I must, look at me). My father has tried for years to get me interested in writing fiction stuff. I've tried to explain that I was too busy living—and you know where I've been these years—however, we can connect the two, feeling and writing, just drop the syntax.

I don't consider myself a writer, an intellectual, really none of the things that can be *isolated*, when I *feel* I'll write (or talk) in an effort to effect and affect, and sometimes on the safety-valve principle, but actually I don't prefer anything as

306

mild as pen and paper. In my fancies I see myself growing up to be a VC type, a Che-type cat with all four paws on the ground, a clear line drawn, a kiss for some, the claw for the malicious. I'm a very simple person at heart. Perfect love, perfect hate, that's the insides of me. It means that I've devided the world's people into two categories only (I reject further classification on the grounds that I will not be confused, manipulated, divided to be conquered). I recognize two distinct types only, the innocent, the guilty.

The innocents, even the ones that I'll meet tomorrow, I love them all equally. I'll be serious with you, Joan, I find it almost impossible to think in terms of digging some more. Do you understand. Think of who you love most, Dan or Liz? Do you dig it? If told, or made to choose which one of my parents should be allowed to live, how could I choose either. I'd *have to give myself.* Follow this line by putting your son against my brother. I *would give myself.* I *will give* myself.

The guilty, I *will give* the folding crane's wing snap—to the temple. Simple.

I saw your mark in the book—I love you—for several very sound reasons—feelings—mainly for understanding. Ironic that we couldn't have lived this several years ago. I'll attack Ardrey of course, he is a nationalist, capitalist, dilettante, just wanted the books so I could do it accurately.

From Dachau with "these feelings."

George

307

JUNE, 1970

3

Dear Joan,

I have your message of June 2 already, and it feels nice to be worried about, I confess. But you can't be my mama, I feel a lot older than Dan (how old is he—in years?). You and yours truly will have to be sister and brother. I insist.

I do all right, I never have been a guy who ate much, I know you understand why. They *allow* us to spend money once a week, I stock up then. My father has provided me with all the money they'll let me spend in the next six months. I'm not really hurting.

I still think of myself as a black, and an African but I can't be satisfied with myself until I am communist *man*, revolutionary *man*,' and this without feeling that I've denied myself, or failed to identify.

Your descriptions of places, things, people, leave nothing to be desired. I was standing right there over you, with you, on the beach. Life can be (could be if) a wonderful experience. I have very mixed feelings about this whole affair, of drawing in and forcing out air. When I think of the very lovely people, the innocent, when I read your descriptions and some others, my mind strays momentarily from the fact that I'll never be safe.

308

At these moments I feel a thrill of promise, but that's only for a moment, the rest of my day is elevated to a pledge I made to myself, a compact that I would never live at ease as long as there was or *is* one man who would restrict my and your self-determination.

Must go, last chance to post this. Tomorrow.

From a guy who really digs you.

George

JUNE, 1970
4

Dearest Anglea,

This is the fifth one of these (on legal paper). I hope one reaches you soon. . . . Very discouraging. But I'll never stop trying.

All of these brothers here with me love you. In fact, every black I've talked with concerning you who had an opinion at all agrees with me about you. . . .

One thing about this bothers me a great deal. Do you know (of course you do) the secret police (CIA, etc.) go to great lengths to murder and consequently silence every effective black person the moment he attempts to explain to the ghetto that our problems are historically and strategically tied to the problems of all colonial people. This means that they are

309

watching *you* closely. I worry. If something happened to you I just wouldn't understand.

It's no coincidence that Malcolm X and M. L. King died *when* they did. Malcolm X had just put it together (two and three). I seriously believe, they knew all along but were holding out and presenting the truth in such a way that it would affect the most people situationally—without getting them damaged by gunfire. You remember what was on his lips when he died. Vietnam and economics, political economy. The professional killers could have murdered him long before they did. They let Malcolm rage on muslim nationalism for a number of years because they knew it was an empty ideal, but the second he got his feet on the ground, they murdered him. We die too easily. We forgive and forget too easily.

Gentle and refined people, aren't we. We'll make good communists, if someone deals with the fascists for us.

That was a little bitter. Pay no attention to stuff like that. I have more faith in our resilience than is healthy for me.

If what I said about M.L. King is true, and I'm going to put it down as if I were positive that it is, he was really on our side (the billions of righteous), his image can be used. I mean we can just claim him, and use his last statements and his image . . . to strengthen ours. And Malcolm can also be "reformed."

I'm working this into my thing right now, I can use anything you have or can get that contains King's public statements or comments to notable people. I'll be easy with it, slip it in, like it was just common knowledge that King was a Maoist.

I sure hope you understand, sister, and hurry. This hour hand is sweeping like the second hand. I don't care. My credo is to seize the pig by the tusks and ride him till his neck breaks. But if fortuitous outcome of circumstance allows him to prevail over me—again—then I want to have this carefully worked-up comment prepared. I want something to remain, to torment his ass, to haunt him, to make him know in no

310

uncertain terms that he did incur this nigger's sore disfavor. I need some facts and figures to dress this passion—*insist* where you have to, but get them to cooperate.

The lights went out an hour ago perhaps an hour and a half. It's 12:45 A.M., June 5, and I love you twice as much as I did yesterday. It redoubles and double redoubles. I'm using the night-light in front of my cell to write this. You may never read it. I make this convenant with myself I'll never again relax. I'll never make peace with this world as long as the enemies of self-determination have the running of things. You may never read this, and I may never touch you, but I feel better than I have for many seasons. You do know that I live, and I hope that by some means you have discovered that I love you deeply, and would touch you tenderly, warmly, fiercely if I could, if my enemies were not *at present* stronger. I'm going to stop here and do something physical, push-ups, finger stands, something quiet and strenuous.

Love to

George

JUNE, 1970

7

Dear Joan,

It's early Sunday morning, 4:05 A.M. These are my favorite hours, it's when I think of my favorite people, this is the only time that it will sometimes settle down here. Bet you're asleep this time.

This is my third day up, I slept for about half an hour yesterday when I fell off at my improvised combination desk-easy-chair. The "uniforms" probably have put me down as insane. They've started to look at me that way. (You probably don't know what I'm referring to, however.) There's a special air and expression reserved for "those crazy N——" a nuance different from the normal disdain. I try not to let them see me in my kata* but they're rather sneaky and they catch me sometimes. I guess it does look strange, a dance without music.

Last week(?) when I mentioned that I felt older than I am, I wasn't referring to my knees or elbows, back or hands, nor did I mean that I felt in any way wise. I feel old, Joan, in the sense that a paper target is old after about an hour on the

---

*Martial exercises mentioned in an earlier letter.

312

Police Academy practice range. Used.

Whatever it was that I lost these last ten years, I lost it suddenly. I can hardly imagine time passing any faster, the same can be said for the years before prison also (I picked up my first two bullet holes at age fifteen), but the prison experience was unique or I should say is unique in that there can be absolutely no emoluments for accepting the risks and responsibilities for hanging on.

I haven't seen the night sky for a decade. During the early sixties in San Quentin, "lockup" meant just that, twenty-four hours a day, all day, a shower once a week, and this could last for months (it's not changed much). On a shower walk one day in '63??, a brother called me to his cell for an opinion on this work he was doing on his walls. He had drawn in *the night sky* with colored pencils and against it, life size, lifelike (he was good), female comrades—some with fluffy naturals like my sister Angie, some with silky naturals like my sister Betsy. He had worked on it for three months. It was enormous—beautiful, precise, mellow. When he finished the last strokes the pigs moved him to another cell and painted over it, gave him a bad-conduct report, and made him pay for the new coat of paint. That brother didn't draw much any more last time I saw him. Some political cartoons, abstracts in book margins. Life's "a tale told by an idiot." Have you read any Shakespeare? I really enjoyed him when I was young. Macbeth is timeless, put him in a Brooks Brothers or a uniform and he'd fit right into the seventies. But you read all that stuff when you were in high school. I keep fogetting your background (class). Forgive me, sister, forgive the parochialism I sometimes slip into, habits formed in being, and addressing myself to, the hindmost.

From Dachau with love—

George

313

JUNE, 1970

7

Dear John, *

    You and your secretary just left. It's Sunday.

    I hope that ham on the tape was satisfactory. I find that sort of thing hard. I'll have to deal with it. I can, I guess, but it's not in keeping with my character. I'm the original shy guy? No ego at all. It's been crushed. I'd feel more relaxed at a shooting scrape than talking at the head of the table. Just not the kind of thing I favor. But if you feel that it may be necessary in the future, I'll work on it; but you're going to have to *convince* me.

    I've always thought in terms of division of labor—John, Huey, Angela Davis, etc., on the political front, cats like me behind them, in the crowd, watching the watchers—neutralizing the watchers. Where I have the nervous equipment naturally for that, the addressing would be strained. You understand, the difference between Fidel and Che. Fidel is at home behind a bank of microphones, Che is at home behind the carbine. Both can switch roles temporarily but Che is really a man of few words. And where would the Cuban revolution have ended were it not for Che and Camilo Cienfuegos.

*John Thorne, one of the author's lawyers.

314

But I'll try. It's merely a question of security, inner confidence, you understand. Will these people want to hear and bother to understand what *I'm* saying?

I feel a little funny about Angela being fired at this time and for that reason. We've fronted them off so often over these last few hundred years. I know they would have fired her anyway but I still feel . . . dependent in a way that damages my ego further. I hope like hell I'll have the opportunity to live up to expectations. She is such an incentive factor . . . how can I fear otherwise.

Thanks—Power to the People.

George

JUNE, 1970
11

Dear Joan,

Nice, very nice surprise for me today, but have you ever experienced a faster half hour. I did have some word for my family, but we got so wrapped up that I forgot. As you were being pulled away (I thought they would dislocate your arm), I was reflecting on how nice it is to hug.

Tell Georgia my case requires her to see me at least once a week, I want to see her now.

She may come up tomorrow—but if so I imagine you'll know.

Adore you—

George

JUNE, 1970
14

Dear G.,

The California Adult Authority board and inmate
Jackson A63837 clashed for the final time in June 1969. When
I was called up in June '70 (the usual arrangement is once a
year), I refused to go. I was already under indictment for the
murder of the pig and it wasn't very likely that I would be
given consideration for anything but the firing squad. The
June 1969 appearance, however, was very significant because
it followed a six-month postponement. I had gone to the
board for the eighth time in December 1968. I was told by the
institution employee who always sits on the board hearings
that I was "granted a parole." I would be back on the street on
March 4. I walked back to my cell telling everyone I had a
"date." I even wrote to my family. Three days later I was
informed that a mistake had been made. Consideration of my
case was postponed for six months. They explained to me that
I would be transferred to Soledad from San Quentin. If I did
well for six months at Soledad, I would be given parole for
certain. When the June 1969 appearance finally took place
different people were on the board panel. No one could find
any reference to the promises made to me by the earlier board.

316

I was denied for another full year.

Something very similar had happened the year before at the December 1967 appearance. At the previous meeting they had promised me that if I had seven or eight clean months I would be released. When I reminded them of their promise, they laughed and stated that "we never make deals like that."

All the other board appearances were tense affairs conducted in an atmosphere of mutual hostility. We argued over conflicting interpretations of the disciplinary reports in my central file. I had been accused of being a Muslim, Communist, agitator, nationalist, loan shark, thief, assassin, and saboteur. Nothing was ever settled, nothing was really exchanged except hostility.

Power to the People.

Comrade George

JUNE, 1970
15

Dear Joan,

I missed a day or two! I will clean up for that soon. I've been extremely busy in here, and then sometimes I get lazy. Then I'll kick back and think about you all. Since you're my eyes, and ears, and interpreter, I find myself with you most of the time.

317

I also missed seeing you today during what may have been the best court session to date. We won one.* The people—on the march. I've lost so many rounds, Joan—it feels good. We love you. You know where I'm at, I've always loved you. But all the rest of these cats down here are starting to feel your presence also.

I have Marie in here now.† Marie was my first love, my first experience. It was tender, I failed her, but if I try real hard now she may forgive me. That's been my thing—for years, to *always* live up to expectations.

And if *you* don't ask me for something very difficult, very taxing, I won't be able to relax from this point on.

We won't have to worry about these here too much longer. How far is San Jose from San Francisco?

Hope they'll let me see you, and perhaps they'll relent and let me see your daughter also. But . . . there isn't much chance of that.

What in your opinion was the principal reason for granting the move? Your opinion helps me anticipate. You understand that's what kept me here among the living with you over these years, anticipating.

Adore you—

George

*The court in Salinas granted a change of venue to San Francisco.

†"Someone sent me a card with a picture of 'The African Mother' done by and named Marie. I was commenting that I and my black male comrades had failed to be fathers and husbands, over the decades."

318

JUNE, 1970
17

Dear Joan,

I may have read a review or quote from Levi-Strauss but that's about all. And the *World*, I love it, send it to me. I'll share it with all the rest here who can still love. But will have to transfer it soon. The day I leave I'll send you a line or two. You let them know.

Western culture developed out of a very hostile environment. Rocks, snow, ice, long periods when the ground was too hard to be worked, when nothing could be produced from the soil, hunting became too important; accumulating, hoarding, hiding, protecting enough to last through the winter, things falling apart in winter, covetous glances at one's neighbor's goods. Would three or four thousand years of that kind of survival influence a culture? Would greed color itself into the total result, in a large way? Hunt, forage, store, hoard, hide, defend, the thing at stake!! Not very conducive to sensitivity, tenderness.

Change the environment, change the man. Simple.

Consider the people's store, after full automation, the implementation of the theory of economic advantage. You dig, no waste makers, no harnesses on production. There is no intermediary, no money. The store, it stocks everything that the body or home could possibly use. Why won't the people hoard, how is an operation like that possible, how could the storing place keep its stores if its stock (merchandise) is free?

Men hoard against want, need, don't they? Aren't they taught that tomorrow holds terror, pile up a surplus against this terror, be greedy and possessive if you want to succeed in this insecure world? Nuts hidden away for tomorrow's winter.

Change the environment, educate the man, he'll change. The people's store will work as long as people *know* that it will be there, and have in abundance the things they need and want (really want); when they are *positive* that the common effort has and will *always* produce an abundance, they won't bother to take home more than they need.

Water is free, do people drink more than they need? There is a reason for the ugliness of Western culture, many reasons I would say, but the fact that it was founded and tied into greed, the need to store so much, and work and fight so hard for something to store stands out from the other reasons.

This man that you work with, I know about cats like him. They never take more than they can give, so that sounds like a near-perfect relationship. You have to ask cats like that for something hard to make them relax.

Love you,

George

JUNE, 1970
27

Dear G.,

The man who has never received a kind message, a gesture, and who has never held anything of value, material or otherwise, if he is healthy, or I should say remains healthy (my persuasion presupposes original innocence), he never becomes so practical as to expect more of the same—nothing. Less but never nothing.

To be denied or rejected means less to this man but never nothing.

And if he is still healthy of mind, he knows he can't be practical, he can't afford practicality. His have-nothing status, the absence of the all-important controls, predisposes him to impracticality, he can never relax, he is or becomes the desperate man. And desperate men do desperate things, take desperate positions; when revolution comes he is the first to join it. If it doesn't come he makes it.

But the significant feature of the desperate man reveals itself when he meets other desperate men, direct or vicariously; and he experiences his first kindness, someone to strain with him, to strain to see him as he strains to see himself, someone to understand, someone to accept the regard, the love, that desperation forces into hiding.

321

This significant feature in the desperate men, and women, people, redeems them, redeems the revolution, alters the sanguine coloring of war, and gives revolution its love motive.

Men who have never received and have had little occasion to express the love theme or original goodness respond in a very significant manner to that first *real, spontaneous, gratuitous* kindness. Those feelings that find no expression in desperate times store themselves up in great abundance, ripen, strengthen, and strain the walls of their repository to the utmost; where the kindred spirit touches this wall it crumbles —no one responds to kindness, no one is more sensitive to it than the desperate man.

I'm trying to say thanks.

Power to the People—

Comrade George

JUNE, 1970
28

Dear Joan,

I knew you were here Thursday before I got the letter informing me of it. Our spirits met right there over the flower beds for a while. Then too I have my spies out, tall tan lady with huge round blue eyes. They have turned away dozens of my visitors, sorry to have put you through that.

322

What exactly did they say?

As soon as you finish with this letter, jump into your auto, find someone who will sell you some envelopes like the ones I generally send these messages in, long, business envelopes, then find some a little larger, go back home, write me a love note. Put the smaller of the two types of envelopes in one of the larger envelopes, include the love and pass to me.

I'm thinking of Jon now. I wish there was some way to talk with him in private. They ran him off too. They certainly must be sure of themselves, I mean sure of being able to convict and hold and get rid of me, because they're not very concerned about making me mad. And they know I don't forget.

It's real early Sunday morning, you're probably asleep. When I'm finished with this I'll join you in that dimension, and you're not shy at all.

Power—Love,

George

JUNE, 1970
30

Dear Joan,

You correctly sensed I am in a terrible rush, all the time. This rush characterizes everything that flows from me. (I'll take my time loving you, but when I come I'll be fresh from some hurried encounter with the Minotaur and related problems.)

I'm not really shy either, a little defensive yet—but no one would listen! That's what happened to me. But it was good in a way. It crushed the egotism, and the egocentric thing. (I only wish to help in the work against the minotaur.) The question is, do these nice people really want to hear what I have to say—as a victim of the first order—will they mistake it—as extreme—can these wonderful gentle people understand that some extreme situations call for extreme remedies; that the only means of ever dealing with a situation that calls for movement is to get ahead of the people and pull, not the reverse!!! Get ahead and pull. You've heard that . . . excuse(?), "Don't get ahead of the people." Bull! And then the others will change if we pull them into something that demands adjustments, breakthroughs. Theotis's job will be to rebuild, after I do my work. You, Minerva, will be his teacher.

You mentioned once—well, you spoke of "Jewish mama instincts"—are you Jewish? And what in your view is a Jew? (That should keep you working for a while.) All these years I've never given it a thought. I mean, I've never noticed anything singular or let's say distinctively different. Except in ways of love, and of course the physical, personal features so pleasing to the inner man.

Your daughter, I could breathe her in with one intake. I was referring to the auto accident when I spoke of her health, I've been worrying since I read that letter. Cuts, face, black eyes!! She has a hundred pounds on that wonderful little body??!! One long slow breath. Tell her I am devoted to her, and although we can't be together now I do want her to stay close as she can to me.

From me come great feelings of warmth and all kinds of love—for Joan.

George

324

JULY, 1970
8

Dear Joan,

This, my lovely one is just a note. Troubled times here that preoccupy your comrad's attentions.

Oh! I'm still here.

They don't like it, however. Fools, to say the least.

I have your two letters of Tuesday here with me now.

I feel closer every—things, people, complexities—each time I see you (two times). I feel a little closer—what if people start talking nasty about us? You with those long legs, and me with these long arms. I never feel shy around my other female army.... You be cool or I'll breathe you in.

I feel so sorry for them both, Georgia and her man. If you say I should, I'll send him a line tonight, but don't think you've twisted me around that white little finger. It will be a while yet before I give in completely to you.

I dig you a lot.

Love,

George

JULY, 1970
28

Dear Joan,

It's certainly nice to have a wonderfully alive, intelligent woman in the hand—every fingertip thanks you.

I've been back in the cell for ten minutes, after waiting forty-five for an escort. I saw you and Jon leave (you're almost as tall as he). I can't help but worry myself for him, not in the same way that his parents worry, actually the opposite of that. My concern is that his development not be retarded. Our immediate family is relating to him in the exact manner that they related to me. Bitter experience has taught them nothing. He's clearly rejected selfish love and restraints. Their attitudes are forcing him to choose between them and the ideal. We oppress each other, smother and confuse with contradictions between the tongue and the act. They're pushing him away from them. You know he's already somewhat withdrawn. Fear responses . . . he said he was leaving the house there in Pasadena. That should cause some tidal waves of emotionalism. I advised him to guide his decisions by necessity first, feelings secondly. I wonder, though, if I was right.

I'm chain-smoking again.

But you, you give me massive doses of relief. Thanks for

326

the confidence, the tears, the love.

   *We will win.

George

*"Anyone who doesn't sense this fundamental power of the people cannot be a guerrilla fighter."

JULY, 1970
28

Dear Fay, Dear Fay,

   The possibility of us, as persons, misunderstanding each other will always rest on the fact that I am an alien. It will always be my fault. The secret things that I hide from almost everyone, and especially the people who are sweet and gentle and intellectually inhibited from grasping the full range of the ordeal of being fair game, hunted, an alien, precludes *forever* a state of perfect agreement. You dig what I'm saying now you've conceded this much. Keep it always in mind, and strain with me.

   I feel threatened. That's where we should begin. Recall how I attempted to explain that feeling, the singular and inclusive sense. Then add to this that even in the days of my darkest confusion, when I was at once myself and not myself, my response to this feeling (and I've always felt threatened) was one from the older section of my brain. Being an alien has never (or seldom) made me feel sheepish!

In the inclusive sense, my politics, you'll find all of the atypical features of my character. I may run, but all the time that I am, I'll be looking for a stick! A defensible position! It's never occurred to me to lie down and be kicked! It's silly! When I do that I'm depending on the kicker to grow tired. The better tactic is to twist his leg a little or pull it off if you can. An intellectual argument to an attacker against the logic of his violence—or one to myself concerning the wisdom of a natural counterviolence—borders on, no, it overleaps the absurd!!

I just don't subscribe to that superman shit, I've seen too many men cry, seen them in all postures of the common infirmity—death. My message to black people and to sweet, gentle, much-loved people like yourself will be the same message I receive from my brain for myself. It will be the same as long as we have the same problem, it will be the same coming from the *living*, loving brain or from the grave.

They just put a new night-light in front of my cell, I'll be able to break up my days as I wish. Or not break them, just keep on going.—Just keep going—straight ahead—right on.

You're like no one I've ever met from across the tracks. I do think a very great deal of you and I'm certain that you do try to understand our problems. Don't mistake this as a message from George to Fay, it's a message from the hunted running blacks to those people of this society who profess to want to change the conditions that destroy life. These blacks are still in doubt as to whether those elements across the tracks want this change badly enough to accept the U.S. being physically brought to its knees to attain it. Will the Weathermen always be a microscopic minority? Working outside the protection of *all* their people, instead of *with* the support of an aggressive political cadre. I dig them, and love you.

Fondly and Always.

Power to the People,

George

328

AUGUST, 1970

9 Real Date, 2 days A.D.

Dear Joan,

We reckon all time in the future from the day of the man-child's death.

Man-child, black man-child with submachine gun in hand, he was free for a while. I guess that's more than most of us can expect.

I want people to wonder at what forces created him, terrible, vindictive, cold, calm man-child, courage in one hand, the machine gun in the other, scourge of the unrighteous—"an ox for the people to ride"!!!

Go over all the letters I've sent you, any reference to Georgia being less than a perfect revolutionary's mama must be removed. Do it now! I want no possibility of anyone misunderstanding her as I did. She didn't cry a tear. She is, as I am, very proud. She read two things into his rage, love and loyalty.

I can't go any further, it would just be a love story about the baddest brother this world has had the privilege to meet, and it's just not popular or safe—to say I love him.

329

Cold and calm though. "All right, gentlemen, I'm taking over now."*

Revolution,

George

*The author quotes his brother's words from the San Rafael courthouse.

APPENDIX:

Introduction to the First Edition by Jean Genet*

Every authentic writer discovers not only a new style but a narrative form which is his alone, and which in most cases he uses up, exhausting its effects for his own purposes.

Many people would be amazed to hear that the epistolary narrative was still capable of affording us a resolutely modern mode of expression; yet if we merely juxtapose (one after another) a certain number of George Jackson's letters, we obtain a striking poem of love and of combat.

But even more surprising, when we read these letters from a young black in Soledad Prison, is that they perfectly articulate

*Brazil, July 1970. Translated by Richard Howard.

331

the road traveled by their author—first the rather clumsy letters to his mother and his brother, then letters to his lawyer which become something extraordinary, half-poem, half-essay, and then the last letters, of an extreme delicacy, to an unknown recipient. And from the first letter to the last, nothing has been willed, written or composed for the sake of a book, yet here is a book, tough and sure, both a weapon of liberation and a love poem. In this case I see no miracle except the miracle of truth itself, the naked truth revealed. George Jackson is a poet, then. But he faces the death penalty. I shall talk about that.

A court of justice, a certain number of jurors protected by uniformed guards, by plainclothesmen, by informers, by the whole of white America, will decide whether Jackson and his brothers killed a prison guard. The jurors answer yes or no. If they answer yes, a very strange operation begins. The judges must pronounce sentence—either a death sentence, a life sentence, or a sentence of time to be served.† What, then, is this intellectual operation which changes a simple act (a murder, if there was one) into something quite different: into another death, or a life sentence or a period of time served?

How these two facts are linked together—the initial and hypothetical murder, and the sentence pronounced—no one knows, no one has yet said. This is because the courts, in America as elsewhere, are tribunals of authority, a crude authority which adapts itself very well to the arbitrary.

Yet this sentence, once pronounced, must be carried out. It

† When this Introduction was written, Genet did not realize that, under California law, the jury usually determines the sentence. In Jackson's case, however, the sentence of death is actually mandatory. In California, convicts serving life sentences who are convicted of assault on a noninmate are automatically sentenced to death.

332

will be carried out by and upon the Soledad brothers, upon George Jackson, and in this way: either by proceeding from his cell to the gas chamber, or by living twenty or thirty years in still another cell.

A guard is discovered—murdered.

A jury answers yes or no to indicate the murderer.

The murderer dies in his turn, or lives in a cell for thirty years in order to justify a sentence that has been *pronounced*.

To understand the significance of this book as a weapon, a means of combat, the reader must not forget that George Jackson is in danger of death.

If a certain complicity links the works written in prisons or asylums (Sade and Artaud share the same necessity of finding in themselves what must lead them to glory, that is, despite the walls, the moats, the jailers and the magistracy, into the light, into minds not enslaved), these works do not meet in what is still called ignominy: starting in search of themselves from that ignominy demanded by social repression, they discover common ground in the audacity of their undertaking, in the rigor and accuracy of their ideas and their visions. In prison more than elsewhere one cannot afford to be casual. One cannot endure a penalty so monstrous as the lack of freedom without demanding of one's mind and body a labor at once delicate and brutal, a labor capable of "warping" the prisoner in a direction which takes him ever farther from the social world. But . . .

It might be supposed that as the site of absolute malediction, prison, and at its heart the cell, would enforce by its misery upon those confined there a kind of solidarity required by that very misery, a merciful harmony in which all social distinctions maintained in the free air would be abolished.

Prison serves no purpose. Do we imagine that at least it can strip its inmates of their wretched social differences, that under the surveillance of a cordon of guards, black or white but armed, there develop behind its walls, in its darkness, certain new relations between the prisoners, whoever they may have been during their moments of freedom?

That is an idealistic hope which we must avoid or get rid of. George Jackson's book tells the brutal truth: in prison, in a cell, the white skin of the prisoners becomes an image of complicity with the white skin of the guards, so that if white guards superintend a hell in which white men are jailed, the white prisoners superintend another hell inside that one in which black men are jailed. Now the security of the guards, their independence—their time off duty, their visits to town, their family lives—grant a certain respite to the white prisoners; but the fact that .these prisoners must be constantly confined, never distracted by the world outside, means that they employ all their time and all their imagination in maintaining the hell in which they confine the black prisoners.

Few prisoners, on the whole, escape the tendency of a complicity with certain guards: it is a kind of nostalgia for the social world from which the prisoner is cut off (a nostalgia which makes the prisoner cling to what seems, in his prison, closest to the social order: the guard. As for the guard, the motives which lead him to accept the game between certain prisoners and himself are many and complex). Now would this complicity have too much importance, when its meaning is abatement, a temporary weakness likely to be revoked, abruptly halted—on the occasion of a riot, for example. But in the United States, this complicity has a different meaning: the complicity of the white prisoners with the guards exasperates and intensifies what constitutes the basis of relations between white men and black: racism.

This racism is scattered, diffused throughout the whole of America, grim, underhanded, hypocritical, arrogant. There is one place where we might hope it would cease, but on the contrary, it is in this place that it reaches its cruelest pitch, intensifying every second, preying on body and soul; it is in

334

this place that racism becomes a kind of concentrate of racism: in the American prisons, in Soledad Prison, and in its center, the Soledad cells.

If, by some oversight, racism were to disappear from the surface of the United States, we could then seek it out, intact and more dense, in one of these cells. It is here, secret and public, explicable and mysterious, stupid and more complicated than a tiger's eye, absence of life and source of pain, nonexistent mass and radioactive charge, exposed to all and yet concealed. One might say that racism is here in its pure state, gathering its forces, pulsing with power, ready to spring.

The extravagant adventure of white America, which is the victorious expansion of Victorian England, is doubtless exhausted, it will dissolve and fade, revealing at last what is cheerfully devouring it: the black nation which was caught within it, itself traversed by liberating currents, liberating movements, producing long screams of misery and joy. What seems new to me in this black literature is that now we hear almost no echoes of the great Hebrew prophets. From Richard Wright to George Jackson, the blacks are stripping themselves of all the presbyterian and biblical rags: their voices are rawer, blacker, more accusing, more implacable, tearing away any reference to the cynical cheats of the religious establishment. Their voices are more singular, and singular too in what they seem to agree upon: to denounce the curse not of being black, but captive.

Is that new?

Incontestably.

George Jackson's style is clear, carefully pitched, simple and supple, as is his thinking. Anger alone illuminates his style and his thinking, and a kind of joy in anger.

A book written in prison—in any place of confinement—is addressed chiefly perhaps to readers who are not outcasts, who have never been to jail and who will never go there. That is

335

why in some sense such a book proceeds obliquely. Otherwise, I know that the man who writes it need only take, in order to fling them down on paper, the forbidden words, the accursed words, the words covered with blood, the unwritten words of spit and sperm—like the ultimate name of God—the dangerous words, the padlocked words, the words that do not belong to the dictionary, for if they were written there, written out and not maimed by elipses, they would utter too fast the suffocating misery of a solitude that is not accepted, that is flogged only by what it is deprived of: sex and freedom.

It is therefore prudent that any text which reaches us from this infernal place should reach us as though mutilated, pruned of its overly tumultuous adornments.

It is thus behind bars, bars accepted by them alone, that its readers, if they dare, will discover the infamy of a situation which a respectable vocabulary cannot reinstate—but behind the permitted words, listen for the others!

If the prisoner is a black man captured by whites, a third thread runs through this difficult web: hatred. Not the rather vague and diffuse hatred of the social order or of fate, but the very precise hatred of the white man. Here again, the prisoner must use the very language, the words, the syntax of his enemy, whereas he craves a separate language belonging only to his people. Once again his situation is both hypocritical and wretched: he can express his sexual obsessions only in a polite dialect, according to a syntax which enables others to read him, and as for his hatred of the white man, he can utter it only in this language which belongs to black and white alike but over which the white man extends his grammarian's jurisidiction. It is perhaps a new source of anguish for the black man to realize that if he writes a masterpiece, it is his enemy's language, his enemy's treasury which is enriched by the additional jewel he has so furiously and lovingly carved.

He has then only one recourse: to accept this language but to corrupt it so skillfully that the white men are caught in his trap. To accept it in all its richness, to increase that richness

336

still further, and to suffuse it with all his obsessions and all his hatred of the white man. That is a task.

And it is a task which seems contradicted by the revolutionary's. The revolutionary enterprise of the American black, it seems, can come into being only out of resentment and hatred, that is, by rejecting with disgust, with rage, but radically, the values venerated by the whites, although this enterprise can continue only starting from a common language, at first rejected, finally accepted, in which the words will no longer serve concepts inculcated by the whites, but new concepts. In a revolutionary work written by a black man in jail, certain traces must remain, then, of the orgiastic and hate-ridden trajectory covered in an imposed solitude.

Having emerged from his delirium, having achieved a cold revolutionary consciousness, Sade still kept something of that obsessional delirium which nonetheless led him to his revolutionary lucidity.

This is also evident in the letters which follow.

In prison, George Jackson must still be sure to fortify in himself what sets him against the whites, and to elaborate a consciousness so acute that it will be valid for all men.

It was almost predictable that having reached this stage of self-discovery, his revolutionary consciousness should meet and come to terms with the Black Panther party. Thus it is without equivocation and without any mystery that he names it and abides by its directives in the course of his last letters. For myself, who have lived with the Panthers, I see George Jackson in his place there, fighting at their side with the same conviction and the same talent as his brothers accused of murder, Huey Newton and Bobby Seale.

If we accept this idea, that the revolutionary enterprise of a man or of a people originates in their poetic genius, or, more precisely, that this enterprise is the inevitable conclusion of poetic genius, we must reject nothing of what makes poetic exaltation possible. If certain details of this work seem

337

immoral to you, it is because the work as a whole denies your morality, because poetry contains both the possibility of a revolutionary morality and what appears to contradict it. Finally, every young American black who writes is trying to find himself and test himself and sometimes, at the very center of his being, in his own heart, discovers a white man he must annihilate.

But let me return to the amazing coherence of George Jackson's life and of his *unwilled* book. There is nonetheless one rather disturbing thing about it: at the same moment he was living his life (a kind of death or higher life), without his realizing it, by letters and certain notations in his letters, he was also writing his legend, that is, he was giving us, without intending to, a mythical image of himself and of his life—I mean an image transcending his physical person and his ordinary life in order to project himself into glory with the help of a combat weapon (his book) and of a love poem.

But I have lived too long in prisons not to recognize, as soon as the very first pages were translated for me in San Francisco, the special odor and texture of what was written in a cell, behind walls, guards, envenomed by hatred, for what I did not yet know so intensely was the hatred of the white American for the black, a hatred so deep that I wonder if every white man in this country, when he plants a tree, doesn't see *Negroes* hanging from its branches.

When this book comes out, the man who wrote it will still be in his Soledad cell, with his Soledad Brothers.* What follows must be read as a manifesto, as a tract, as a call to rebellion, since it is that first of all.

*In late June 1970, before the publication of this book, the Soledad brothers were transferred to San Quentin.

It is too obvious that the legislative and judiciary systems of the United States were established in order to protect a capitalist minority and, if forced, the whole of the white population; but these infernal systems are still raised against the black man. We have known for a long time now that the black man is, from the start, natively, the guilty man. We can be sure that if the blacks, by the use of their violence, their intelligence, their poetry, all that they have accumulated for centuries while observing their former masters in silence and in secrecy—if the blacks do not undertake their own liberation, the whites will not make a move.

But already Huey Newton, Bobby Seale, the members of the Black Panther party, George Jackson, and others have stopped lamenting their fate. The time for blues is over, for them. They are creating, each according to his means, a revolutionary consciousness. And their eyes are clear. Not blue.

JEAN GENET